the

GREAT
RESET

the

GREAT RESET

HOW NEW WAYS OF LIVING AND WORKING DRIVE POST-CRASH PROSPERITY

RICHARD FLORIDA

RANDOM HOUSE CANADA

Library and Archives Canada Cataloguing in Publication

Florida, Richard L.
    The great reset : how new ways of living and working drive post-crash prosperity / Richard Florida.

Includes bibliographical references and index.

ISBN 978-0-307-35829-5

    1. Human geography—Economic aspects—United States. 2. Economic geography. 3. Economic policy. 4. Creative ability—Economic aspects—United States. 5. Global Financial Crisis, 2008–2009. 6. United States—Economic conditions—21st century. I. Title.

HC106.84.F56 2010   330.973093   C2009-906617-3

Design by William Ruoto

Printed in the United States of America

10 9 8 7 6 5 4 3 2 1

For Zak

Contents

Part III: A New Way of Life

Preface

t isn't as though we didn't see it coming. To many of us, it may feel as though our society turned almost overnight from prosperity to chaos. But in fact the financial crisis that stopped the economy in its tracks in 2008 and 2009 was years, perhaps even generations, in the making. It's easy to point fingers, to scapegoat the high-flying bankers and mortgage lenders whose high-risk shenanigans leveled the financial markets. But that would perhaps be like blaming fast food for obesity.

We've been bingeing for a long time. For twenty-five years or more, the U.S. economy grew and grew, feasting on the unchecked consumption of a never-ending cascade of real estate, goods, and gadgetry. The United States used to be revered for its innovative capacity, its so-called American ingenuity, but all that somehow got refocused on overly risky financial innovation. The economy became a giant bazaar, fueled by easy credit. At the same time, the financial markets, once a haven for investors, mutated into rolling casinos, where many of our most brilliant minds gambled recklessly, making bets of dizzying complexity. It's been nearly ten years since Alan Greenspan revised his description of "irrational exuberance," replacing it with the more condemning phrase "infectious greed" as he watched the house of cards rise higher and grow ever more precarious.

Inevitably, it all came crashing down, but this isn't news to anyone. Nor is it anything *new*. We've been here before. Not just now, but at two other critical times in the last 150 years—in the 1870s and the 1930s—the economy caved in and depressions ensued. Both times, however, we emerged from those dark times healthier and wealthier than before. And it can happen again.

Enough time has already been spent uncovering the roots of this crisis and predicting the depths to which the economy may or may not fall, and at which point it will rebound. The real point of looking backward is to learn for the future, and we have much to learn from the crises and recoveries of the past. These were eras of real devastation and pain that left gaping holes in our economy and society. Nature always abhors a vacuum. For every institution that failed, for every business model that outlived its usefulness, new and better ones rushed in to fill the void. Past periods of crisis eventually gave rise to new epochs of great ingenuity and inventiveness. They were the times when new technologies and new business models were forged, and they were also the eras that ushered in new economic and social models and whole new ways of living and working.

The clock of history is always ticking. We can cross our fingers and hope for the best, or we can take steps now to move toward a better, more prosperous future. We've weathered terrible crashes and depressions before, and we've always picked ourselves up and unflinchingly remade our economy and society, setting the stage for longer-term prosperity. As times have changed, we've embraced new ways of working and living and new ways of organizing our cities, providing the foundation for growth and recovery. Time and again, we've come out of the crises surely "stronger in the broken places," richer in ways both tangible and intangible. In *The Great Reset*, I look back on the key elements of our previous epochs of crisis and change, in the hope that it can help us better identify the key elements of our current transformation and provide a framework for guiding us toward a new era of lasting prosperity.

Part I

PAST AS PROLOGUE

Chapter One

The Great Reset

I can't help wondering what my parents would be thinking right now. Born in the 1920s, my mother and father lived through many of the greatest upheavals of the twentieth century, from the Great Depression of the 1930s to the roaring recovery of the decades that followed the Second World War. Both grew up in Newark, New Jersey's Italian district, my father's home absent a refrigerator or indoor plumbing. They recounted stories of the bread lines and tent cities and government-issued clothing that marked the urban misery of the Depression years. My dad left school at age thirteen and took up work in an eyeglasses factory, combining his wages with those of his father, mother, and six siblings to make a family wage. At Christmas, his parents, unable to afford new toys, wrapped the same toy steam shovel, year after year, and placed it for him under the tree. But thirty years later, they were able to follow countless contemporaries to the greener pastures of the suburbs, buying first a house all their own, then a shiny new Chevy Impala, a washing machine, and a television, and raising their children in relative security. My father saw his low-wage job—in the very same factory—turn into good, high-paying work that could support our entire family.

The economic peaks and valleys that my parents experienced are part of the life cycle of any society. They can be difficult, sometimes horribly painful, but just as trees shed their leaves in the fall to make room for the new growth of spring, economies *reset* themselves. Times of crisis reveal what is and isn't working. These are the times when obsolete and dysfunctional systems and practices collapse or fall by the wayside. They are the times when the seeds of innovation and invention, of creativity and entrepreneurship, burst into full flower, enabling recovery by remaking both the economy and society. Major periods of economic transformation, such as the Great Depression or the Long Depression of the 1870s before it, unfold over long stretches of time, like motion pictures rather than snapshots. Likewise, the path to recovery can be long and twisted—the better part of three decades in the case of those two previous crises. Seen in the greater context of history, economic crises inevitably give rise to critical periods in which an economy is remade in ways that allow it to recover and begin growing again. These are periods I call Great Resets.

Sitting at his perch in the British Museum, Karl Marx wrote trenchantly about the violent shift from an older agricultural economy to a modern capitalist one. Capitalism, the most innovative, revolutionary economic system of all time, was also prone to financial panics and economic crises. Despite the massive deprivation and human suffering they caused, these crises played a fundamental role in propelling the economy forward. They were critical moments when existing economic and social arrangements were remade, enabling new periods of economic growth. Born in the same year that Marx died, the great theorist of innovation and entrepreneurship, Joseph Schumpeter, used the phrase "creative destruction" to describe how economic crises sweep away old firms and outmoded economic systems and practices, clearing the way for entrepreneurs to introduce new technologies and even entirely new industries and setting into motion a new era of growth. John Maynard Keynes saw in these crises the need for government spending to essentially protect capitalism from itself. With the private sector flat on its back, government spending was the only way to keep capitalism going and get the economy back on its feet. Each of these important thinkers described the part of the process by which busts slowly turn around and lead to booms, but real, lasting recovery requires more than bursts of technological innovation and new roles for government.

President Barack Obama's chief of staff, Rahm Emanuel, likes to quote Paul Romer's now-famous maxim about "a crisis being a terrible thing to waste."[1] The fact of the matter is that we're wasting it, big time. The whole approach of throwing trillions of public dollars at the old economy is shortsighted, aimed at restoring our collective comfort level. Meaningful recovery will require a lot more than government bailouts, stimuli, and other patchwork measures designed to resuscitate the old system or to create illusory, short-term upticks in the stock market, housing market, or car sales. Government spending can't be the solution in the long run. Though government can fill in gaps for a while, it simply lacks the resources to generate the enormous level of demand needed to power sustained growth.

"This economic crisis doesn't represent a cycle. It represents a reset. It's an emotional, raw social, economic reset," said General Electric CEO Jeffrey Immelt. "People who understand that will prosper. Those who don't will be left behind."[2] *Webster's New Collegiate Dictionary* defines "reset" as "to set again or anew." The *Oxford English Dictionary* defines it as "to set again or differently."

Great Resets are broad and fundamental transformations of the economic and social order and involve much more than strictly economic or financial events. A true Reset transforms not simply the way we innovate and produce but also ushers in a whole new economic landscape. As it takes shape around new infrastructure and systems of transportation, it gives rise to new housing patterns, realigning where and how we live and work. Eventually, it ushers in a whole new way of life—defined by new wants and needs and new models of consumption that spur the economy, enabling industry to expand and productivity to improve, while creating new and better jobs for workers.

Economic systems do not exist in the abstract; they are embedded within the geographic fabric of the society—the way land is used, the locations of homes and businesses, the infrastructure that ties people, places, and commerce together. These factors combine to shape production, consumption, and innovation, and as they change, so do the basic engines of the economy. A reconfiguration of this economic landscape is the real distinguishing characteristic of a Great Reset. After the Great Depression, suburbs expanded, creating new demand for automobiles, appliances, televisions, and other goods, allowing the golden age of mass production to come into full flower. The resolution to the economic crisis of the late nineteenth century involved the rise not only of new industries and technologies but of massive industrial cities.

Geographers call it the *spatial fix* of a problem.[3] By what they destroy and what they leave standing, by the responses or new activity they catalyze, and by the space they clear for new growth, such big economic shocks ultimately leave the landscape transformed. Technological innovation leads to new forms of infrastructure, which lead to revolutions in where and how we live and work. Whether it's pipes and cables or trains and bridges, the new systems expand the reach of energy and the efficiency of communication and transportation, accelerating the flow of goods, people, and ideas. A powerful movement of people ensues as cities, as well as nations, rise and decline, as major population centers massively expand, and as the economic landscape is developed ever more intensively. Every major economic era gives rise to a new, distinctive geography of its own. This Great Reset will likewise take shape around a new economic landscape and a whole new way of life that is in line with the emerging economic and social realities of our time.

We're still very early on in the current economic Reset, so it's difficult to fully grasp how it will ultimately play out. But we can all sense that our way of life is changing and our economic landscape is too. These changes are emerging—and have been emerging—organically, in fits and starts, for some time now. They don't result from top-down policy or programs, though government can encourage or discourage them by what it does or does not do. One thing is certain: this emerging new way of life, which some already refer to as an impending "new normal," will be less oriented around cars, houses, and suburbs. We'll be spending relatively less on the things that defined the old way of life. We'll have to, if we expect to have money left over to sustain the new industries that will emerge in the Great Reset and usher in an age of renewed prosperity. During the Great Depression of the 1930s, as we will see, the amount of money families spent on food fell dramatically, as did the percentage of Americans working in agriculture to directly produce that food. The same kind of transformation has to happen today. Before we can nurture the new industries of the future, develop new forms of health care and biotechnologies, or even explore new forms of education or more experiential forms of entertainment and recreation, we first have to free up capital by producing the goods of the old industrial order more cheaply and efficiently.

We've reached the limits of what George W. Bush used to call the "ownership society." Owning your own home made sense when people could hope to hold a job for most or all of their lives. But in an economy that revolves around mobility and flexibility, a house that can't be sold becomes an economic trap, preventing people from moving freely to economic opportunity. Not only has that piece of the American Dream grown dark, but it's also clear that financial excess in the housing sector was one of the central causes of the economic crisis. Housing sucked up far too much of the nation's and the world's capital, and too many people—already overextended by the purchase of outsized houses—used those homes like virtual ATMs to finance carefree consumption. Every Great Reset has seen our system of housing change, and this one is no different. The rate of home ownership has been on the decline for some time now. Many of those who still choose to buy homes will choose smaller ones, while many more will opt for rental housing.

Our new way of life is likely to depend a whole lot less on the car. In October 2009, the *New York Times* reported, "The recession and a growing awareness of the environment are causing many people to reassess their automobile ownership. After more than a century in which an automobile represented the American dream, car enthusiasm may no longer be a part of Americans' DNA."[4] Car culture no longer exerts the powerful pull it once did. More and more families are deciding to share cars, and young people are putting off buying them and using public transit, bikes, their feet, or Zipcars or other auto-share services instead. It's not just that oil and gas have become expensive, it's that traffic and gridlock have become a deadweight time cost on us and our economy.

One constant in the history of capitalism is the ever-more-intensive use of land, as mercantile towns replaced agricultural villages, major industrial cities replaced those towns, and massive complexes of suburbs, exurbs, and edge cites expanded the boundaries of those cities. The change we are living through is much more than a movement from suburbs to denser urban communities. What we are seeing is the rise of a new, bigger, and denser economic landscape than ever before—the rise of vast megaregions such as the corridors stretching from Boston to New York and Washington, D.C., around greater London, and from Shanghai to Beijing.

These trends are in their infancy but will imprint themselves ever more forcibly on future generations. We need to understand them so that we can best adjust to them in ways that nurture broadly shared prosperity. My goal in this book is to provide a deeper understanding of the forces that are reshaping our economy and society and to provide a framework that can better direct our effort to guide or accelerate them, while ameliorating their most onerous dislocations and human costs. Resets are complex, organic processes—progress in one area of life triggers changes in another and so on down the line. Looking backward, I aim to unpack and distill the main factors and forces that have emerged during past crises and have shaped previous Resets, ultimately driving whole new eras of growth and prosperity. Looking ahead, I seek to identify the already emerging tendencies in our economy and society that can come together as core elements of yet another Great Reset—new consumption patterns that are less centered around houses and cars, new forms of infrastructure that once again speed the movement of people, goods, and ideas, and a radically altered and much denser economic landscape that will provide the springboard for a whole new way of life and drive the development of new industries and jobs. We need to anticipate and understand the trends that are already under way so that we can develop strategies that will speed their onset, shrink the time it takes to move from crisis to enduring recovery, deal most effectively with the dislocation and pain they bring about, and ultimately create a broad new era of prosperity.

Chapter Two

■

The Crisis Most Like Our Own

The historian Scott Reynolds Nelson writes that today's crisis most closely resembles the Long Depression of 1873.[1] Our "current economic woes look a lot like what my 96-year-old grandmother still calls 'the real Great Depression,'" he says. "She pinched pennies in the 1930s, but she says that times were not nearly as bad as the depression her grandparents went through. . . . It looks much more like our current crisis." That nineteenth-century downturn began as a banking crisis brought on by insolvent mortgages and complex financial instruments (sound familiar?) quickly spread to the entire economy, leading to widespread and prolonged unemployment.

As long and as painful as it was, that crisis spurred a period of incredible inventiveness. When one economist mapped patented U.S. inventions back through the early nineteenth century, he found a huge spike in the 1870s. These innovations revolutionized existing industries, helped create new ones, and generated powerful economies of scale that made possible a series of new industries that were bigger than anything the world had ever seen.[2]

A revolution in transportation technology was occurring. One of the earliest examples of the industrialized mass production of wheeled transportation was, in fact, the bicycle. Primitive bicycles had been developed in the middle of the nineteenth century, but it wasn't until the invention of the Rover Safety Cycle in 1885, with its balanced seating and easy steering, that the bicycle we know today came onto the scene. The bicycle freed many from the need to own a horse, and became a sensation particularly among women, for whom it represented a tangible form of liberation. Advances in the steam turbine by Gustaf de Laval and Charles Parsons in the mid-1880s made it possible to build much larger ships. Inventors had been working on variants of the internal combustion engine since the early part of the nineteenth century. But it was in 1877 that a German inventor, Nicolaus Otto, built a modern gas-powered four-stroke engine. And in 1885, the Germans Gottlieb Daimler and Karl Benz introduced an Otto-type gas-burning engine with a modern carburetor to mix air and fuel.[3]

This revolution in transportation could not have happened in a technology vacuum; without the progress made in materials, especially steel, in the systems of manufacturing, none of these ingenious inventions could have become practical realities. Henry Bessemer had revolutionized steelmaking with his invention in 1850 of a process for refining iron ore that enabled the first mass production of steel. But Bessemer steel was of low quality. A series of new inventions led to the development of an open-hearth process that enabled higher-quality steel to be made in large quantities. By 1900, Andrew Carnegie declared the open-hearth process the future of the steel industry.

The First Reset engendered a fundamental shift in the organization of production itself. The invention of new technologies is one thing, but the ability to organize them into a workable system can lead to massive gains in output and efficiency that can revolutionize the economy. The new systems are, themselves, key factors of a Reset. The mid–nineteenth century had seen the rise of a powerful new system of production based on interchangeable parts, dubbed the "American system of manufacture."[4] This system was a huge advance over the older system of a craftsman working independently to make parts with a chisel and file, replacing that time-honored practice with machine-made parts. But it advanced only slowly, in fits and starts, and was used mainly at first for military production. Advances made during the First Reset enabled the system to spread from "firearms, then in clocks, pumps. Locks, mechanical reapers, typewriters, sewing machines, and eventually bicycles and engines," notes the economic historian Joel Mokyr.[5] Adding to this were major strides forward in continuous-flow technology, initially pioneered in the huge meat-processing factories of Chicago, where it was initially used to speed up the disassembly of livestock, which paved the way for modern mass production à la Henry Ford.

These innovations, and many others that were developed during the First Reset, actually helped shape Schumpeter's theory of creative destruction. Innovation does not slow down during crises, but because the economy is depressed, they tend to accumulate and bunch up. They then come bursting forward as the economy recovers.[6] "Well, one reason why upturns follow downturns is that downturns tend to overshoot," explains the Nobel Prize–winning economist Edmund Phelps regarding the way that crises spur invention and lead to the formation of new businesses. "[E]ntrepreneurs keep on waiting to produce new things [so] that there's an accumulation of as-yet-unexploited new ideas that keeps mounting up. . . . Things can get only so bad. People want to eat, so at some point they resist further cuts to their consumption—it's not a bottomless pit. There's a rising stockpile, a mound of fuel developing, to power new projects and new investment activity. . . . A lot of new projects are being deferred because of uncertainty, but as the downward spiral peters out the uncertainty will wane."[7]

The technological revolution of the First Reset gave rise to powerful new energy systems creating an unparalleled infrastructure for growth on an unprecedented scale. As a case in point, the era saw a whole series of crucial inventions that revolutionized electricity: Paul Jablochkoff's arc lamp, Charles Brush's high-tension direct-current lamp, Thomas Edison's electric lightbulb and advances in alternating current (AC), Nikola Tesla's alternating-current motor, and George Westinghouse's electric transformer and advances in direct current (DC). These were used in new products from electric blankets to hot plates. But they also helped usher in the modern system of electric power transmission and distribution that today lights our homes, powers our industries, and runs our cities.

These inventions provided the backbone of a massive and critical wave of what the historian of technology Thomas Hughes dubs "systems innovation."[8] Thomas Edison was a systems builder par excellence who had the foresight to understand the interplay among science, engineering, and commerce. Contrary to popular belief, Edison didn't actually "invent" the lightbulb. In fact, by the late 1870s, the grand Avenue de l'Opéra in Paris was already lit by large electric arc lamps. But no one had come up with a durable design that would make lightbulbs practical and affordable, and that was the problem on which Edison focused his efforts. The genius of his approach was that he got his own infrastructure into place first, setting up the Edison Electric Light Company so that he could own, and later license, whatever patents he and his laboratory team might achieve. Once the technology of the lightbulb itself was perfected, Edison turned his attention to developing a complete infrastructure to generate and distribute electricity, without which the lightbulb would have been little more than a novelty gadget. Every component of that electrical system—generators, switches, fuses, sockets, and so on—was the product of Thomas Edison's brain trust.

Edison created the United States' first citywide electrical system in 1882. His Pearl Street Station power plant in New York City, the first large-scale construction of the Edison Electric Illuminating Company, was based on direct current and distributed electricity only over short distances at low voltages, using large copper wires. "Edison invented systems," writes Hughes. He devoted most of his efforts to invention but sought to "relate everything to a single, central vision," and to do so he had to "reach out beyond his special competence to research, develop, finance and manage his inventions." And he formed companies as needed to push his inventions to market and to make the market for them, one for research and development, others to make components, and still another to operate the system.

Edison also gave us a new system for organizing research and invention and applying it directly to the development of new commercial products. He opened the doors to his Menlo Park, New Jersey, laboratory in 1876, dubbing it his "invention factory." His goal was to create a system that could regularly churn out "useful things every man, woman, and child in the world wants . . . at a price they could afford to pay."[9] Within a decade he had turned it into a mammoth invention factory sprawling over two city blocks, stocked with technical staff, library resources, machine tools, scientific instruments, and electrical equipment. Essentially, he "merged the machine shop with sophisticated electrical and chemical laboratories," writes the Rutgers University historian Paul Israel, "and employed teams of researchers who could experiment on all aspects of his inventions and move them rapidly from research to development and commercialization."[10]

The application of science and invention to industry was a massive spur to productivity. "The first industrial revolution—and most technological developments preceding it—had little or no scientific base," writes Mokyr. "It created a chemical industry with no chemistry, an iron industry without metallurgy, power machinery without thermodynamics."[11] By applying science to invention directly and systematically to industry, inventions were generated that vastly increased productivity and brought all this technological innovation into the daily lives of the middle class and the working class.

George Westinghouse was another great systems-builder. Inspired by Alexander Graham Bell's invention of the telephone and recognizing the inefficiencies inherent in Edison's use of direct current, Westinghouse assembled teams of experts, including the great Serbian engineer Nikola Tesla, who developed signaling and switching systems and transformers, all of which allowed for faster and more widespread distribution of electricity. He also established companies to manufacture and market his new technologies. Westinghouse's work was easily transferrable to railroads, spurring even further improvements to infrastructure in the 1880s. Westinghouse was a master of integrating technologies coming literally from everywhere. When English inventors came to visit his Pittsburgh factory to see what his companies had accomplished, they were astonished that he had been able to fashion their individual inventions into such a powerful system. "It is not a very complimentary reflection for European electricians and capitalists," an English technical journal lamented in 1887, "that although all ideas and experimental work needed have come from Europe . . . it should be reserved for an American firm to take up the system and make it the commercial and practical success which the Westinghouse Company is now doing."[12]

"The war of currents," as some historians describe the competition between Edison and Westinghouse, ultimately worked to the greater good, by clarifying which systems would be the most efficient and thus benefit the public most. In that effort we can see a crystal-clear example of innovation progressing toward infrastructure that could become the foundation of a Great Reset.

Electrical power was just one system to come out of the First Reset. There were others, many of which transformed what we now call communications and information technology. Alexander Graham Bell introduced his telephone in 1876. Edison invented the phonograph in 1877. The period also saw major advances in wireless technology for transmitting sounds. The 1880s saw the emergence of linotype technology for printing newspapers and ultimately books.

The great systems innovations of the First Reset did not take place just anywhere but arose in particular places. Edison's lab in central New Jersey, and clusters of innovation in Pittsburgh and Cleveland, functioned as veritable Silicon Valleys of their time,[13] with those labs and companies incubating new technologies and siphoning off new branches. They also became centers of early and informal forms of venture finance. Andrew Mellon actually relocated a number of the companies he invested in to Pittsburgh. The First Reset reinforced the position of those innovative centers and allowed them to leapfrog over others to become among the largest and wealthiest cities in the United States.

The First Reset also saw major advances in transportation infrastructure. By the 1830s and 1840s, the first mass transit systems were moving people around some of the world's biggest cities. Early incarnations of what we now know as buses, called "omnibuses," essentially big horse-drawn stagecoaches, charged low fares and ran along fixed routes. More efficient horse-drawn streetcars running along fixed steel rails could carry more passengers and required less horse-power—literally. San Francisco's cable cars were the first successful effort to replace horses as the primary mode of transportation. Introduced in 1873 by Andrew Smith Hallidie, cable cars latched onto a steam-powered cable running between the rails, which would then pull the cars along the route. By the 1880s and 1890s, cable cars were moving people around San Francisco, Chicago, and other big cities. Writing in 1888, Harriet Harper declared, "If anyone should ask me what I consider the most distinctive, progressive feature of California, I should answer promptly, its cable-car system. And it is not alone; its system which seems to have reached a point of perfection, but the amazing length of the ride that is given you for the chink of a nickel."[14] In 1888, an Edison protégé, Frank Sprague, installed a complete system of electric streetcars in Richmond, Virginia. And thereafter cities across the country turned to electric-powered streetcars, which were dubbed "trolleys."[15]

Rudimentary systems like these were in place prior to the 1873 crisis. The railroad was developing, and there were early water and sewer systems in some large cities. But those systems expanded enormously during the resetting period of the Long Depression. That crisis, notes Mokyr, "turned the large technological system from an exception to a commonplace."[16] And as the next chapter will show, the new infrastructure systems would come together to drive the growth of much bigger cities, establishing the spatial fix that would help unleash the power of the industrial machine.

This kind of hard, physical infrastructure is one thing, but there is another type of infrastructure, another large-scale systems' innovation that is crucial to Great Resets: education and the infrastructure that supports it. The vision of large-scale public education in America dates back to Thomas Jefferson; Pennsylvania provided free universal education as early as 1834, and Massachusetts and New York established public school systems in the 1850s. But up until the First Reset, public school systems varied widely by location, and long-term schooling was still the province of the wealthy. By the 1870s, the burgeoning factory system created a much greater demand for mass public education, which would help provide the growing class of factory workers with basic reading, writing, and arithmetic skills and provide the discipline and socialization required of them. This new demand for literacy was made more urgent by the massive influx of foreign immigrants into those factories. The 1880s saw the rise of John Dewey and the Progressive Education movement, and by the turn of the century mass public education was commonplace in America's cities. The number of days per year an American child spent in public school education more than doubled from 1870 to 1950, rising from 78 to 157.[17]

Factory workers required just the basics and typically went no further than elementary school, but higher education was required for the growing ranks of administrative and professional workers. The federal government helped expand higher education with the Morrill Acts of 1862 and 1890, which established the system of great state land-grant universities—by essentially providing federal land to the states for higher education. College enrollments grew from 63,000 to 238,000 students between 1870 and 1900.[18]

The First Reset saw the rise of large-scale engineering education. Industrial capitalism needed bright, well-trained engineers to help make its factories run as well as to create new innovations. MIT was founded as Boston Tech in 1865 but established its first course in electrical engineering in 1882. Purdue was established in 1874, Case Western Reserve in 1880, and Georgia Tech in 1888. The number of engineering schools grew from just 6 in 1862 to 126 by 1917, and the number of engineering graduates grew from 100 in 1870 to 4,300 at the outbreak of World War I.[19]

It was more than individual innovations that powered the First Reset, but rather the combination of innovations into broader systems. This resetting period engendered new kinds of infrastructure—from electric power and transportation to mass public education—that set the stage for a new round of prosperity and growth, one that could fully harness the productive power of industrial capitalism. These new infrastructure systems generated broad productivity improvements and fundamentally changed the way we live and work, giving rise to massive industrial cities—the spatial fix of the First Reset.

Chapter Three

Urbanism as Innovation

magine living in the mid–nineteenth century. Whether in Europe or in North America, people overwhelmingly lived in the countryside, on a small farm, or in a small town. The typical family grew most of its own food and raised its own livestock, taking whatever surplus it might generate to the nearest market town for sale or barter. The cities of the period were small, even tiny, by today's standards, no more than a few miles around and all but the very largest housing perhaps 50,000 or 100,000 people. In the 1860s, eight of ten people in the United States lived in rural areas, with less than 20 percent living in urban centers.[1] America's five largest cities, all along the East Coast, were New York, with 813,000 people; Philadelphia, with 565,000; Brooklyn, with 266,000; Baltimore, home to 212,000; and Boston, with 177,000. The future great industrial cities of Pittsburgh, Cleveland, and Detroit each held less than 50,000 people.[2] When the economic crisis of 1873 hit, not a single American city was home to a million people.

Great Resets are defined not just by innovation but by massive movements of people. Such shifts of people are essential to creating a new, more productive landscape. During the First Reset, as the last chapter has shown, major industries such as railroads, petroleum, and steel were consolidated, new industries and new systems innovations took shape, and the way was paved for a period of remarkable industrial growth. By the turn of the twentieth century, the economic landscape was also transformed.[3] Between 1870 and 1900, the populations of urban areas exploded. New York City's population more than tripled, rising from 942,000 to 3.4 million people. Philadelphia expanded from 550,000 to 1.3 million people, and Chicago swelled from 300,000 to 1.3 million. Manufacturing employment in these three cities grew by 245 percent over the same period.[4] The period also saw the rise of a new set of massive industrial cities. Pittsburgh grew from 86,000 people in 1870 to more than 320,000 in 1900; Detroit from 79,000 to 285,000; Cleveland from 92,000 to 382,000. Across the nation, the number of Americans living in urban areas surged by more than 20 million, as the share of the population counted as urban rose from 25 to 40 percent.

O f course, civilization is about people, not just technologies, industries, and places. Great Resets also involve major population shifts, especially in the clustering of what we now refer to as talent or human capital. These are times when talent flows out of some places and into others. In the case of the First Reset, this included everyone from migrating farmers and immigrants looking for better work to inventors and entrepreneurs seeking new places to launch their enterprises. These talent Resets thus shift the balance of power among cities and regions as well as among nations. Locations rise or fall based on their ability to attract, retain, and productively use talent of all sorts—from brilliant innovators to unskilled laborers.

While Resets push some regions to the fore, others decline. Growing regions grab hold of new technology and attract new talent. But as these leading regions grow and evolve, some eventually fall victim to what the late economist Mancur Olson called "institutional sclerosis."[5] Committed to old behaviors and social systems, old technologies, and, even more important, outmoded and hard-to-change institutions, organizations, and business practices, they are either too slow or literally unable to change. This is what stymied growth in many of the early manufacturing cities, such as Paterson, New Jersey, the mill towns of Massachusetts and upstate New York, and older

Rust Belt cities in our time. It's why, Olson argued, new technologies and new economic systems so often arise in locations that were previously less prominent. In this way, economic Resets provide the jolt that hastens these geographic shifts.

The First Reset drew people from far beyond the United States. The turn of the twentieth century also saw great waves of immigration. This is the time my own grandparents migrated from southern Italy through Ellis Island and ultimately to Newark, New Jersey. During this period, between 1881 and 1930 to be exact, 27.6 million immigrants came to America.[6] Immigrants made up a greater share of the population—14 percent—than they do today. Hailing primarily from Italy, Austria-Hungary, Russia, and Eastern Europe, they manned America's factories and in many cases were the moving entrepreneurial force behind those businesses, such as Andrew Carnegie, the Scottish steel magnate; Adolphus Busch, the German-born brewer; and Joseph Pulitzer, the Hungarian-born newspaper giant, to name just a few.[7]

For the great majority of the huddled masses getting off ships in the port cities of the east, there was enough employment close at hand in the nearby manufacturing centers that only a small fraction kept pushing on to the relatively empty farmlands of the American breadbasket. By 1890, immigrants made up more than 40 percent of the population in eight of the country's fifty largest cities, including New York, Chicago, and Detroit.[8] These immigrants not only helped swell the populations of the growing urban centers but brought with them cultures and lifestyles that contributed vastly to transforming the character of those regions (think opera and pizza, hot dogs and polka). As the conditions of the First Reset settled into daily reality, the great cities of America became vibrant meccas, drawing new residents from both within and outside the country.

Great industrial cities not only grew larger; as their boundaries expanded, they also became more complex, with distinct areas for work and homes and different residential areas for workers, managers and professionals, and capitalists. Before the First Reset, cities were extremely compact. Most city dwellers tended to live where they worked: craftsmen and artisanal producers lived on top of or close to their shops, lawyers and doctors used their homes as offices. Pubs and cafés became neighborhood social centers or meeting places for subcommunities within large and diverse urban populations, a purpose they still serve today. New transportation systems—trolleys, streetcars, subways, and early commuter trains—enabled cities to expand. Average travel speeds doubled from four miles an hour in 1850 to eight miles an hour in 1900.[9] As improved transportation allowed people to live ever further from the centers of employment, the lifestyle of the average worker began to evolve. The now-common distinction between home and work, for example, is a direct product of the spatial fix of this period. For increasing numbers of people, gone were the days when your house was but one part of the complex that included your barn, your fields, your stables, or your orchards. If your job was in a factory or in some retail concern in the city, "work" was now a place to go to, a separate world outside the home. Cities became more differentiated into areas for working, living, and shopping. Driving this evolution was the rise of the factory as the center of economic life. "The main elements in this new urban complex," wrote the fabled urbanist Lewis Mumford, "were the factory, the railroad and the slum. . . . The factory became the nucleus of this new organism. Everything else was subordinate to it."[10]

Early factories were concentrated in and around the core of the city. But as the scale of production grew larger, some moved to the outskirts of towns where larger plots of land could be assembled. Pittsburgh's steel industry, for example, developed along its three great rivers. Boston's shoe, machinery, and textile producers spread out as well into a series of suburban industrial districts. Ever-expanding factories pushed the boundaries of the city farther and farther outward in city after city, from Philadelphia to Baltimore, Buffalo to Cleveland, and elsewhere. If industrial factories had previously been "close enough to the centre to be confused for a single manufacturing core," write the geographers Richard Walker and Robert Lewis, "by the turn of the century, urbanization had reached the metropolitan scale." By the late nineteenth century, they add, "the North American city had grown largely through the accretion of new industrial districts at the urban fringe."[11] The compact city of the past was turning into a farther-flung and more sprawling metropolis.

The city was also being reshaped internally. At it expanded out-ward, the industrial city began to divide up into separate districts and different types of neighborhoods, increasingly segregated by class. More affluent groups—including the growing ranks of the managerial class—fled the congestion and pollution of the center city, moving outward to the suburbs springing up along the streetcar lines.[12] Workers were crammed into tenement housing surrounding the factories where they worked. The center of the city—its business district—began to change too. Once a hurly-burly area filled with factories, shops, and stores, the city reorganized itself as these ac-tivities started to physically separate from one another. Department stores arose in the heart of the city, and self-contained shopping dis-tricts emerged. Zoning codes were eventually developed to segment land uses and protect upscale shopping districts from encroaching on factories.

With this major shift in the location and working lives of the pop-ulation came significant changes in lifestyle and consumption—the rise of a new way of life. Days and weeks were more clearly delineated into work time and home time. Leisure time was now a more common phenomenon for many, part of every day and not relegated merely to Sundays. This was, perhaps, the birth of the hallowed "weekend." And, of course, new forms of entertainment, many of them fueled by technological advances, arose to fill that time. Lodges and dance halls, billiard parlors and entertainment arcades sprang up across the country. Crowds flocked to nickelodeons and the thrilling new movie houses. Professional sports leagues and other spectacles attracted thousands of paying customers to stadiums and arenas. Baseball be-came "America's pastime." Attendance at games increased from 3 mil-lion in 1900 to 9.6 million by 1920. Amateur sports associations such as bicycling clubs and softball leagues took off even faster. Beginning in the 1890s, membership in everything from church clubs and sports leagues to fraternal organizations and civic associations grew rapidly.[13] The then-novel concepts of distinct leisure time and of entertainment outside the home took solid hold as the ever-denser population centers became destinations not just for employment but for culture and entertainment.

Ironically, some of the amazing new labor-saving inventions and innovations of this period actually added to the burden of work in the home, mostly for the women of the time. Geographer Roger Miller examines the effect of the vacuum cleaner on women's work in the home. "In short, standards became more stringent as the means for meeting them became generally available," he writes. "Thus the ability to wash clothes more efficiently did not mean that the wash would be done in less time; it meant that the same clothes could be washed more frequently. The Hoover brought the rug out of the attic, where it was stored between social events, and put it down permanently to be trampled and vacuumed every week. Women had to rationalize their schedules with those of the new machines they tended."[14] We tend to look back at this moment in history and see images of suffragettes, of women gaining independence and claiming their rightful place in society, but in truth, many women found themselves increasingly tied to the home by the very trappings of modern life that should have liberated them.

This new more urban lifestyle spurred changing consumption patterns. In 1874, the average family spent 56 percent of its budget on food; by 1901 this number had fallen to 47 percent. (It would decline considerably further during the Great Depression and Second Reset.) This shift opened up the space for the beginnings of a consumer society. By the turn of the twentieth century, the U.S. government added three new categories to its survey of household spending—home furnishings, health care, and recreation, which now stood alongside the traditional ones of food, shelter, and clothing.[15] This is another key feature of Great Resets: they bring about shifts in consumption that fuel rising industries.

This new way of life suited the spatial fix and helped propel an era of renewed expansion and growth, completing a proverbial circle of growth by providing new outlets for increased inventiveness and improved productivity. The factories were humming, and the new population living in larger and larger cities generated a demand for the goods being produced. Times were good, at least for a while, until the cycle reasserted itself in the next major crisis: the Great Depression.

Chapter Four

The Most Technologically Progressive Decade

T
he specter of the Great Depression of the 1930s hovers over us to this day. It's difficult to read today's headlines about the bankruptcies of once-great corporations, whether they are venerable investment banks or automobile companies, and not feel haunted by the stock market crash of 1929 and the subsequent bank failures that wiped out both personal and corporate wealth—some 9 million Americans saw their savings simply evaporate—and brought the economy to a standstill.[1]

In fact, there was quite a lot about the economic landscape on the eve of the 1929 stock market crash that we today would find eerily familiar. Picture Jay Gatsby and his cronies, decked out in tuxedos while cavorting in opulent seaside homes filled with the latest consumer enticements. By the end of the 1920s, vast fortunes had been made through risky investment instruments and wild real estate speculation. The gap between the middle class and the super-rich was widening, with an ever-increasing percentage of overall wealth in the hands of a privileged few. The nation was sitting on a huge bubble not unlike the one that burst in 2008.

The similarities extend even to the terms we use to describe these times. We refer to the current crisis as the Great Recession, because it sounds a lot less bad than depression. Herbert Hoover latched onto the term "depression" because it was less alarmist than terms such as "panic" and "crisis," which had been used to describe previous crises.[2] Whatever it is called, the great crash of the 1930s brought on a period of tremendous hardship, and images of breadlines, huddled masses, Hoovervilles, and hobos are powerfully etched in our collective memory.

It's hard to imagine, but this period also sparked a period of far-reaching and dramatic technological innovation. The economic historian Alexander Field concludes that the 1930s were the "most technologically progressive" decade of the twentieth century.[3] Its technological dynamism, according to Field, outpaced even the great high-tech revolution of more recent times. I believe that the innovative outburst of the 1930s was absolutely comparable to that of the Long Depression in terms of its profound impact on the nature and structure of capitalism.

Not that it felt that way to anyone living through those dark times. The zeitgeist of the period was one of panic in the face of economic decline and "secular stagnation," to borrow from the language that the Harvard economist and adviser of Franklin D. Roosevelt, Alvin Hansen, used to describe the tendency of the economy to stay depressed as people save money, even hoard it, rather than buy and invest in a manner that might create jobs or otherwise increase the general economic health. By the late 1930s, Hansen argued that secular stagnation had permanently paralyzed the American economy. It would never grow rapidly again, he believed, because all the ingredients for growth, including technological innovation and population growth, had been exhausted, and deficit spending by the government was the only way out.

The Great Depression set the stage for the Second Great Reset. Just as Hansen and others were advancing this theory and capturing the attention of policy makers and the public, his Harvard colleague Joseph Schumpeter was developing his own, more accurate assessment of the role of innovation in overcoming economic crises. Schumpeter, notes Field, had a much "better fix on what was going on. He developed his homage to the power of creative destruction against the backdrop of what has turned out to be the most technologically dynamic epoch of the twentieth century."[4]

Field's contention about the innovativeness of the Second Reset is based on detailed and meticulous research. Delving deeply into the statistical record, he tracks trends in innovation and in total factor productivity over the entire twentieth century, and examines in detail the rise of specific new technologies. "Total factor productivity" is a term economists use to describe the output of production not attributable to the amount of inputs used in production, which is to say that it reflects efficiency—how well the available inputs are used in production. Total factor productivity, Field finds, grew fastest during the Depression years, when it increased at a rate of 2.3 percent annually. This rate was better than both the "boom years" of the twenties—when productivity grew at a 2 percent annual clip—and the golden era of postwar expansion, the years spanning 1948 to 1973, when productivity grew at 1.9 percent annually. Field shows how the tremendous innovativeness of the Depression era—and not other factors, such as a substitution of higher- for lower-skilled workers—fueled those productivity gains.

Field even argues that the 1930s were more innovative than the recent high-tech boom of the 1990s. Productivity grew during the Great Depression at a rate roughly three times greater than during that latter-day period. His detailed analysis shows that productivity growth during the 1990s was confined to a narrow group of high-tech industries such as semiconductors, communications and computers, logistics and transportation, and securities. "This technical advance," he writes, "although undeniably dramatic in many ways, was more localized and smaller in aggregate impact than what took place in the 1930s." The 1990s high-tech boom was more fiction than reality, Field argues, "with spiraling equity of the 1990s propelled by human fallibility and one of the most formidable marketing machines ever assembled." The conclusion that the 1930s were a period of unparalleled innovation is supported by the economists Michelle Alexopoulus and Jon Cohen, whose careful analysis of publications about new technologies solidly backs up Field's claims.[5]

What accounted for these achievements in the face of such economic adversity? For starters, the Second Reset, like the First Reset before it, saw massive improvements in economic efficiency. Advances in machinery and the introduction of modern assembly lines generated huge economies of scale. Power generation improved, and companies got better at capturing and using what before had been wasted energy. Parts that previously had been made of wood or flimsy metals were replaced by better ones made of new metal alloys or new plastics that were more resilient, lasted longer, and could do bigger jobs. Better motors and instruments improved efficiency and saved both capital and labor. Older factories that were based on multistory buildings near the city center were replaced by bigger ones laid out on one floor that were better suited to long assembly lines. Together, these sorts of innovations created the new, ever-more-powerful system of Fordist mass production, named after Henry Ford, who introduced it, which combined Frederick Taylor's scientific management with assembly-line technology to bring about a quantum leap in economic productivity. Productivity growth during the Depression, Field adds, was "characterized by advances across a broader frontier of the economy," spurred by technological and organizational improvements in a wide range of manufacturing industries, combined with advances in transportation and communication and gains in utilities and wholesale and retail distribution.

Research and development expanded significantly during the Second Reset. Although many see it as an easy target during budget cutbacks, spending on research and development actually doubled over the course of the 1930s. More research and development labs were opened in the first four years of the Depression than in the entire preceding decade—seventy-three compared to sixty-six. The number of people employed in research and development quadrupled, increasing from fewer than 7,000 in 1929 to nearly 28,000 by 1940, during a period of double-digit employment overall. Spending on research and development doubled over the course of the 1930s.[6]

The Second Reset also brought about the enormous upgrading and expansion of America's educational infrastructure. More and more Americans attended public school and more completed high school, with the percentage of high school graduates increasing from around

20 percent to more than 50 percent between 1920 and 1950.[7] While it was common for teenagers during the Depression to leave elementary school to go to work, after the Second World War a high school education became the norm. Colleges and universities similarly blossomed in the Second Reset. The G.I. Bill provided tuition assistance for returning veterans to attend college. After the Second World War, the federal government created the National Science Foundation and committed enormous sums of funding to university-based scientific research. The National Defense Education Act, passed in the wake of *Sputnik*, provided new federal funding for math and science education. In 1940, about 500,000 Americans attended college, about 15 percent of their age group. By 1960, however, college enrollment expanded to more than 3.5 million, exploding to more than 7.5 million by 1970, 40 percent of all college-age adults. Twenty years later, the number was closer to 17 million.[8]

The United States and other advanced nations had learned a critical lesson: that a skilled and talented workforce is a cornerstone of economic competitiveness. Spirit, drive, and a willingness to work would no longer be enough. Inquisitiveness and analysis, knowledge and invention were the necessary tools of the modern world. That same imperative exists today, and a transformation in our educational priorities as profound as that of the Second Reset is critical to the long-term health of our economy.

By the time the United States entered the Second World War, the essential components of the Second Reset were in place. The massive, well-oiled manufacturing machine was stoked and manned; a new and expanded system of education was in place. At the close of the war, society was primed for the last piece of the Reset puzzle, to reshape itself once more with the suburban spatial fix.

Chapter Five

▦

Suburban Solution

When my father was a boy in the 1920s and 1930s, his immigrant parents made almost everything they ate from scratch; my grandmother did the wash—for nine people—by hand with a scrub board and a clothesline. Their humble apartment had a simple stove but lacked a refrigerator, never mind a toaster or a washing machine. The Second Reset changed all that. The period saw a massive diffusion of new home technologies. While consumer spending on big ticket items like houses and new cars fell drastically, just the opposite occurred with smaller household appliances, as Megan McArdle shows in an essay for the *Atlantic*. "In 1926, 20 percent of American households had radios," she writes. "That figure reached 50 percent in 1929—and 75 percent two years later, in the depths of the Depression. Refrigerators were in 20 percent of households in 1932 and 50 percent in 1938."[1] A new way of life was slowly emerging, creating new sources of demand for new products.

The 1920s are often referred to as the Jazz Age, when people rushed to embrace anything and everything that smacked of modernism, from telephones and airplanes to wailing trumpets and pounding drums, relaxed sexual mores, and even radical politics. The onset of the Great Depression brought with it a retrenchment, not just economically but in terms of social behavior and cultural development. With no cash in their pockets and grim prospects for the future, young people saw little chance to marry, establish a home, or start a family. Marriage and childbirth rates declined significantly in the 1930s. Even casual dating seemed problematic. Marriage might have been out of the question, but young men and women will do what they have always done, and at the height of the Depression, there could have been no more disastrous news than an unexpected pregnancy.

Social historians have noted that during these years, people returned to entertainments inside the home. The vibrant nightlife of the 1920s faded rather quickly into memory as families began spending more and more time together. "Families gardened and used their backyards more (the 1930s saw a renaissance in badminton); in the evenings they gathered around the radio, worked on jigsaw puzzles (another 1930s craze), played cards and, of course, Monopoly (an irony-heavy product of the Depression)," writes Benjamin Schwarz in a recent review of the social and cultural impacts of the Great Crash. "And—that free and quintessentially homebody activity— they read. Between 1929, the last year of the boom, and 1933, the nadir of the Depression, Muncie's public library circulation more than doubled, as did the average number of books each patron borrowed."[2]

My grandparents took great pride in their radio and Victrola, an early crank phonograph. My grandfather would place the speaker in the window so that his relatives and neighbors could listen to the great opera star Enrico Caruso or *Major Bowes' Amateur Hour*, on which young Frank Sinatra got his start, or a heavyweight boxing championship. My grandparents' family was part of a much larger group of Depression-era radio purchasers. As it turns out, "radio boasts the second-shortest interval between introduction and adoption by 75 percent of U.S. households," McArdle writes, "topped only by the black-and-white television, even though radio completed the last third of that journey during a major financial crisis." Radios were a big-ticket item for Depression era families like my father's, costing $133 on average at a time when the average American produced just $850 worth of goods or economic output annually. Still, McArdle notes, it was a smart purchase. Families bought radios because they offered tremendous entertainment value for the dollar. The radio could in effect substitute for a wide range of other activities, from concerts and sporting events to newspapers and movies. Amortized over time, it provided cheap entertainment.

The Great Depression did more than destroy wealth and eliminate jobs, according to Schwarz; it destroyed expectations for the future. "The defining characteristic of the middle classes has always been their orientation toward the future," writes Schwarz. "The Depression ruined schemes for such baubles and pleasures as the new car and the winter vacation. But it also at best disrupted and at worst (and often) destroyed carefully wrought plans for so-called investments in the future: the substantial house in the stable neighborhood, the savings account, and, most important, what was then and remains the cynosure of American middle- and professional-class family life—a college education, or a certain kind of college education, for the children. . . . Disaster was always imminent; the future was at best chancy and diminished."

Families pulled together and became working units. Children took on adult responsibilities. "Half of all boys in one survey had part-time jobs, and both girls and boys took on more household chores," notes Schwarz. "Whether or not they worked outside the home, these children believed they had productive roles to perform for the family's betterment, and saw the Depression as a family problem they had to help face—an attitude that pulled them ever more strongly into the family circle." It took every member of the household, adults and children alike, to scrape together the living wage of one person and keep the family afloat. As often as not, that group effort extended beyond the immediate household. How many of us have grown up hearing about the old neighborhood of their parents' or grandparents' generation: aunts and uncles and cousins and grandparents living up and down the block or around the corner, all part of a unified support system. That, however, would change with the new economic geography of the Second Reset, as more and more people moved away from these dense and cohesive enclaves to find more privacy and freedom—their private piece of the dream in the new suburbs.

■ ■ ■

S uburbanization had actually begun in the first few decades of the
century. As electrical power grids, along with rail and streetcar
lines, extended beyond old city limits, construction and population
followed. Street and road systems grew as well, as did auto production. The number of registered cars exploded from just 8,000 in 1900
to more than 20 million by the late 1920s, and the number of trucks
increased from virtually none to more than 3 million over the same
period. And though thousands and thousands of people lost their
homes during the Great Depression, the share of Americans owning
their own homes actually increased from 27 percent in the late teens
to 30 percent at the height of the Depression.[3]

The Roosevelt administration sought ways to ease the path to
home ownership for average working Americans. The Federal Housing Administration was set up to guarantee more affordable long-term
mortgages, and it was followed by the Federal National Mortgage
Association—Fannie Mae—to ensure that funds were available to
mortgage lenders. Not only were houses becoming available, but the
money to purchase them was within reach.[4]

With the war effort of the early 1940s, the great manufacturing
engine kicked into high gear and so was primed to keep pumping out
goods in peacetime. And though the captains of industry were nervous
that the end of the war would see the return to a depressed economy,
any number of government actions helped sustain consumption—and
prosperity. Whereas young men a decade earlier had feared the financial
burdens of marriage and family, returning veterans found they had access to college, unemployment insurance, business loans, and mortgage
guarantees through the G.I. Bill and the Veterans Administration.

Even without all that assistance, workers after the war found their
lot in life greatly improved. The Wagner Act, passed during the Depression years, prohibited unfair labor practices and gave workers the
rights to organize and bargain collectively. Its passage helped spur
wage increases as the economy recovered, especially in the years after
World War II. My father told me that before the war, his factory job

was low paying, but when he got home after the fighting, he found that he had a good job with decent pay and benefits, which enabled him to buy a house and a car and send his sons—my brother, Robert, and me—to college.

Another significant factor in the suburban boom, of course, was the spreading of roads and highways in the years after the war. The Defense Highways Act of 1956, which provided funds for more than forty thousand miles of new roads across the country, expanded the opportunity to develop new housing and new communities that could be reached through the use of the automobile. The number of cars on the road exploded from roughly 20 million in the 1930s to more than 60 million in 1960 and more than 100 million by the early 1970s. And the average speed for moving people and goods surged from eight miles an hour in 1900 to twenty-four miles an hour in 1950.[5]

The Second Reset was propelled by rising home ownership. Home ownership became a cornerstone of economic life primarily because decades of policy put it there. No longer was owning a home something just for affluent Americans; now it became something available to the ranks of the working and middle classes. For much of U.S. history, odds were you did not own the home you lived in unless you were a farmer. The percentage of Americans owning their home increased from 27 percent before 1920 to 45 percent by 1950, reaching more than 60 percent during the 1960s—the exact year my working-class parents bought a suburban home of their own.[6] For my immigrant grandparents and their peers, the American Dream meant one thing: economic opportunity. But the Second Reset redefined and broadened that dream, making owning your own home a central part of it.

Most of all, home ownership radically transformed the way people consume. The amount of money the average family spent for food fell from almost half at the turn of the twentieth century to a third in 1950 and less than a fifth by the mid-1980s. Spending on basic needs—that is, food, shelter, and clothing combined—declined from more than three-quarters of family budgets at the turn of the century to less than half by 1960. With the economy humming and wages rising, immense tranches of income suddenly came free to be spent on the products of the assembly line. Spending on home furnishings and equipment increased from 4 percent during the Depression to 7 percent in 1950, while vehicle expenses climbed from around 5 percent to 12 percent in 1950 over the same period, before reaching almost a quarter of family spending by 1970.[7]

B efore the Great Depression, in 1920, nearly half of the U.S. population lived on farms or in rural areas. By the close of the crisis, in 1950, nearly two-thirds of Americans lived in cities and their surrounding suburbs, climbing to three-quarters by 1970. America was becoming a suburban nation. In 1910, just 7 percent of the population lived in suburbs. Central cities and suburbs then grew rapidly alongside each other until the stock market crashed. Suburban growth surged during the Second Reset. From 1940 onward, suburbs grew considerably faster than cities, and by the early 1960s, the population of suburbanites exceeded that living in cities.[8]

This period also saw the decline of many inner cities, from Newark and Philadelphia to St. Louis and Detroit, as more affluent, largely white residents fled older urban neighborhoods for the safety and comfort of suburbia. The abandonment and decay of so many of these once-great inner cities was a tragic development by any standard— one that was made worse by the ravages of government-sponsored urban renewal. I never got to see my father's boyhood home, which was demolished in one of Newark's major urban renewal projects. But the growth of the suburbs stretched out the boundaries of metropolitan areas. The city of Detroit exploded from some 40 square miles in 1910 to 139 square miles by 1950, not counting its rapidly growing suburban rings, a fact that could be easily traced in the ascending names of its major roadways: Six Mile Road, Seven Mile Road, and Eight Mile Road, continuing on to Nine Mile Road, Ten Mile Road, and all the way to Eighteen Mile Road and beyond in the suburbs.

At first, many remained close to their roots in the new suburbs of their home cities, like my parents and aunts and uncles, who ended up in the new suburbs of Bellville, Montclair, the Oranges, North

Arlington, and other towns around Newark. As time went on, people started moving farther and farther out. As my cousins married and had families of their own, many moved considerably further out to newer developments in central and southern New Jersey.

Eventually, others ventured much farther afield to the booming areas of the Sunbelt, as the country turned its eyes to the south and west. In my own extended family, one of my father's sisters and her family made the trek to California. Between 1940 and 1983, the broad swath of territory referred to as the Sunbelt—stretching from coast to coast below the 37th parallel—increased its population by 112 percent. Together, the South and West accounted for two-thirds of all U.S. population growth in the twentieth century, with virtually all of it occurring since 1950.

Phoenix exemplifies the Sunbelt's rapid rise. Home to just 100,000 people in 1950, barely cracking the ranks of the country's hundred largest cities (it was ninety-ninth), it saw its population quadruple to 439,000 by 1960 and then almost double again to 789,000 in 1980, placing it among the ten largest American cities. Since 1950, five Sunbelt cities—Phoenix, San Diego, Houston, Dallas, and San Antonio—have displaced five northern ones—St. Louis, Boston, Baltimore, Cleveland, and Washington, D.C.—in the ranks of America's ten largest cities.

This shift led a major study by the U.S. Census Bureau to conclude: "One of the most significant demographic trends of the twentieth century has been the steady shifting of the population south and west."[9] In 1900, the majority of Americans—62 percent—lived in the Northeast and Midwest. By 2000, the majority (58 percent) resided in the South and West. When you map it out, the mean center of gravity of the U.S. population has shifted 324 miles west and 101 miles south over the past century.[10]

Much has been made of the great suburban and Sunbelt migrations of the postwar years, but it continues to bear closer examination, exemplifying the role of the spatial fix in an economic reset.

Chapter Six

The Fix Is In

T he hit television show *Mad Men*, which debuted in 2007, paints a fascinating and detailed portrait of the society produced by the Second Reset. Among other cultural phenomena, it chronicles the aggressiveness with which the new suburban dream was packaged and pounded into the collective unconscious. None of those new homes was considered complete without a television, still so novel and exciting that it was rarely turned off. And on that flickering screen— from *Father Knows Best* and *Ozzie and Harriet* in the fifties to *Leave It to Beaver* in the sixties and *The Brady Bunch* in the seventies—were safe and tidy domestic dramas, played out in pristine suburban homes on tree-lined streets. Naturally, the programming was underwritten by the very companies that made that lifestyle possible: Procter & Gamble and Hallmark, Philco and Maytag, Ford, General Motors and Shell Oil, and many, many others. All these factors came together in the fifties and sixties in an almost perfect storm of opportunity, driven by private investment and aggressive corporate opportunism, in tandem with timely adjustments to governmental policy. The economy came roaring back stronger than ever. The Second Reset, the roots of which were established during Roosevelt's New Deal, became reality only through the transformative power of suburbia—the spatial fix of the postwar era.

The idea of the spatial fix was first advanced by the geographer David Harvey in the mid-1970s "to describe capitalism's insatiable drive to resolve inner crises through spatial expansion and geographical restructuring." We're all familiar with the concept of a technological fix—the idea that not only technological problems but economic and social problems as well can be solved by new innovations and technological progress. Harvey argued that technological fixes are insufficient to solve economic crises and that the solution also always involves new patterns of real estate development and of economic geography broadly. The spatial fix effects a way out of crisis by creating a physical framework for development and further geographic expansion.[1] It thus "provides a way to productively soak up capital by transforming the geography of capitalism," adds the economic geographer Erica Schoenberger. The spatial fix induces massive investment in and expansion of infrastructure and the built environment, which effectively freezes "a significant tranche of accumulated capital in the earth, while using it to support the further accumulation of capital."[2]

Spatial fixes work for a while, but they are not permanent solutions; rather, they are part of an ongoing cycle. Spatial fixes initially overcome crises and channel capital into more productive uses. But eventually those spatial fixes reach their limit, and new bubbles appear and then burst, giving way to renewed cycles of growth, and the process repeats itself in a predictable cycle. We've all seen the results in our own time, when the collapse of the housing and mortgage market brought down the financial industry. It happened a century ago, in the period leading up to the crash of 1873, when shaky mortgages and other complex financial instruments led to economic and financial collapse. And it was a key factor in the crisis of 1929 and the Great Depression.

The 1920s saw a huge boom in industrial production, as companies such as Ford, General Motors, and General Electric helped power renewed economic expansion. But guess what was the biggest single contributor to the nation's total stock of capital and investment? Not companies, not railroads, not industrial buildings, but housing. Residential homes—mainly in the form of new developments—made up the largest single component of the nation's capital stock—factories, buildings, roads, and more—and its largest single source of net investment flows. Investment in everything from small apartment blocks and commercial buildings to early suburban subdivisions and Florida retirement communities surged during the decade. "White elephant apartment buildings, poorly located and with low occupancy rates, figure prominently in accounts of the boom, and were certainly a feature of the late 1920s," writes Alexander Field.[3] But 80 percent of this residential investment went into one- to four-family structures.

The problem went beyond rising prices and declining affordability, which played their roles. There was also the disconnect between the single-family housing construction boom and the infrastructure of the period, which from lax building codes and zoning ordinances to underdeveloped water and sewer systems, roads, and highways, simply could not support the housing that was being built. Some of the new construction was located too far away from urban hubs and transport connections; some simply lacked good utility hookups. The "urban system" was insufficiently developed to support the housing being built. And then the whole thing collapsed.

Spatial fixes take a long time to come together and an even longer time before they can reset the economy. Consider this startling set of facts. The bubble was so big in the 1920s that after it popped during the Great Depression, it would take twenty-two years for nonresidential construction investment to regain its pre-crash peak and twenty-four years for real spending on residential construction to recover to its pre-crisis highs, notes Field, the historian. Anyone who thinks we'll be able to reset the current housing market quickly needs to pay close attention to this.

In each and every case, we find that spatial fixes are key to Great Resets. It's a cycle that unveils itself in five distinct phases. In the first stage, as crisis sets in, old institutions break down and business and consumers cut back their spending. But eventually, in the second stage, new innovations emerge and begin to be introduced into the market. Third, those new technologies are forged together by entrepreneurs into bigger and better technological systems. As we get to the fourth stage, new public and private investments in energy, transportation, and communication infrastructure provide the broad skeleton of a new economic landscape and increase the speed and velocity of urban life. Ultimately, in the fifth stage, a new spatial fix emerges, creating a new economic landscape that is more closely in sync with the improved productive capacities of the underlying economy. This provides nothing less than the physical representation of a new way of life, unleashing powerful new kinds of consumption that can power economic growth.

Though spatial fixes can and do shape the rise of a new economic system, they are, by nature, *temporary* solutions. They work for a time but ultimately come up against their own limits. And then the cycle starts over again. As is the case today.

Chapter Seven

Unraveling

N ow, we all know what it feels like to live through the bursting of a huge economic and financial bubble. We can literally feel the demise of the old suburban way of life all around us. But how exactly did it come to this?

Others have chronicled the financial shenanigans and policy blunders that led to the collapse of Lehman Brothers and the onset of the economic and financial crisis. But, to a surprising degree, the causes of the crash are also geographic in nature. The bursting bubble that sparked this crisis signaled a system of economic organization and spatial fix long past its sell-by date. Suburbanization worked well for a time. The lifestyle that played out on millions of television screens was much more than a cultural phenomenon; it made people's lives better and did much to keep the engines of American mass production humming. Though we've come to think of suburbs as dull and homogeneous, many of the bland "organization men" whom William Whyte wrote about actually came out of traditional communities and ethnic neighborhoods. Families walked away from environments where neighbors and relatives knew everyone's business in pursuit of a freer, more cosmopolitan life in the then-new suburbs.

The cities of the early and mid–twentieth century were dirty, smelly, and crowded, while commuting from the first, close-in suburbs was fast and easy. As manufacturing became more technologically stable and product lines matured during the postwar boom, suburban growth dovetailed nicely with the pattern of industrial growth. Business began opening new plants in greenfield locations that featured cheaper land and labor; management saw no reason to continue making now-standardized products in the expensive urban locations where they'd first been developed and sold. Work was outsourced to the suburbs and the emerging areas of the Sunbelt, whose connections to bigger cities by the highway system enabled rapid, low-cost distribution. This process brought the Sunbelt economies, which had lagged behind since the Civil War, into modern times and sustained a long boom for the United States as a whole.

At the very center of the great golden era was the rise of home ownership as the ultimate middle-class aspiration. For the generation of penny-pinchers raised during the Great Depression, policies that encouraged home buying through easy credit were sensible enough, as they allowed the economy to grow faster. The dream of owning a sub-urban home of your own encompassed so much more than comfortable shelter; the house represented a better life with more personal freedom to be who you wanted to be and to raise your family as you saw fit. But for ensuing generations, born into relative prosperity and raised in a culture of seemingly risk-free credit, a house came to seem both an entitlement and an investment vehicle. By 2004, at the height of the boom and of President George W. Bush's ownership society, almost seven in ten American families owned their home. For many, owning a home came to be not just an end in itself but a means to quick financial gain. Innovations in finance such as adjustable-rate mortgages and securitized subprime loans expanded home ownership further, kept demand high, and turned the family home into a sort of personal bank. During the bubble years, Americans extracted on average about twenty-five to thirty cents on the dollar of home value or home equity value from their homes, which they used to pay for home improvements and to fuel consumption. And with home prices climbing so steeply over such a prolonged period, most people saw their homes as among the easiest, most lucrative investments they could make.[1]

As the real estate frenzy took hold, more and more people started speculating in real estate. Just as the promise of capturing dotcom profits fueled the tech bubble, all sorts of people jumped into the real estate game with both feet, seeing the chance to get in and get out fast, flipping properties for quick profit. In places such as Miami and Las Vegas, it seemed that every hairdresser, masseuse, and waiter owned a condo—or several; people such as the Miami resident Rula Giosmas, featured in a segment of *60 Minutes*, who said she had bought six properties in five years as investments, financing all of them with adjustable-rate mortgages. When the market turned, she found herself catastrophically underwater. Giosmas confessed that she had been too busy to read the paperwork. "My full-time job is, I'm an acupuncturist. So this is just a side thing."[2] The real question is, who in their right mind would have lent her the money to make those purchases?

On one level, the crisis has demonstrated what we've all known for a long time: Americans have been living beyond their means for years, using illusory housing wealth, the easy credit peddled by retailers and credit card companies, and huge slugs of foreign capital to consume far more than their incomes should have allowed and far more than we've produced. The crash has presumably signaled the end to that; the adjustment, though painful, is necessary.

However, another crucial aspect of the crisis has been largely overlooked, and it might ultimately prove more important. Because people's tendency to overconsume and undersave was intimately intertwined with the postwar spatial fix—with housing, suburbanization, and the countless forms of consumption they create—the economy became horribly distorted. These imbalances showed up in everything from how we choose where to live to how we invest our money.

In the three decades spanning 1980 through 2007, residential investment and consumer spending in the United States rose from two-thirds to three-quarters of gross domestic product, or GDP. The debt burden faced by families skyrocketed. In 1960, the ratio of personal debt to disposable income was about 55 percent, according to a study by the Federal Reserve Bank of San Francisco.[3] It rose to 65 percent by the mid-1980s. From that point on, however, personal leverage literally exploded, reaching an all-time high of 133 percent in 2007. The total of outstanding personal debt reached a mind-boggling $5.3

trillion in March 2009. The money had to come from somewhere: as people spent more than they produced, the country's current-account balance went from a slight surplus of 0.4 percent of GDP in 1980 to a deficit of almost 6 percent by 2006. This buying and credit binge left the United States critically dependent on foreign funds, especially from China, creating enormous imbalances on a global scale.[4]

Ultimately, the suburban solution came smack up against its own internal limits. The whole balance between industrial mass production and suburban mass consumption was thrown out of whack. This imbalance worsened as production was outsourced to emerging economies such as China, India, and others, where labor was much cheaper. Stagnating real wages for the middle and working classes meant less money to consume with. And low-wage workers in emerging economies certainly did not have the income to fill the gap. As the ranks of the rich and the super-rich grew ever richer, the imbalances grew ever worse. In 2007, the top 1 percent of all U.S. earners took home nearly a quarter of all income, continuing a three-decade increase. There are only so many luxury homes, German cars, Himalayan vacations, and aged single-malt whiskies the new rich can buy. Not only did economic inequality grow wider and wider, the incomes and purchasing power of the broad mass of Americans began a long decline. Between 2000 and 2008, according to Dartmouth economist Matthew Slaughter, just 2 percent of all American workers—those with a professional postgraduate degree such as doctors, lawyers, and MBAs—saw gains in their "mean real money income." Every other group, including college graduates and those with PhDs, saw their income decline.[5]

At the same time that they used credit to maintain their standard of living, Americans drew down whatever savings they had and then eventually stopped saving altogether. The rate of savings as a percentage of disposable income fell from a respectable 10 percent in the 1980s to close to zero by the mid-2000s. "The combination of higher debt and lower saving enabled personal consumption expenditures to grow faster than disposable income, providing a significant boost to U.S. economic growth over the period," the Federal Reserve Bank of San Francisco concluded. But, it added, "In the long run, however, consumption cannot grow faster than income because there is an upper limit to how much debt households can service, based on their incomes."[6] It's even more telling that the rate of personal bankruptcies went through the roof in the 1990s, and though it dropped by roughly half when the federal bankruptcy laws were revised in 2005, the rate began to climb again in the mid-2000s, hitting more than 40 percent in 2008 and rising an additional 35 percent in the first nine months of 2009.[7]

Almost a century ago, the Austrian economist Rudolf Hilferding identified this very fact as a fundamental contradiction of modern capitalism.[8] Capitalist economic development stands on a shaky foundation, he argued in his aptly titled *Finance Capital*. Workers always produce more than they can consume, more even than society as a whole can consume. Or, as the blogger Yves Smith at Naked Capitalism put it, "The US needs to wean itself of unsustainable overconsumption, and since consumption has come to depend on growth in indebtedness, a reversal, however painful, is necessary. Our excesses have been so great that there is no way out of this that does not lead to a general fall in living standards."[9]

A t a deeper level, the financial meltdown also signaled the rise of a new economic system broadly. The Long Depression was the crisis of the First Industrial Revolution. The massive growth and productivity of the textile, steel, and railroad industries could not be contained by the larger, mainly rural society of the period. The United States' spatial fix transformed it from a largely rural country dotted with trading centers and mill towns to a country of giant industrial cities that concentrated production, generated a great wave of innovation, and created a new way of life and a landscape of economic growth.

The Great Depression was the crisis of the Second Industrial Revolution. That crisis was brought on by the inability of early cities and early industrial society to contain the productive capabilities of the large-scale, mass production economy. Suburbanization was the spatial fix for the industrial age—the geographic expression of that economic model. Henry Ford's automobiles had been rolling off assembly lines since 1913. After making auto production cheaper and more efficient, Henry Ford realized that a bigger market for his assembly-line cars was needed, so he boosted workers' wages and introduced the "five-dollar day." But true Fordism, the combination of mass production and mass consumption, didn't emerge as a full-blown economic and social model until mass suburbanization—the spatial fix of post–World War II America.

Our own collapse, in the early years of the twenty-first century, is the crisis of the latest economic revolution—the rise of an idea-driven knowledge economy that runs more on brains than brawn. It reflects the limits of the suburban model of development to channel the full innovation and productive capabilities of the creative economy. The places that thrive today are those with the highest velocity of ideas, the highest density of talented and creative people, and the highest rate of metabolism. "Velocity" and "density" are not words that many people use when describing suburbia.

Due to its very nature, the pain of this recent economic crisis has been felt unevenly throughout the United States and the world. As the crisis spread outward from the financial crash in New York, it settled much more heavily on some places than on others. For each of the first eight months of 2008, every single one of the nation's 372 metropolitan regions saw its unemployment rate increase. But the burden of unemployment fell most heavily on older Rust Belt cities, devastated by the tremendous blow suffered by the manufacturing sector, and it also surged in sprawling Sunbelt metropolitan areas in the wake of the housing collapse.[10] Housing prices also plummeted as the bubble burst, falling by a third or more from their 2006 peak.[11] And while prices fell in virtually every city and region, again the brunt of the decline was felt in older Rust Belt cities and sprawling Sunbelt locations. The crisis accelerated and cast into concrete several trends that were already altering the economic landscape, marking the end of a chapter in economic history and, indeed, of a whole way of life. Over the next few chapters, I'll look at the factors that will likely determine the fates of many cities. I'll identify the places that have exhibited real resilience in the face of crisis and those that face more difficult circumstances.

Part II

REDRAWING THE ECONOMIC MAP

Chapter Eight

Capital of Capital

A t first glance, few cities would have seemed to be more obviously threatened by the crash than New York. The Big Apple shed nearly 100,000 jobs in the year following the financial crash, including more than 35,000 high-paying finance jobs. Its unemployment rate surged to more than 10 percent by September 2009, when more than 400,000 New Yorkers were out of work.[1] Its financial and insurance industry shrank for the first time in sixteen years. The spillover was horrendous. The city's tax revenues plummeted, forcing a curtailment of public services and creating obstacles to near-term economic growth. With their well-heeled clientele disappearing, countless small businesses, from restaurants to dry cleaners to health clubs, closed, meaning that even more jobs were lost.

Pundits around the world were ready—some almost eager—to see the sun set on New York's preeminence. "Farewell Wall Street, Hello Pudong?" began one article, suggesting that the world's financial capital was shifting from the marble-columned edifices of Manhattan to the more futuristic skyscrapers of Shanghai's business district.[2] Others said that New York was not alone on the slippery slope but would be joined by London. As Michael Lind of the New America Foundation put it, "New York, London, and other financial centers were heavily dependent on financial-sector profits," he argues, citing Frankfurt as another example. "Throw in the technology-driven collapse of the publishing and broadcast industries headquartered in such places, and those cities are likely to suffer devastating blows."[3] Lind sees a brighter future for cities such as Paris and Tokyo, which mix a significant governmental presence with banking and commerce. These, he says, will adjust better to the new era, that of the hybrid state-capitalist world. "Without the obscenely rich investment bankers and the legions of well-paid retainers who supported their lifestyles," he notes, "formerly flourishing parts of these former financial capitals may become as derelict as Detroit or the crumbling industrial towns of northern Britain and Germany's Ruhr region."

Lind paints a grim picture, but I'm not convinced he's right. In *Capitals of Capital*, the economic historian Youssef Cassis says that financial capitals, once established, "have incredible staying power."[4] Amsterdam, for instance, stood at the center of the world's financial system in the seventeenth century; its place was only taken by Paris and then London a couple of hundred of years later, in the early nineteenth century. It took another hundred years for New York to take over London's role in the twentieth. But even when a city declines as a global financial center, it never falls entirely off the map. Over time, Frankfurt, Amsterdam, Zurich, and others have played roles in finance—and they still do. In a 2009 ranking of global financial centers, London placed first, followed by New York, Singapore, Hong Kong, Zurich, Geneva, and Chicago. After all these years, Amsterdam still numbered among the world's top twenty-five financial centers.[5]

The rise of major financial centers correlates with the rise of the nation's economic power, but with a considerable time lag. Global financial centers rise to preeminence only after their nation's economic might has been well established. Amsterdam, London, and New York all gained the financial prominence following the rise of their national economies. In 1700, when Amsterdam ruled finance, the per capita income of Holland was 50 percent higher than that of England. By 1860, when England took the mantle, per capita income in England was more than twice as high as that of any other European country. By the middle of the twentieth century, America's economic output was twice that of all of Europe combined. Only then did New York take its place as the financial capital of the world. And there is a considerable lag between a nation's decline as an economic power and the eclipse of its global financial center. Although the United Kingdom lost its position to the United States as the world's largest economy in 1872 and the largest exporter in 1915, it was not until after two world wars and the Great Depression that New York unseated London as the world's financial center. Asia has likewise become an economic powerhouse, yet its major financial centers, most notably Tokyo, Hong Kong, and Singapore, have not yet come close to New York and London.

This is how it may remain for some time. In 2009, New York and London still appeared to be strengthening their positions atop the global financial system, according to the Global Financial Centres Index (GFCI), a metric based on surveys of financial experts and professionals.[6] London and New York are not only "resilient," notes the GFCI, but the only "truly global financial centres." Indeed, the ratings for these two fell only slightly during the financial crisis. London's resiliency is remarkable, considering that it sits in a British economy that has been declining for several generations. What's particularly amazing is that London was giving New York a serious run for its money in the late 1990s and early 2000s. By the mid-2000s, London was the leading center in cross-border lending, foreign currency transactions, asset management, Eurobond issues, and foreign bank offices.[7]

The most troubling question is not how much of New York's finance industry will migrate to other places but how much may simply vanish altogether. Finance jobs are among the best-paying. Set aside the stratospheric seven-figure-plus bonuses at the high end of the spectrum: the average New York financial job paid nearly $300,000 (exact figure: $280,872) in 2008.[8] At the height of the recent bubble, New York depended on the financial sector for roughly 22 percent of local wages.[9] Most economists agree that, at that point, the financial economy had become bloated and overdeveloped and was likely to shrink substantially. Whatever the reduction, a sizable portion of it would be felt in Manhattan.

Lean times undoubtedly lie ahead for New York's financial indus-try, but even if it wilts for a while, it will not bring the overall economy of the region down with it. It is true that New York has the nation's largest number of financial sector jobs—620,000, about twice as many as Los Angeles or Chicago, three times as many as Boston or Dallas, and about six times as many as San Francisco, Minneapolis, Atlanta, Washington, D.C., or Miami. However, financial positions account for only about 8 percent of all the jobs in the greater New York area—only a few points above the national average of 5.5 percent.

By contrast, many smaller regions have a greater percentage of the population working in the financial sector than New York does, even if the actual numbers of workers are smaller. Financial jobs make up 28 percent of all jobs in Bloomington-Normal, Illinois; 18 percent in Des Moines; 13 percent in Hartford; 10 percent in Sioux Falls, Charlotte, Omaha, and Columbus. By this measure, many of these regions are more vulnerable in the economic downturn than New York. If you include insurance jobs in the financial sector, as many observers do, the combination accounted for roughly 15 percent of the greater New York economy in 2006. This is less than half the level of the equivalent numbers in Charlotte, where finance and insurance made up 31 percent of the local economy, and significantly less, by percentage, than those of many smaller cities, from Des Moines to Hartford to Winston-Salem.[10] Urban planners assess a region's reli-ance on certain industries by determining its *location quotient*, or LQ, which compares a region's specialization in a given industry to that of the country as a whole. An LQ of 1 means a place is at the national average. New York's LQ for the financial industry overall is a modest 1.5. That's about 50 percent more than the national concentration and about the same as those of Philadelphia, Tampa, and Madison.

Still, the financial industry generates an enormous amount of the wealth that circulates around New York, and that has helped to sup-port the city's vibrant culture for a long time. But New York has al-ways been much more than a financial center. Elizabeth Currid's book *The Warhol Economy* provides detailed evidence of New York's diver-sity.[11] In her research, Currid found that finance accounts for only nine of the top fifty of New York's leading professional and creative occupations and only one of the top ten. By this measure, New York is more of a mecca for fashion designers, musicians, film directors, artists, and, yes, psychiatrists than it is for financial professionals. New York's continued success—its uncanny knack for renewing itself again and again—is based on the diversity of its industries and its ability to attract the best and brightest across a wide range of fields.

Writing in the 1960s and 1970s, the great urbanist Jane Jacobs was among the first to identify cities' diverse economic and social structures as the true engines of growth.[12] More than two hundred years ago, the great moral philosopher and economist Adam Smith showed how the organization of tasks and the fine-grained division of labor in his now-famous pin factory powered economic efficiency and so undergirded a healthy capitalist economy. But Jacobs added depth and dimension to that picture, arguing that cities play a critical role in organizing the division of innovative labor: the jostling of many different professions and different types of people, all in a dense environment, is essential to the creation of things that are truly new. Innovation, in the long run, is what keeps cities vital and relevant. The counterintuitive idea in all this, then, is that the financial crisis may ultimately *help* New York.

The extraordinary tranches of cash pulled in by investment bankers, traders, and hedge fund managers over the past two decades skewed the city's economy in some very unhealthy ways. In 2005, I asked a top-ranking official at a major investment bank whether the city's rising real estate prices were affecting his company's ability to attract global talent. He responded simply, "We are the cause, not the effect, of the real estate bubble." As it turned out, he was only half right. Still, housing prices in greater New York have declined more modestly than in ailing Rust Belt centers such as Detroit or housing bubble–driven Sunbelt cities such as Phoenix, Las Vegas, or Los Angeles, for that matter. While housing prices in those regions and others have declined precipitously since the bubble burst, New York–area prices remained more than 75 percent above 2000 levels in summer 2009—the highest of the twenty metropolitan areas tracked by the widely used Case-Shiller Home Price Index.

Still, stratospheric real estate prices have made New York less diverse over time and arguably less stimulating. When I asked Jacobs some years ago about the effects of escalating real estate prices on creativity, she told me, "When a place gets boring, even the rich people leave." With the end of the hegemony of the investment bankers, New York now stands a better chance of avoiding that sterile fate. In fact, to give creativity a boost, New York mayor Michael Bloomberg's administration decided to subsidize garage-like spaces to help laid-off financial professionals create new tech- and media-based start-up companies. "Rather than write them off as losers in the casinos of capitalism," the *New York Times* wrote of the $45 million program, "city officials are encouraging them to start over, the Silicon Valley way."[13]

And there's another fact to consider: New York is the hub of the country's largest megaregion, the Boston–New York–Washington corridor, with 50 million–plus people and more than $2 trillion in economic output. The Big Apple is at the center of this diverse and innovative economy, one built around a broad range of creative industries, from mass media to design to arts and entertainment. "A man born in New York 40 years ago finds nothing, absolutely nothing, of the New York he knew" is how *Harper's Monthly* put it in 1846, at the dawn of the Industrial Revolution.[14] That holds true even to this day.

Chapter Nine

Who's Next?

"One thing seems probable to me," said Peer Steinbrück, the German finance minister, in September 2008. As a result of the crisis, "the United States will lose its status as the superpower of the global financial system."[1] In September 2009, World Bank president Robert Zoellick told an audience at Johns Hopkins School of Advanced International Studies that "The United States would be mistaken to take for granted the dollar's place as the world's predominant reserve currency." "Looking forward," he added, "there will increasingly be other options to the dollar."[2] You don't have to strain too hard to see the financial crisis as the death knell for a debt-ridden, overconsuming, underproducing American empire—the fall long ago prophesied by Yale historian Paul Kennedy.[3]

Big international economic crises—such as the crash of 1873 and the Great Depression—have a way of upending the geopolitical order and hastening the fall of old powers and the rise of new ones. In *The Post-American World*, published some months before the Wall Street meltdown, Fareed Zakaria argued that modern history's third great power shift was already upon us—the rise of Western Europe in the fifteenth century and the rise of America in the nineteenth century being the two previous sea changes.[4] But Zakaria added that this transition is defined less by American decline than by "the rise of the rest." "We're to look forward to a world economy," he wrote, "defined and directed from many places and by many peoples." That's surely true.

Much has been written about the roaring tigers of the Asian economies, especially now that China has asserted itself as a major economic player on the world stage. But before you jump to the conclusion that Hong Kong, Singapore, Tokyo, and Seoul will soon challenge New York and London for global financial supremacy, consider this startling fact: Singapore, Hong Kong, and Zurich—the three centers behind New York and London—saw their ratings on the Global Financial Centres Index nose-dive in the six months following the October 2008 crash. Tokyo fell out of the top ten, slipping to fifteenth place from seventh. New York and London have surely fallen on hard times, but most of the second-tier financial centers fared even worse.

John Pender of the *Financial Times* commented that perhaps only Shanghai—with its well-capitalized banks and government backing—could possibly eclipse New York and London by 2020 as the world's premiere global financial center. In January 2010, Shanghai overtook Tokyo as Asia's largest stock market by trading volume.[5] The economic historian Angus Maddison predicts that China's economic output will *surpass* the United States' by 2015.[6] China, which holds the title of the "world's factory," is already well on its way to becoming the world's largest exporter. That said, it will be a long, long time before China—or more specifically one of its or any of Asia's other financial centers for that matter—eclipses New York or London. Shanghai, China's industrial and financial center, ranks thirty-sixth on the GFCI—roughly equivalent to the British Virgin Islands and the Bahamas. As fast-growing as it is, China as a whole remains an emerging economy in every sense of that phrase: it ranks thirtieth on the Davos Competitiveness index, eighty-first on the U.N. Human Development Index, and thirty-sixth on my own Global Creativity Index—a measure of global innovation, openness, and competitiveness. It will be some time until it can compete with the more established economic powers of the world, never mind the United States.

While some Chinese observers seem to be cautiously optimistic about their financial prospects, others are less so—a fact conveyed in this headline from the China Digital Times: "Shanghai as World Financial Capital? Maybe Next Century."[7] Helmut Reisen, a professor of International Economics at the University of Basel, predicts that it will be quite a while before China's currency displaces the dollar. "[T]he Chinese renminbi can be expected to replace the US dollar as a reserve currency around 2050."[8] He adds that in the interim, the Chinese will have to solve some problems. They will need to lift the current restrictions on money leaving and entering the country and ensure that the currency is fully convertible, meaning it can be freely bought and sold around the world without the permission of a central bank. Pressures from within its own borders, as well as from the outside, are likely to impede China's ascendancy. Internally, persistent and crippling poverty continues to be a fact of life, as is the increasing disparity between the newly wealthy entrepreneurial class in the cities and the rural poor. Infrastructure concerns and the ever-present shadow of political unrest add to the instability.

If not China, surely there are other rising centers waiting in the wings. Singapore, a city-state of almost 5 million people, is also a significant financial center. To be sure, the country is trying to invest in creativity—its "cool quotient" recently increased upon its inclusion in the hipper-than-thou *Wallpaper* series of city guides. Yet Singapore remains a top-down, socially engineered society. Though I would not go as far as one recent visitor who said, "It feels like Atlanta, only Asian," it's also a far cry from the diversity and street-level energy of New York, London, or Toronto.

Hong Kong seems to have the best shot. It has long been an expatriate center and is a player on the global scene. It is tied to China—the world's fastest-growing economy. While it has a highly developed IPO market, it lacks many of the other capabilities—such as bond, foreign exchange, and commodities trading—that make New York and London global financial powerhouses. But what also holds Hong Kong back is the intense competition among Asia's financial centers—itself, Tokyo, Singapore, and Shanghai—and also its ability to become a truly open, global center for talent on a par with New York and London. So perhaps a combined "Shang-Kong" center can emerge over time, as the cities are two and a half hours apart by air.[9]

Shanghai has the industrial muscle and economic size and scale, while Hong Kong brings openness and attractiveness to global talent.

The Middle East is another matter altogether. Dubai placed forty-fourth on a recent ranking of global financial centers—about the same as Edinburgh, Bangkok, Lisbon, and Prague—and that's before the collapse of Dubai World. Meanwhile, religious intolerance is common, and homosexuality is illegal. Without openness, the region lacks the ability to attract the diverse talent required to play at the top of global finance. It is hard to imagine these places achieving the combination of openness and fluidity required to compete for talent on a world-class scale.

That's true of virtually all of the rising financial centers outside New York and London. They are not particularly open to global talent, nor are they places where global talent prefers to be (barring the occasional subsidized boondoggle). Language barriers and quality of life, not to mention immigration restrictions, remain real issues. The ability to attract talent has long been a defining characteristic of leading financial centers. "The crucial contributory factor in the financial center's development over the last two centuries, and even longer," writes Cassis, "is the arrival of new talent to replenish their energy and their capacity to innovate." Cassis explains that the migration of Germans and Swiss bankers to Paris shaped the Parisian merchant banks (*maisons de Haute Banque*) in the first half of the nineteenth century; that London benefited from inflows of international financiers such as the Rothschilds from across Europe; and that in New York, "an entire area of investment banking was built up by German Jewish immigrants during the second half of the nineteenth century."[10] On the other hand, Berlin saw its position as a global economic center undermined by two world wars, the rise of fascism, and its subsequent isolation during the Cold War.

Rising financial centers in Asia and the Middle East are not nearly as inviting to foreign professionals as New York or London. Tokyo, for instance, is a wonderful city, with marvelous infrastructure, incredible shopping, and according to some leading guides, the world's best restaurants. And Japan itself is an innovative and advanced economy. But Japan admits fewer immigrants than any other member of the Organization for Economic Cooperation and Development (OECD), a group of thirty market-oriented democracies. Non-Japanese-looking people are so uncommon as to seem out of place when seen on the street or in the subway. Just 1 percent of Japan's entire workforce is made up of foreign workers (and that includes illegal as well as legal workers), the lowest rate of any of the advanced OECD countries.[11] As Jane Jacobs wrote in *The Economy of Cities*, "[t]he diversity, of whatever kind, that is generated by cities rests on the fact that in cities so many people are so close together, and among them contain so many different tastes, skills, needs, supplies, and bees in their bonnets." It is difficult to envision such a cacophony of voices and needs among the office towers and shopping districts of Tokyo and Singapore—at least Tokyo and Singapore as we know them now.

A former assistant U.S. Treasury secretary, Edwin Truman, notes the enduring advantage for the big financial players. In finance, "there is a huge network and agglomeration effect," he told the *Christian Science Monitor*, an advantage that comes from having a large critical mass of financial professionals, covering many different specialties, along with lawyers, accountants, and others to support them, all in close physical proximity. Truman noted that it is extremely difficult to build up these dense networks from scratch and very hard for up-and-coming cities to achieve a position of prominence in global finance without them.[12] "Hong Kong, Shanghai, Singapore, and Tokyo are more important than they were 20 years ago," he said. "But will they reach London and New York's dominance in another 20 years? I suspect not."

Financial leaders and institutions in these centers acknowledge as much. A key element of their growth strategy has been to go offshore—to New York and London—to gain access to world-class talent where it already lives. One way these foreign firms are acquiring talent is by buying up Wall Street institutions. Nomura Holdings, the giant Japanese brokerage firm, did just that when it bought out the bankrupt Lehman Brothers' operations in Asia, the Middle East, and Europe. In 2008 and 2009, Nomura hired the former head of global equities away from Bank of America, Goldman Sachs' chief currency strategist, and two top Citigroup executives, among its hundreds of new hires in the United States and Europe. India's Ambit Holdings Pvt. Ltd., a small Mumbai-based investment bank with fewer than two hundred employees, poached three top bankers from Merrill Lynch. "We see this situation as an opportunity to source some of the best available talent in the industry," is how a top executive at Tata, the Indian conglomerate, put it, noting that the company was intent on ramping up its investment banking and private-equity operations.[13]

The ability to attract global talent helps explain why the dominant financial centers such as New York and London are likely to stay on top. It is somewhat ironic that in this era of supposedly frictionless communication and highly mobile talent, the local cultural and social life still determines who gets the talent. Even though talent is mobile and can flow freely, the issue remains: where does it want to go? That's why I'm betting that New York and London will remain the key global financial centers for the foreseeable future.

"Financial crises tend to trigger overwrought predictions of major economic shifts—and then debunk them. Today's global economic meltdown is no different," notes Peking University professor Michael Pettis in *Newsweek*.[14] "In recent months, it has become popular to predict that New York and London (or Ny-Lon, as they're together known) will ultimately lose market share as cities in the emerging world use the crisis to wrest away dominance. But history suggests that the opposite is more likely—that New York and London will actually increase in importance over the decade to come." In fact, Pettis argues, when crises come—and liquidity dries up—big financial centers gain an even greater advantage over smaller centers and seize the opportunity to attract the bigger investors.

What's even more certain in my mind is that as the economic crisis and subsequent recovery ultimately play out, we will see the rise of certain cities and regions *within* the United States—and the decline of others.

Chapter Ten

Fire Starter

I grew up putting my boyhood savings in a local thrift or savings and loan institution, which was specialized in taking in local savings and making local mortgages. The bank, Kearney Federal, took its name from the small New Jersey working-class town where it was based. This kind of institution, immortalized both by old Mr. Potter's bank and George Bailey's savings and loan in the classic film *It's a Wonderful Life*, was a fixture of most small towns in America. For much of its history, in fact, America's financial industry was largely decentralized. But since the Second World War, the financial industry has grown more concentrated. Bigger banks and firms gobbled up smaller ones, and then the resulting newly swollen companies began to merge with one another. The quiet little local banks slowly vanished from the landscape, replaced by branches of national and global institutions. The "big eight" accounting firms became the "big six" and then the "big four"; Chemical Bank was bought by Chase Manhattan, which merged with J. P. Morgan to become J. P. Morgan Chase. This has occurred in fits and starts; consolidation has been spurred both by innovations, such as electronic funds transfers and mortgage-backed securities, and by the regulatory response to various crises.

In 2006, the top three financial centers were New York, Los Angeles, and Chicago, which accounted for 16 percent of all financial firms, 20 percent of financial workers, and a third of all financial payrolls—

a figure that will undoubtedly grow higher on the other side of the Reset. The top ten financial centers accounted for roughly a third of all financial companies, 39 percent of financial jobs and half of all financial payrolls. The consolidation of the financial industry has followed a pattern seen across many areas of corporate commerce, from retail and restaurants to entertainment, as national chains have either absorbed or eliminated smaller local competitors: Home Depot and Pottery Barn, AMC Theaters and Clear Channel, Barnes & Noble, Starbucks. You don't have to be enamored of notions such as "power elite" or "monopoly finance capital" to understand that another round of massive consolidation is occurring today.

My own assessment is that most of America's large financial centers outside New York will come out in reasonably good shape. This will have less to do with how the financial industries they house fare over time and more to do with the fact that they are large, relatively diverse economies. Chicago, which is one of the world's top five financial centers, has emerged as a center for industrial management and consulting and a regional talent center that has absorbed many business and financial functions from smaller midwestern cities and towns. Los Angeles is a big, diversified region and a global player in entertainment. Silicon Valley retains its place in high-tech venture capital financing. Even Miami, which has been crushed by housing speculation, remains the financial and business hub for Latin America. For these cities and others, success, and in some cases survival, will turn on their ability to diversify and to develop healthy industries beyond finance.

A decade or two ago, many experts argued that a broad economic sector dubbed FIRE—finance, insurance, and real estate—was the next stage in the evolution of capitalism. The story went more or less like this: capitalism's most dynamic markets have historically evolved to higher and higher orders of economic functions—from trading posts and ports during the eighteenth and early nineteenth centuries, for instance, to manufacturing centers late in the nineteenth century, to high tech in the 1970s, to economies powered by a combination of FIRE industries today. This is a component of the shift to what the great Harvard sociologist Daniel Bell called "postindustrial" society.[1] Looked at this way, the crisis was not merely a crisis of banking and finance, but a broader crisis of FIRE as a whole. As the venture capitalist Eric Janszen wrote in *Harper's*, "As more and more risk pollution rises to the surface, credit will continue to contract, and the FIRE economy—which depends on the free flow of credit, will experience its first near-death experience since the sector rose to power in the early 1980s."[2]

The place that stands as perhaps the best exemplar of the FIRE economy is Charlotte, North Carolina. At the height of the boom in 2006, FIRE comprised a whopping 45 percent of its economy; only Naples, Florida, was higher, with 47 percent. Yet the crisis of the FIRE economy did not devastate Charlotte's economy. Its effect paled in comparison to the way that the collapse of manufacturing pummeled older Rust Belt regions. There's a big difference between a FIRE economy such as Naples, a resort destination where real estate is the only game in town, and a larger city such as Charlotte, which is tilted much more toward finance and is home to large global banks. The "RE" part of the FIRE economy was hit much harder than the "FI." According to my number-crunching colleague Charlotta Mellander, there was no statistical relationship at all between metropolitan areas with high concentration of jobs in FIRE industries and the unemployment rate. It's hard to say exactly why so many FIRE economies have weathered the storm, especially given the massive blow to that sector, but one reason may be that metropolitan areas with large shares of finance and insurance jobs are economically more diverse. Finance and insurance workers also have higher levels of education, more skills, and greater flexibility than workers in manufacturing fields, enabling them to shift jobs and find new work in other fields more easily.

The television show *60 Minutes* once speculated that Charlotte's financial complex might someday come to compete with that of New York. But the numbers simply don't add up. Before the crisis, the city ranked as the sixteenth largest U.S. financial center in terms of total number of jobs, behind Houston, Detroit, and Tampa. And it ranked seventeenth in total financial payroll behind Detroit, Houston, and Phoenix and thirty-second in number of financial institutions behind Indianapolis, Sacramento, Las Vegas, and Columbus, Ohio.[3] Charlotte is to banking and finance what low-cost manufacturing was to the Sunbelt a generation ago.

The financial crisis surely hindered Charlotte's ascent up the financial ladder. The crisis left Wachovia, the other major national bank based in the city, ailing; in 2008, Wachovia was acquired by San Francisco–based Wells Fargo. Meanwhile, acquisition of Merrill Lynch saddled Bank of America with more debt than its management had anticipated. On the flip side, the moment when your competitors are retrenching is the perfect time to grow your market share. Deborah Strumsky, an economist at the University of North Carolina at Charlotte, told me that Charlotte came out much better than initially expected. Wells Fargo's acquisition of Wachovia not only kept it afloat but ultimately led to a much lower level of job loss than many had predicted. Wachovia had a very competitive retail banking arm but had branched into other areas of finance that were less lucrative, she said. "Wells Fargo was happy with the low price to get the physical retail banking facilities in the buyout. Wachovia stated again and again they were going to clean house, but as they interviewed, evaluated, and re-interviewed personnel in Charlotte, they decided to keep many more Wachovia employees than they thought they would. Wachovia was going to clear out the huge northeast Charlotte campus and the downtown offices entirely, but they decided instead to 'consolidate' their work force to just the northeast Charlotte campus. While this was a blow to real estate rental prices in the handful of towers downtown, it meant many more people have kept their steady jobs than anyone initially thought." While job losses of as much as 80 percent were anticipated, they ultimately came in at less than 20 percent, Strumsky points out. Bank of America took "to the banking crisis like a shopaholic with a new credit card—bargain hunting and cutting some astonishing deals," Strumsky adds. It was also slow to cut jobs, because North Carolina law mandates that so-called mass layoffs must be publicly announced, which created worry about the effects of job cuts on the company's already troubled stock price, she said. Instead the company "picked and chose personnel carefully and laid off about twenty workers a week and held the stock price steady, eliminating only their lowest-performing workers, since they had to apply some serious scrutiny to who was let go." Ultimately, Strumsky says, the squeeze on financial sector profits benefited Charlotte in the short run and perhaps in the long run as well. It caused several New York banks and financial firms to shift some midlevel activities to Charlotte as cost-saving measures. "Big financial firms cannot relocate anywhere; they need a high skill labor force experienced in the banking sector," Strumsky said. "Welcome to Charlotte."[4]

The city has built up its downtown, incubated cultural activities, and improved its overall talent base of educated professionals. Charlotte's leaders have made some good moves over the years, but in the midst of the crisis of 2008 and 2009 the city had something less tangible—and more valuable—than that: a run of good luck.

But there is one class of places that has weathered the storm better than any other. And as the next chapter will show, they could not be further from the freewheeling centers of market-based capitalism.

Chapter Eleven

Big Government Boomtowns

emember company towns?" *Newsweek* asked rhetorically in March 2009. "From Detroit to Wolfsburg, Germany, home to Volkswagen," it continued, "they used to be places where you could count on a job for life. Now, they are mostly places where you count your unemployment checks. But as the global economy shrinks . . . and the public sector expands to cope with the fallout, there's a new kind of boomtown—the government town." Capital cities like Washington, D.C., Ottawa, Brussels, and Brasilia are the places where, according to the magazine, "not only are new jobs being created, but home sales are rising, incomes are up, car dealerships are full, and new malls, shops, luxury hotels and gyms can't be built fast enough."[1]

That certainly seems to be the case in Washington, D.C. The District of Columbia itself had the second-fastest-growing job market of any state in 2008. And greater D.C.—which includes northern Virginia and southern Maryland—is a hefty economic entity. With $275 billion in economic output, it's America's fourth largest regional economy, almost the size of the state of Massachusetts—only New York, Los Angeles, and Chicago are bigger—and would rank among the top twenty-five economies in the world, bigger than Denmark, Norway, Ireland, or Hong Kong.[2]

Washington, D.C., has emerged as a powerful talent magnet, drawing in huge numbers of young, highly educated, and ambitious people. More than 46 percent of greater D.C.'s adult population has at least a college degree and 22 percent have a graduate degree, ranking it first among the country's largest metropolitan areas on these measures. Nearby counties in Virginia and Maryland have among the highest income levels in the country and the highest levels of educational attainment and human capital as well. Six of the eight most-educated counties in the country are a part of the greater D.C. region. It is, in some ways, the definitive postindustrial city, with some 43 percent of its population in professional, knowledge-based, or creative occupations—first among large metro areas.[3] Even longtime residents of the Washington, D.C., region are surprised to learn that government is not the biggest sector of the local economy—technology is. The region is second only to San Jose in high-tech electronics industries and ranks third nationally in total software employment. Greater D.C. is a player in the biotech industry, as well, and one of the leading centers of broadcast media in the country. It boasts large concentrations of computer scientists, software workers, and mathematicians, as well as political scientists, lawyers, economists, and policy wonks.

At the height of the crisis, greater D.C. boasted one of the lowest rates of unemployment in the United States—roughly 6 percent, a full 4 percentage points below the national rate—and close-in neighborhoods saw only a modest drop in housing prices, with the bulk of price declines hitting remote suburbs and exurbs.

One observation that may rankle D.C. loyalists, however, is that greater D.C. is close enough and well connected enough to New York City to make it a veritable suburb. It's a four-hour drive or a two-and-a-half-hour trip on the Acela train—high-speed rail would cut the trip to less than ninety minutes. And, of course, the air shuttle flies back and forth every half hour. This is not to say that D.C. has in any way become dependent on New York. It is, in fact, more of a symbiotic relationship; with goods, services, ideas, and people moving back and forth in both directions, the nation's capital has benefited from its relationship with the bigger, more global city to the north.

The quality of life is high, and at a reasonable cost. In one of my earlier books, *Who's Your City?*, I ranked greater Washington, D.C., as number one among large regions for families with children and number two for young singles (only San Francisco does better). It's also among the best places for gays and lesbians.[4] Residents express a high degree of satisfaction with the region and would recommend it "highly" to others, according to a survey I conducted with the Gallup organization.

The D.C. region faces difficult problems. It suffers from some of the worst commutes and traffic congestion in the nation and is plagued by deep and rising urban inequality, devastating poverty in certain quarters, and a lack of affordable housing. But it continues to weather the economic crisis about as well as any other U.S. city. I continue to believe it has just about the biggest upside of any U.S. region, not only because of federal spending but because it is attracting talent and business as a livable and relatively affordable node in the gigantic Bos-Wash megaregion.

Canada has a new government boomtown of its own: Ottawa, its national capital. Its unemployment remained low during the crisis, and housing prices were relatively stable. More than 40 percent of the population works in knowledge, professional, and creative occupations, placing it ahead of Austin, Texas, and the North Carolina Research Triangle and slightly behind Silicon Valley on this measure. And 25 percent of its workforce is concentrated in an even more specialized group of science, technology, arts, and media occupations I call the supercreative core—roughly twice the rate of North American cities.

Greater Ottawa boasts large concentrations of communications equipment, information technology, business services, and education and knowledge creation industries. It is a classic postindustrial city, like D.C., offering a high quality of life. In the rankings for the Canadian edition of *Who's Your City?*, it placed first for young professionals, first for families with children, first for retirees, second for young singles (after Calgary), and second for empty-nesters (after Toronto).[5]

College towns are miniversions of government boomtowns. With their economies bolstered by large universities, high levels of state funding, and jobs markets with high concentrations of "meds and eds"—that is, stable medical and education jobs—college towns have considerable resilience. They are, by definition, talent magnets, attracting bright young students and faculty from the United States and around the world. This is why none other than the *Wall Street Journal* proclaimed that college towns were "looking smart" in the face of the crisis.[6] Just twelve U.S. metropolitan areas had unemployment rates below 5 percent in September 2009—a time when the overall national rate was 9.5 percent. But three of them were college towns—Morgantown, West Virginia, the home of West Virginia University; Logan, Utah, the home of Utah State University; and Ames, Iowa, the home of Iowa State University.[7]

Whether a state's economy was struggling or thriving, its college town seemed to do better. For instance, while unemployment reached 17 percent in greater Detroit and was well above 20 percent in the city proper, just 8 percent of the population was unemployed in Ann Arbor, less than an hour's drive away. College Station's and Austin's unemployment rates were 4 and 4.8 percent, respectively, compared to 7 percent for Dallas. Across the country, college towns from Lawrence and Manhattan, Kansas to Athens, Georgia; Lansing, Michigan; Bloomington, Indiana; and Champaign-Urbana, Illinois, all had relatively low rates of unemployment and relatively stable housing markets at the height of the crisis. Even in California, where in 2009 the state's budget crisis led to cutbacks and staff furloughs in the state university system, college towns such as Santa Barbara and San Luis Obispo have fared better than average regarding unemployment. And these advantages are compounded in places like Austin, Texas, and Madison, Wisconsin, which are home to state capitals as well as large research universities.

"Some areas aren't just miraculously better able to handle the downturn," says the Harvard economist Edward Glaeser. "Longstanding features of the urban landscape can explain the bulk of the variation in today's unemployment rates." Glaeser conducted an analysis of several factors thought to shape regional unemployment—using the percentage of college graduates in the region as a proxy for its skill level. "While the disparity in unemployment rates is enormous, it isn't random," he adds.[8] He found that places with more highly educated people—those with college degrees—had lower levels of unemployment. This was true of places that had higher percentages of college graduates in 2000, but places that had higher levels of college graduates way back before the Second World War also had lower levels of unemployment today. "Given the enormous gap in unemployment between skilled and unskilled workers," he writes, "it isn't surprising that skills best explain today's metropolitan unemployment rates." Conversely, he found that unemployment was highest in manufacturing centers.

Manufacturing cities and regions—the ones with the rusting steel beams and the pigeons roosting in the rafters—weigh most heavily on the minds of economists and policy makers. Will the lost jobs ever come back? Can they be replaced? Can we reclaim our industrial might? What's really in store in those places?

Chapter Twelve

Death and Life of Great Industrial Cities

There's a long history of writers extolling the virtues of blue-collar work. From Leo Tolstoy's Levin finding happiness alongside his field hands in *Anna Karenina* to Robert Pirsig's *Zen and the Art of Motorcycle Maintenance* in 1974, our greatest intellects have repeatedly been surprised to discover the simple joys of hard physical labor. In his best-selling book *Shop Class as Soulcraft*, Matthew Crawford, a University of Chicago philosophy PhD, walked away from his knowledge-work career in a boring think-tank job and, following in Pirsig's footsteps, found far more satisfying work in a motorcycle repair shop. Richard Sennett's *The Craftsman* similarly explores the honest satisfaction of craft work.[1]

I can practically hear my father, my uncles, and our neighbors laughing at the idea that college guys are making money writing books about working with their hands. My relatives could fix anything. I never recall seeing a repairman in the house. All of the kids watched and helped and learned from the grown-ups, so that we could take apart and rebuild our bicycles or fix the musical instruments and amplifiers we used in our band.

As a teenager, I spent my summers doing factory work, working in machine shops. It was monotonous, mind-numbing, beyond boring. And it was dangerous. You could lose a finger or an arm in the machinery or get your nose broken by an older guy who didn't like your attitude. Nonetheless, I developed a deep appreciation for the talent and skill of physical workers. I vividly remember visiting the Newark eyeglasses factory where my father worked. "Richard," he would say, "the factory does not run itself. It is those incredibly skilled men who are the heart, soul, and mind of this factory."

Sadly and unjustly, the places likely to suffer the most from the crash are, to a great extent, the ones just like those my father knew so well. This is all part of an ongoing shift in the structure of our economy. Since 1950, the manufacturing sector has shrunk from 32 percent of nonfarm employment to less than 10 percent. The percentage of the workforce employed in blue-collar jobs peaked at 39 percent in 1951 and has declined to 19 percent today.[2]

This decline is the result of such long-term trends as increasing foreign competition and especially the relentless replacement of people with machines. The inescapable reality is that a lot of manufacturing can be done more cheaply overseas. Many of those jobs are gone now, and a good number of them aren't coming back. As the son of a factory worker, as someone who has seen with his own eyes the economic and human devastation in Newark and Detroit, and even in Pittsburgh and Boston before those cities remade themselves, I am heartbroken by what so many workers, their families, and their communities have had to endure in this time of catastrophic job losses.

According to an analysis done by Michael Mandel, formerly the economics editor at *BusinessWeek*, 1.8 million jobs were lost in blue-collar fields between December 2007 and November 2008. The unemployment rate in manufacturing more than doubled from 6.3 to 13.7 percent between April 2008 and April 2009. Certain kinds of blue-collar jobs dried up faster than others, with the unemployment rate hitting 15.6 percent for production workers and 19.7 percent for those in construction jobs.[3] Job losses in manufacturing were concentrated regionally. Paul Krugman noted that the "Slump Belt," heavy with manufacturing centers, running from the industrial Midwest down into the Carolinas, is the epicenter of the crisis.[4] In 2009, the unemployment rate topped 10 percent in eleven of fourteen Michigan regions, nine of thirteen in Ohio, six of thirteen in Indiana, and seven of fourteen in North Carolina.

■ ■ ■

Detroit has become the poster child for the economic trauma of the crisis. Though some cities have higher rates of unemployment, no major city in the United States looks more beleaguered. In October 2008, the average home price in Detroit was $18,513, and some 44,000 of the 65,000 homes that went into foreclosure between 2007 and 2009 remained empty.[5] A YouTube video from November 2008 showed someone leafing through 137 pages of foreclosure listings in Detroit's Wayne County.[6]

Nearly a million people have left the city since its peak at midcentury. And in 2000, Detroit became the first city in U.S. history to see its population slip from 1 million people to below that mark. Its housing prices declined some 40 percent from the peak and, by late 2009, were less than 70 percent of 2000 levels, falling back to levels not seen since the mid-1990s, even before adjusting for inflation.

The city's public school system, facing a budget deficit of more than $400 million, was taken over by the state in December 2009; dozens of schools have been closed since 2005 because of declining enrollment. Not a single national grocery chain operates a store in the city; only four Starbucks are located there (compared to one on virtually every street corner in many Chicago neighborhoods); and Borders, which opened its first store only a generation ago just down the road in Ann Arbor, closed its last city branch in spring 2009. While the official unemployment rate for the city itself was a staggering 27 percent in October 2009, Mayor Dave Bing told a jobs forum in Washington, D.C., that the real figure "might be closer to 50 percent," because so many workers had simply given up looking for jobs.[7]

If talent is a key driver of the emerging economy, Detroit faces a major deficit. Just 10 percent of the city of Detroit's adult residents are college graduates, and 30 percent are on food stamps. Detroit ranked as the single hardest-hit metropolitan region in the country on the Brookings Institution's MetroMonitor Index. "It's a depression—not a recession," an eighty-one-year-old retired surgical technician, Warlena McDuell, told the *Associated Press* with the authority of someone who lived through the great one. "It will get worse before it gets better."[8]

As anyone who has seen Clint Eastwood's *Gran Torino*, a movie that was set there, knows, parts of Detroit are abandoned, literally wiped clean of their former urban glory. There are forty-eight large vacant buildings—buildings at least five stories tall or occupying ten thousand or more square feet—in Detroit's central business district, according to a detailed examination by the *Detroit News*. Never mind that records kept by the U.S. Postal Service document a jaw-dropping sixty-two thousand vacant lots or uninhabited buildings across the city as a whole.[9] In 2009, Detroit put up for auction almost nine thousand decayed or abandoned houses and properties. "Taken together, the properties seized by tax collectors for arrears," Reuters reported, "represented an area the size of New York's Central Park." Total vacant land in Detroit now occupies an area almost the size of Boston, according to a *Detroit Free Press* estimate. Despite rock-bottom prices, less than a fifth of the land was sold during the auction. The article paints a very grim picture. "After five hours of calling out a drumbeat of 'no bid' for properties listed in an auction book as thick as a city phone directory, the energy of the county auctioneer began to flag."[10]

Detroit is not just bombed out; it's handicapped by its very model of sprawling, auto-dependent growth. This is how a June 2009 *New York Times Magazine* story, "G.M., Detroit and the Fall of the Black Middle Class," described it.[11]

Unlike most major metropolitan areas in the Northeast, which were designed for maximum density, Detroit rose in the age of the automobile. This helped create a sprawling city of detached, single-family homes. As . . . I drove through it, I saw the images of the postapocalyptic city to which we've all become accustomed: the deserted streets, overgrown lots and empty storefronts with boarded-up windows and faded signs for long-closed stores and restaurants like Pick 'n Party, Jet King Chop Suey and African hair braiding. As familiar as these images have become (just punch "Detroit" and "urban decay" into YouTube to see them), it's only when you're actually riding around Detroit and can see that this goes on for block after block, mile after mile, that the profundity of this idea—the death of a city—really sets in.

When work disappears, city populations don't always decline as fast as you might expect. Even though it has lost more than a million people since its midcentury peak, greater Detroit remains, astonishingly, the eleventh largest metropolitan region in the United States. But much of that remaining population is stuck—unable to relocate for financial reasons. Greater Detroit has seen a streaming outmigration of its young, talented, and ambitious people. Many of those who remain either lack the skills and resources to move or are trapped by houses that are so far underwater, they're unable to get out. "If you no longer can sell your property, how can you move elsewhere?" asked Robin Boyle, an urban planning professor at Wayne State University. But then he answered his own question: "Some people just switch out the lights and leave—property values have gone so low, walking away is no longer such a difficult option."[12]

As difficult as it is to even imagine, other Rust Belt cities have fared even worse than the Motor City: the greatest pain has been felt in the smaller, second- and third-tier communities in this industrial belt. Greater Detroit's regional unemployment rate was not the highest in Michigan; unemployment was higher in the smaller cities of Flint and Monroe. The same was true in Ohio, where unemployment was worse in Akron, Canton, Toledo, Youngstown, and Mansfield than in Cleveland. With a rate of 17.8 percent, the little-known blue-collar town of Elkhart, Indiana, had one of the highest rates of unemployment in the entire country.[13]

Detroit and places like it have reached an inflection point. I'd certainly expect them to shrink more quickly in the next several years than they have in the past few. But many people will stay—those with close family ties nearby or personal connections to the area; young professionals and creative types looking to take advantage of the city's old industrial buildings and cheap real estate; as well as those whose houses are underwater or whose meager means make it impossible to relocate. Still, as population dips even lower, the struggle to provide services and prevent blight across an ever-emptier landscape will only intensify.

This is a challenge many Rust Belt cities share: how to manage this kind of economic hardship without literally collapsing. The task is doubly difficult because as the manufacturing industry shrinks, the local services it once supported—the marketing firms, advertising companies, consulting companies, and law firms—diminish as well.

That said, not every factory town is locked into inexorable decline. You need only look at the geographic pattern of December 2008's Senate vote on the auto bailout to realize that some places, mostly in the South, will benefit from the bankruptcy of GM or Chrysler. Marysville, Ohio; Georgetown, Kentucky; Smyrna, Tennessee; Montgomery, Alabama; Canton, Mississippi: these are a few of many small cities, stretching from South Carolina and Georgia all the way to Texas and up to Indiana and Ohio, that have benefited from the establishment, over the years, of plants that manufacture foreign cars.[14] Those benefits will likely grow over the coming years and decades as U.S. automakers streamline and consolidate their production.

But there will surely be far fewer manufacturing jobs in America after the crisis. And, given the forces of global competition, its manufacturing landscape will become even more uneven, as many older industrial centers are further diminished, too many of them devastatingly so.

Many older manufacturing cities have tried to reinvent themselves in different ways, with varying degrees of success. Pittsburgh, for instance, has sought to reimagine itself as a high-tech center and has met with more success than just about any other city.[15] I know the city well, having lived there for seventeen years while teaching at Carnegie Mellon University. Pittsburgh's much-ballyhooed renaissance has brought innumerable calls for it to stand as a model for Detroit—a comparison fueled perhaps by the Pittsburgh Steelers' victory in 2005's

Super Bowl XL, which was played in downtown Detroit, as well as the nail-biting 2009 Stanley Cup Final between the Pittsburgh Penguins and Detroit Red Wings.

Newsweek's Howard Fineman, a Pittsburgh native, has taken to invoking Pittsburgh as a model for remaking older industrial cities and even for urban policy in the age of Obama.[16] "Before jetting off to the Middle East and Europe," in early spring 2009, Fineman wrote, "President Obama took care of another piece of international diplomatic business: He announced the city in which the United States will host the next G20 summit in September. His choice drew laughter and puzzlement from reporters and diplomats alike." Fineman continued, "Pittsburgh? Are you serious? As a proud native, I understand and agree with the president's decision. Pittsburgh's story is inspiring and impressive. It was a rusting steel-making behemoth that, through struggle, pain and creativity, retooled itself as a surprisingly vibrant, 21st-century leader in education, computer science, medical research, sports entertainment and boutique manufacturing. By most measures—unemployment and foreclosure rates, to name two—Pittsburgh is an island of calm in the raging recession."

Fineman is right to take pride in his hometown's achievements. While Detroit ranked as the single worst-performing economy on the Brookings MetroMonitor, Pittsburgh ranked as one of the top twenty strongest-performing metro regions on this score in spring 2009, in the middle of the economic crisis. Pittsburgh and Detroit have glaringly obvious similarities. Both cities bear the legacy of heavy industry towns that lost their core industries—autos in Detroit, steel in Pittsburgh. Both numbered among the nation's largest cities. In 1940, Detroit was America's fourth largest city, Pittsburgh its tenth.

But Pittsburgh and Detroit are different in many ways. "I'm dubious about the next step in the White House's reasoning," Fineman added. "Pittsburgh's success, officials say, offers hope that Obama's own economic policies will work for Detroit and other beleaguered cities and industries. No, in fact, it doesn't. Simply put, what worked in Pittsburgh won't work for the auto industry, and what the president wants to do for Detroit isn't the kind of thing that worked in my old hometown. Pittsburgh's rebirth is about the grit, sacrifice and the hustle of locals—not the sweeping plans and power of federal bureaucrats."

That's an important point. Pittsburgh, for one, rose to industrial supremacy earlier than Detroit. It was a city of the First Reset. Sure, its core industry was steel. But Pittsburgh benefited from a more diverse industrial base than Detroit—with Westinghouse, Pittsburgh Plate Glass, Alcoa, Heinz, and other powerhouses diversifying its economy. The Mellon banking empire was founded in Pittsburgh as well and provided the venture capital needed to attract technology to the city. Pittsburgh is also home to the University of Pittsburgh, with its massive medical complex, and Carnegie Mellon, which conducts leading-edge research into computer science and software.

To be sure, Pittsburgh's population has declined from a high of almost 700,000 in the middle of the twentieth century to roughly 300,000 today. Still, Pittsburgh's downtown core has remained intact. It remains a center for regional commerce and employment. More people work in downtown Pittsburgh than downtown Detroit—298,429 and 241,627, respectively—though it has one-third the population. Much of the worst of the Pittsburgh region's decline occurred in the older mill towns dotting the rivers outside the city limits. Numerous affluent and middle-class neighborhoods are home to professionals, academics, younger people, artists, and the creative class. The city has several excellent urban public schools.

Fineman credits this urban miracle to local boosterism and the benefits of education: when the mills closed in the 1970s and 1980s, people in Pittsburgh went out and got training and college degrees. It was not a federal action, not a top-down solution, he notes, but a grassroots groundswell, using state and city money and individual contributions. Today, the skies over Pittsburgh no longer glow red from the steel mills. It's a college town now, with one of the highest ratios of students to full-time residents in the nation.

I know Detroit personally almost as well as I do Pittsburgh; it's where my wife's family is from, and I've spent a good deal of time there. The devastation of Detroit may be rooted in the inability of the U.S. auto industry to remain competitive, but the city's sprawling, highly segregated economic landscape allowed the tremendous misery to become concentrated in the city's almost completely hollowed-out core. Pittsburgh was quite literally formed in the First Reset. It has a relatively compact geography. Its core is quite functional, and there are numerous, stable working-class, middle-class, and affluent neighborhoods in the city. Detroit is a city and region of the Second Reset built along multilane roads and highways that radiate out of the city core. The city and region witnessed massive white flight during the late 1960s and 1970s, leaving the city core almost abandoned. Large swaths of the city are burned out. Poverty is highly concentrated. The landscape is postapocalyptic—with a small area of secured "Renaissance" towers, casinos, and stadiums ringed by abandoned lots and burned-out buildings. Not only did middle-class and immigrant families leave for the suburbs in search of lower crime and better schools, Detroit lost many of its young professionals, its gay community, and its creative class to older suburbs such as Ferndale and Royal Oak.

So does Detroit have anything at all to work with? Of course it does. The metropolitan area is home to 4.2 million people, making it the nation's eleventh largest. It has a world-class airport that is logistically well placed. Though two of its major universities—the University of Michigan and Michigan State—are outside the city, they and other local universities provide levels of research that are substantially greater even than Pittsburgh's. Greater Detroit is also home to Cranbrook, a world-class center for architecture, art, and design. The region also has suburban areas, such as Birmingham in Oakland County, which have levels of human capital and education that mirror those of Bethesda, Maryland, and the northern Virginia suburbs—and even Washington, D.C., itself. Detroit has a long legacy of immigration, a large Arab population, and an industry that though diminished continues to function. Greater Detroit is home to some of the world's most advanced engineering technology and design facilities, with important ties not only to the Big Three U.S. auto companies but to most of the world's major carmakers. Fiat's purchase of Chrysler in the summer of 2009 has brought an injection of new foreign, in this case Italian and other European, talent to the region.

Detroit has a substantial creative spark. The city that gave us Motown, Mitch Ryder, Iggy Pop, Bob Seger, and the White Stripes remains home to one of today's most propulsive music scenes, spanning rock, electronic music, and hip-hop. While some of Detroit's musical greats have migrated away from the region, many, such as Kid Rock and Eminem, remain and the city stays at the cutting edge and incubator of emerging musical trends. It has greater diversity and, in my estimation, a higher "coolness factor" than many other places. And Detroit's downtown core is revitalizing, albeit slowly. Beyond the new stadiums and casinos a more organic grassroots kind of redevelopment is taking place. A designated "creative corridor" around Wayne State University and the city's cultural institutions is springing back with coffee shops, art galleries, new restaurants, even a bed-and-breakfast. Young tech firms and design and architectural companies are converting old factories and warehouses into office space. New generations of young professionals and even some young families are moving back downtown into revitalized districts such as the city's fabled Lafayette Park, a seventy-eight-acre development with an amazing mix of verdant open space and modern high-rises and town houses designed by one of the original "star-chitects," Mies van der Rohe. Across the city, acre upon acre of once-useless vacant lots are being turned into vibrant urban farms. One writer even claimed that the city was turning into a veritable laboratory for innovative approaches to urban revitalization.[17]

So how long will it take Detroit or any other hard-hit Rust Belt city to come back? It's a big question—for which there are no easy answers. Some cities are quite resilient: places like New York and London seem to be able to remake themselves endlessly. Others fail and never bounce back, becoming essentially ghost towns. Detroit is going to need more than these few small pockets of hope to overcome the disappearance of its industrial legacy. It is likely to take a generation, probably two, for Detroit to bounce back from this economic crisis. That's about how long it took Boston to recover from the manufacturing crisis of the 1970s, or for Pittsburgh to undergo its renaissance. One thing is for certain: the Detroit—or the Cleveland or Buffalo or

Scranton—that emerges from this mess will bear little resemblance to the city it once was.

Greater Boston launched its efforts to remake its economy all the way back in the 1940s, in the wake of the decline of its textile and boot and shoe industries. It began with the creation of the early venture capital fund American Research and Development, which invested in Digital Equipment Corporation. When I studied there in the early 1980s, the MIT campus was still surrounded by derelict manufacturing buildings, which have now been remade into a complex of high-tech laboratories.

Pittsburgh is seeing the payoff now from revitalization efforts that were under way by the 1970s. As John Craig, the former editor of the *Pittsburgh Post-Gazette*, writes in the *Washington Post*, "So when I think about the lessons that the Steel City's 30-year economic transformation may hold for Detroit, another town built on an industry beaten by competition and confronting bankruptcy, I have to say that the first and hardest lesson for the Motor City is this: Fundamental change will be much longer in coming than you can imagine." He added, "You'll survive. But there'll be no 'getting over' your past, only moving beyond it."[18] Fineman offers similar advice. Pittsburgh suffered for two decades, "its wounds salved by the Steelers and other local sports teams, but the pain was very real," he says. The lesson from this, he continues, is to pick yourself up and get back to work. Don't expect the federal government or anyone else to save your city or bring back your industries. "It is that the old world will inevitably disappear, and that creating a new one is up to you, not someone else."

One response to the problems of rusted-out industrial cities such as Detroit has been a new urban reclamation effort called "shrinking cities."[19] The idea, perhaps inspired by Pittsburgh, has caught on in smaller cities in the American Midwest, such as Youngstown, Ohio, and Flint, Michigan, and their European counterparts. The basic notion is that older industrial cities need not grow to improve. They can be better places by making do with less, by focusing on improvements in the quality of life for their residents, and by bringing their level of infrastructure and housing into line with their smaller populations. A June 2009 story in the U.K. newspaper the *Telegraph* bore the wince-inducing headline "U.S. Cities May Have to Be Bulldozed to Survive."[20]

The concept that certain places would be better off by shrinking has been around for a while. The notion of "planned shrinkage" was originally proposed in the 1970s by then New York housing commissioner Roger Starr. The late Senator Daniel P. Moynihan once suggested that benign neglect could be part of an urban policy. Though Moynihan meant to focus attention on dying cities—a cause he worked on over his entire career—the term "benign neglect" ultimately came to represent the Nixon administration's neglectful attitude toward America's urban centers: let hopeless neighborhoods fall to dust, and support the healthier areas that remain standing.[21]

Today's shrinking-cities advocates are much more sensitive to the issues facing older industrial communities. They recognize how globalization and market forces work against some older communities and sensibly suggest that such places would be better served by proactively managing the process of economic transformation and adjustment and by devising strategies to enable those communities to improve their quality of life and realign with the new economic and fiscal realities.

The most successful examples of shrinking, such as Pittsburgh's, result not from top-down policies imposed by local governments but from organic, bottom-up, community-based efforts. While Pittsburgh's government and business leaders pressed for big-government solutions—new stadiums and convention centers—the city's real turnaround was driven by community groups and citizen-led initiatives. Community groups, local foundations, and nonprofits—not city hall or business-led economic development groups—drove its transformation, playing a key role in stabilizing and strengthening neighborhoods, building green, and spurring the development of the waterfront and redevelopment around the universities. Many of Pittsburgh's best neighborhoods, such as its South Side, are ones that were somehow spared from the wrath of urban renewal. Others, such as East Liberty, have benefited from community initiatives designed to remedy the damage done by large-scale urban renewal efforts that left vacant lots in place of functioning neighborhoods and built soulless public housing high-rise towers. That neighborhood is now home to several new community development projects, including a Whole Foods Market, which provides local jobs as well as serving as an anchor for the surrounding community. This kind of bottom-up process takes considerable time and perseverance. In Pittsburgh's case, it took the better part of a generation to achieve stability and the potential for longer-term revival.

The sad but unavoidable fact is that overall, and with few exceptions, places in the United States and in other advanced nations where the regional economies are based on blue-collar industries are headed for trouble. In my detailed statistical studies on hundreds of cities and regions, I found that those regions with large working-class concentrations have lower levels of economic output, lower incomes, lower levels of innovation, and lower levels of happiness. Our studies found this to hold true in a comparison of the fifty states and across the nations of the world, in a sample of more than one hundred countries.[22] Stop for a moment and think about that. In both the nations of the world and U.S. states, locations with large working-class concentrations are far less happy. In fact they appear downright unhappy. Perhaps Marx was right after all about the alienation that comes from industrial work, or, for the purposes of our discussion, the unhappiness found in working-class locations.

The bigger question, then, is this: Should public policy toward hard-pressed, economically strapped cities focus on people, not just by encouraging retraining but also by helping them relocate to places with a better job market? Or should policies focus on places, by fostering geographically targeted reinvestment? For many urban economists the answer is simple—put people first. "While regional diversity within the United States might prompt politicians to pursue policies that target aid to distressed regions," writes Harvard's Glaeser, "that seems likely to be counterproductive. America has always dealt with regional economic disparities through migration. . . . Today's recession will also prompt mobility, probably toward more skilled, more centralized cities with less historical commitment to manufacturing."[23] My own view is that in most cases it makes sense to put people first. At the end of the day, people—not industries or even places—should be our biggest concern. As Clyde Prestowitz, president of the Economic Strategy Institute, aptly put it, "The plight of these people is also in a way our plight."[24] We can best help those who are hardest hit by the crisis by providing a generous social safety net, investing in their education and skills, and encouraging them, when necessary, to move from declining places to ones that offer better opportunity. Especially in tough economic times, we're all better served by helping people. People need education and skills to shift from old industries to new jobs. And since these jobs are often in different places, they have to be able to move where the jobs are. This imperative is strongest for members of less-advantaged groups in declining areas, who we must prepare for new economic realities. There are times when it's simply better for families to relocate to where the jobs are than to wait for longer-term efforts to rebuild declining industries to take hold.[25]

That does not mean we should give up on places altogether. There is intelligent help we can offer to declining places that wish to turn around or at least stabilize themselves. First and foremost, their elected officials need to get over their love affair with big renewal projects. If we've learned anything over the past generation or two, it's that large-scale top-down government projects to revitalize communities do not work and frequently do more harm than good. Bailouts of old industries are also a poor use of limited resources, because they simply forestall the inevitable and do little to bolster the prospects for older industrial regions.

So what can be done? Instead of spending millions to lure or bail out factories, or hundreds of millions and in some cases billions to build stadiums, convention centers, and hotels, use that money to invest in local assets, spur local business formation and development, better employ local people and utilize their skills, and invest in improving quality of place. One leading economic developer, who has extensive experience in economic revitalization in the United States, Canada, and Europe, explained the shift in economic development toward older industrial regions this way: "Urban revitalization based on luring so-called big game projects no longer has a place in the advanced countries," he said. "If economic developers want to do that today, they should move to China. That's where all the big corporate projects are or are heading. Revitalizing older cities in North America and Europe increasingly depends on being able to support lots of smaller activities, groups, and projects." He talked about how efforts to support local entrepreneurship, build and nurture local clusters, develop arts and cultural industries, support local festivals and tourism, attract and retain people—efforts that he and his peers would have sneered at a decade or two ago—have become the core stuff of economic development. When taken together, seemingly smaller initiatives and efforts can and do add up in ways that confer real benefits to communities. These are the kinds of initiatives that Jane Jacobs and others have advocated as plain old good urbanism. And as chapter 21 will show, one of the most effective things the federal government can do to help revitalize older Rust Belt cities and regions is to invest in a high-speed rail network that would better connect them to one another and to other, more thriving economic hubs, shrinking the distance between them and building economic size and scale required to compete more effectively.

Cities can take bold steps beyond the remaking of their physical space. One brilliant and beautiful example can be found in the City of Brotherly Love, an initiative called "Graduate! Philadelphia." I've been making the point for years that cities with a higher percentage of college graduates in their populations are better positioned for long-term prosperity. The city of Philadelphia recognized this, too, and also knew it ranked poorly among cities in the level of educational attainment of its residents. Civic leaders also knew, however, that a very high percentage of the people, although they had no college degree, had accumulated some credits along the way. A partnership among the city government, foundations, and other private institutions formed to offer guidance and support to any Philadelphian who wanted to go back to school and get a degree. Quite a few nearby colleges and universities became partners in the project. A related project, Campus Philly, has worked to make the city and region more attractive to college students and to retain as well as attract recent college grads. And the city's major universities, especially the University of Pennsylvania, devised new, more cooperative approaches for revitalizing their surrounding neighborhoods by investing in local schools, supporting home and storefront improvements, and making their own health centers and facilities open to residents as well as students and faculty. Here is a city looking toward the future, developing a strategy to raise its competitive position by preparing more of its people to succeed in the postindustrial, knowledge-based economy of the Great Reset. It seems to be paying off. In 2009, while older Rust Belt and sprawling Sunbelt cities were literally hemorrhaging people, the city of Philadelphia saw its population increase.

As with so many things in life, the small stuff really can make a difference to the people living in cities. That sounds like an easy thing to say, but there is considerable research to back it up. The quality of life in the place we live is a key component of our happiness, according to surveys of tens of thousands of people conducted by the Gallup Organization. There are three key attributes that make people happy in their communities and cause them to develop a solid emotional attachment to the place they live in. The first is the physical beauty and the level of maintenance of the place itself—great open spaces and parks, historic buildings, and an attention to community aesthetics. The second is the ease with which people can meet others, make friends, and plug into social networks. The third piece of the happiness puzzle is the level of diversity, open-mindedness, and acceptance: Is there some equality of opportunity for all? Can anyone—everyone—contribute to and take pleasure from the community?[26] My own work with cities across the United States and Canada and around the world convinces me that none of these things can be accomplished by government-sponsored megaprojects. Instead, they are organic in nature and require real leadership and the active engagement of the community.

Chapter Thirteen

Northern Light

've come to know several cities intimately in my lifetime: Newark, Boston, Washington, Pittsburgh, Detroit. Now I have a new adopted hometown: Toronto, where I've lived since 2007. In some key ways, Toronto is a classic Frostbelt city; like nearby Buffalo, Cleveland, and Detroit, it borders the Great Lakes. Its early growth was powered by trade and industry, particularly its role as a food-processing center, which earned it the nickname "Hogtown." But while other Frostbelt cities have been declining for decades, Toronto has not only grown steadily; it has also weathered the economic crisis and maintained steady growth in the face of it.

There are several reasons for Toronto's resilience. For one, it's a big city which gives it the size and scale to do many things. With 2.5 million people living in the city itself, only three U.S. cities—New York, Los Angeles, and Chicago—boast larger populations. And more than 5.5 million total fill the greater Toronto area—or GTA, as it's called. Toronto is also the hub of a great megaregion that stretches west almost to Detroit, east to the capital, Ottawa, and Montreal, and south to Buffalo and Rochester. This area is home to 22 million people and represents $530 billion in economic output.

Toronto's size makes for a diverse economic structure, one that's less like Detroit's or even Chicago's and more a mix of those of New York, Los Angeles, and even San Francisco, with heavy concentrations of finance, media, film, and entertainment. It also has more than its share of information technology and biotechnology, with more within commuting distance—in Waterloo, home to Research in Motion (the BlackBerry company) and numerous other high-tech firms. Toronto ranked tenth on a recent *Forbes* ranking of the world's most economically powerful cities and eleventh in a separate comprehensive report on urban competitiveness.[1]

Toronto also benefits from a steady stream of immigration, which has made its population among the most diverse of any city in the world. Nearly half (some 46 percent) of Torontonians were born outside Canada's borders, making it one of the most ethnically diverse cities in the world. Though Miami may have a slightly greater percentage of foreign-born residents, the vast majority of them are from Latin America and the Caribbean, not the comprehensive, global spectrum of countries from which Toronto welcomes its new arrivals. Neither Miami nor Los Angeles nor New York City can compete with Toronto's cosmopolitan credentials.

But in contrast to American cities, even the best performing of them, Toronto's downtown core is loaded with middle-class families of roughly the same demographic that would live in, say, Bethesda, Maryland, as well as working-class and immigrant families. Toronto provides a workable model of an "urban family land" that stands in sharp relief to American cities, which are heavy on singles, childless couples, empty-nesters, and gays. Such diversity reflects the region's ability to attract top talent from around the world, providing a powerful spur to innovation and growth.

Toronto also benefits from a great quality of life and typically ranks atop the lists of the world's best places to live. It's been rated the fifth most livable city in the world—this according to the Economist Intelligence Unit in a report last year. The *Economist* found that Toronto is wealthy, healthy, well educated, and much safer than any American city of comparable size. In 2008, its murder rate was 1.9 per 100,000 residents, which makes it less than half as deadly as Des Moines, Iowa, one of the safest cities in the United States.[2]

Toronto's economic success is reflected in its housing prices, which are more like those of Boston or Washington, D.C., than Cleveland, Pittsburgh, or Detroit. After taking a slight hit at the apex of the crisis, its housing market bounced back quickly. In fact, the prices of Toronto homes rose 10 percent and sales were up 28 percent between September 2008 and September 2009, a time when the housing market in virtually every U.S. city was still tanking.[3] On a brisk October weekend in 2009, I noticed an open house sign on my street; the following Tuesday it was replaced by one that read "Sold." That very same week, a *New York Times* story pronounced that Toronto's financial district was in the midst of an unprecedented "building boom."[4] At a time when American cities were dotted with abandoned construction sites, the city's downtown was experiencing what the *Times* called an "unusual burst of construction," including three new energy-efficient, "green" office towers and three high-rise condo-hotel towers worth more than a billion dollars. "Toronto's real estate investment fundamentals and its place as Canada's financial capital are more sound than most international capitals—New York included," Blake Hutcheson, a partner and the head of global real estate investing at New York's Mount Kellett Capital, told the *Times*.

Part of the reason is that Toronto and all of Canada actually managed to avoid the humongous housing bubble and financial irresponsibility that plagued the United States. "Guess which country, alone in the industrialized world, has not faced a single bank failure, calls for bailouts or government intervention in the financial or mortgage sectors?" asked Fareed Zakaria after visiting Toronto for an economic roundtable with the country's leading young professionals and financial leaders. "Yup, Canada."[5] Zakaria notes that in 2008, the World Economic Forum ranked Canada's banking system as the most stable in the world, while the United States stood at fortieth. Tighter government regulations (including legal requirements that preclude buyers from walking away from underwater homes) and higher capital requirements helped Canadian banks stay profitable during the crisis. Canada's biggest banks have posted about $20 billion or so in write-downs and credit losses since 2007, a fraction of the $1.6 trillion losses taken by global financial services firms in the period, according to Bloomberg. As a result, they've been able to cut less and grow more. Canada's five biggest banks have pared 3,135 jobs, or about 1.1 percent, of their staff since the onset of the crisis. During this same time, Bank of America alone has eliminated 46,150 jobs, Citigroup has cut 38,900 positions, and Lehman Brothers lost 13,390 employees.[6]

"Canada has done more than survive this financial crisis," Zakaria adds. "The country is positively thriving in it." In fact, as he added, Canadian banks are well capitalized and poised to take advantage of opportunities that American and European banks cannot seize. The Toronto Dominion Bank, for example, which was the fifteenth-largest bank in North America in 2008, jumped to fifth place in 2009; the Royal Bank of Canada rose to fourth place. Only J. P. Morgan Chase, Wells Fargo, and Bank of America were larger among North American banks. Of course, as Toronto Dominion Deputy Chairman Frank McKenna mirthfully concedes, his bank's surge in the rankings was due less to the bank's actions than to the fact that U.S. banks shrank dramatically. Toronto Dominion ranked seventeenth based on market capitalization in 2009, while the Bank of Nova Scotia was twenty-fourth, and the Royal Bank of Canada was thirteenth, ahead of the traditional giants Barclays and Credit Suisse.[7]

All of this has meant good things for Toronto. Canadian financial institutions, clustered in Toronto's Bay Street financial district, have brought in more global talent, attracting top people in New York and London. "The profile of the Canadian banks on the global scale has been heightened exponentially over the course of the last year," a Toronto-based headhunter doing the recruiting told Bloomberg News. "They look more powerful and are able to attract talent that was historically not available to them."[8]

None of this is to say that Toronto has somehow sidestepped all the stubborn problems that infect most rapidly growing metropolitan centers. Income inequality is increasing, and the population is becoming more segmented by class, ethnic, and racial lines, according to a landmark report on the "three Torontos" by the University of Toronto's Centre for Urban and Community Studies.[9] The study paints a stark portrait of a city increasingly divided into three distinct geographic regions: a wealthy core; inner suburbs increasingly characterized by disadvantage, disconnection, and poverty; and outer suburbs populated by a shrinking mix of working- and middle-class families. And it points out that the growing economic polarization is overlaid with ethnicity. Despite this, Toronto is nowhere near as segmented and unequal as New York, Los Angeles, or Chicago.[10]

Still, I'm convinced that Toronto has a tremendous upside potential coming out of the current crisis. It won't topple New York or London as a financial center, nor will it dethrone Los Angeles as the international entertainment capital, but with banks this big and this stable, numerous knowledge-based industries thriving in the surrounding megaregions, and an increasingly diverse population, it will gain ground. And with employment opportunities in the largest centers eroding, it can make a big move on top global talent. It stands as a model of an older, once heavily industrial Frostbelt city that has not only turned itself around but continues to grow and thrive.

█

Chapter Fourteen

Sun Sets on the Sunbelt

For a generation or more, no area of the United States has seen more mad, unchecked growth than the Sunbelt, the massive swath stretching across the entire southern United States from South Carolina and Florida all the way to Arizona, Nevada, and southern California. A good deal of that growth made sense: Los Angeles grew up as the world's center for media and entertainment; San Jose and Austin developed significant, innovative high-technology industries; Houston became a hub for energy production; Nashville enjoyed a unique niche in low-cost music recording and production; Charlotte emerged as a center for cost-effective banking.

But in the heady days of the housing bubble, some Sunbelt cities and regions experienced an irrational boom, centered largely on real estate and construction. Phoenix and Las Vegas are the most extreme examples: with sunny weather and plenty of empty land, they got caught in a classic boom cycle. Across Florida too, developers put up new condos and communities seemingly on every available acre. Rather than being built for workers employed in growing industries, housing became the central industry itself. At the height of the boom, the combination of real estate, housing, and the construction-related industries accounted for more than a quarter of the entire economies of Las Vegas, Miami, and Phoenix; more than 30 percent of Orlando's; and upward of 40 percent of that of Naples, Florida.[1] In these places, real estate, mortgage finance, and construction literally became the economy, making up a bigger piece of it and employing more workers than manufacturing, government, health care, and education combined.

This created what I like to call the great growth illusion of development for development's sake. New housing development brought new shopping malls, with chain restaurants, big-box stores, and the like providing at least the semblance of expanding jobs and growth. Of course, all these new homes needed furniture, electronics, appliances, granite countertops, window treatments, and more, necessitating even more retail. And the people flocking there needed more and more cars, which meant more car dealerships and ultimately more roads. The syndrome spilled over to the public sector. Cities grew, tax coffers filled, spending increased, and the people just kept coming. Yet the boom neither followed nor resulted in the development of sustainable, scalable, highly productive industries or services. It was fueled and funded by housing, and housing was its primary product. In this debt-intoxicated, crazy real estate bubble era, whole cities and metro regions became giant Ponzi schemes.

Phoenix, for instance, grew from 983,000 people in 1990 to more than 1.5 million in 2007. One of its suburbs, Mesa, exploded out of nowhere to more than half a million residents, filling with more people than Pittsburgh, Cleveland, or Miami. As housing starts and housing prices rose, so did tax revenues, and the fattened public coffers allowed for a major capital spending boom throughout the Greater Phoenix area. Arizona State University built a new downtown Phoenix campus, and the city expanded its convention center and constructed a twenty-mile light-rail system connecting Phoenix, Mesa, and Tempe.

Then the bubble burst, and the Phoenix area registered the largest decline in housing values in the country. By April 2009, Phoenix housing prices dropped to less than half of their peak. Mortgages Ltd., the state's largest private commercial lender, filed for bankruptcy. While images of mass foreclosures in Rust Belt cities like Detroit are common, Phoenix saw more than seventy-five thousand foreclosures between 2005 and 2009.[2] The debt-fueled, speculative binge extended well beyond residential housing, however, affecting Phoenix's hotel industry as well. "Phoenix suffers from the dual challenges of over-building and shrinking demand due to the national drop-off in corporate conferences," said David Loeb, a hotel industry analyst, told the *Wall Street Journal*. "All of this means that Phoenix's hotel market has experienced one of the steepest downturns among the big markets."[3]

Overstretched and overbuilt, the region experienced an economic double whammy: on top of its decline in house values, many of its retirees (some 21 percent of its residents are over age fifty-five) saw their retirement savings decimated. "We had a big bubble here, and it burst," Anthony Sanders, a professor of economics and finance at Arizona State University, told *USA Today* in December 2008. "We've taken Kevin Costner's *Field of Dreams* and now it's 'Field of Screams.' If you build it, nobody comes."[4] The economic crash quickly turned into a fiscal crisis of government. The city's budget deficit swelled some $200 million, prompting the city government to petition for federal funds to help it deal with its financial mess. The state of Arizona even resorted to trying to sell its state office buildings to cover the growing financial gap, lampooned in a side-splitting segment on Jon Stewart's *The Daily Show*.

Phoenix wasn't alone among the Sunbelt sufferers. By late 2009, housing prices had fallen more than 50 percent off their peak in Las Vegas. Florida, the other great American retirement destination, also felt the sharp pop of the housing bubble as real estate prices tumbled more than 40 percent from their peak in Miami and Tampa. The crisis decimated the Sunbelt's nouveau riche, many of whom had made their pile in real estate. Phoenix lost 34 percent of its high-net-worth individuals, those with more than $1 million in assets apart from their home; Las Vegas lost 38 percent; Miami and Orlando, 42 percent each; and Tampa, 51 percent.[5]

Plummeting home prices triggered a cascading series of related problems. Sunbelt cities developed the nation's highest concentration of homes underwater—those where the amount owed exceeds the current value. Las Vegas led the nation with 67.2 percent of its homes underwater in May 2009. In Stockton and Modesto, California, more than half of all homes were underwater. Phoenix, Orlando,

Reno, Riverside, Vallejo and Merced, California, and Port St. Lucie, Florida, rounded out the top ten with more than 40 percent of their homes underwater, roughly twice the national average.[6] Some places, like people, never learn. In late 2008 and early 2009, foreclosures and other distressed sales made up a huge percentage of housing in hard-hit Sunbelt cities. In Phoenix, for example, so-called absentee buyers—that is, buyers who were not going to live in the home they purchased—accounted for nearly four of every ten homes sold in April 2009, leading the *New York Times* to conclude, "Real estate got just about everyone into trouble in Phoenix, and the thinking seems to be that real estate is going to get everyone out."[7]

It's obvious now that housing was an unsustainable engine of economic growth. Too many cities simply lacked the underlying economic base and productivity to support high housing prices. Historically, housing prices have been about three times income, but by 2006 they had soared to more than five times income. In Irvine, California, the housing-price-to-income ratio hit a peak of 8.6.[8] There's a measure I like even better: the housing-to-wage ratio. It shows the enormous disparity between housing prices and wages that existed in the Sunbelt. Six regions, all in the Sunbelt, posted ratios of 15 or greater. Another twelve metropolitan areas, again all in the Sunbelt, had ratios above 10. Las Vegas' ratio was 9, Miami's 8.4, and Phoenix's 7.2, all sky-high by any standard.[9]

With their debt-fueled economies driven by housing, it's no surprise that the housing crisis has brought severe economic pain to many Sunbelt cities. According to a study by the Brookings Institution, of the twenty worst-performing regions in the country, fourteen were in the Sunbelt, including Las Vegas and Miami.[10] Both Las Vegas and Phoenix saw their economic Stress Index value—a composite measure of economic hardship developed by the Associated Press—more or less double between December 2007 and March 2009.[11]

At the peak of the crisis the Sunbelt states and cities witnessed something that had once been unthinkable: after a century of unchecked growth, many locations had their first taste of mass outmigration and population decline. "The housing collapse and economic crisis are dramatically transforming the population and political landscape of the nation by ending the Sunbelt boom that dominated growth for a generation," wrote *USA Today*'s Haya El Nasser and Paul Overberg.[12] During the peak years of the real estate boom, from 2004 to 2006, the state of Florida was growing by 1,100 people *a day*. But by 2009, for the first time in more than a century, more people left Florida than moved there. The Sunshine State, long leading the nation in attracting people from other states, now had more people going the other way. "It's dramatic," Stanley K. Smith, a University of Florida professor who tracks the state's population, told the *New York Times*. "You have a state that was booming and has been a leader in population growth for the last 100 years that suddenly has seen a substantial shift." "It's got to be a real psychological blow," added William H. Frey, a leading demographer at the Brookings Institution. "I don't know if you can take a whole state to a psychiatrist, but the whole Florida economy was based on migration flows."[13]

I f a picture is worth a thousand words, here's one that has to be worth ten thousand: online video of a bulldozer razing brand-new homes in a suburban Sunbelt development. I call it the "suburban bulldozer"—a tip of the hat to the much older phrase "federal bulldozer," which referred to the government-sponsored demolition of inner-city neighborhoods during the heyday of federal urban renewal in the 1950s and 1960s.[14] The story behind the video was that Guaranty Bank of Austin had taken over the homes in foreclosure—four in the suburban Texas development and another twelve in California. The bank said it was tearing them down to create a "safe environment" for the neighbors. It's interesting to pause there and note that brand-new homes, standing empty, could be seen as posing a danger to a neighborhood. In fact, just as youths squatted in abandoned tenements in the South Bronx and bohemians homesteaded the empty lofts and factories of Brooklyn, many of the empty McMansions of the Sunbelt are providing shelter to homeless and jobless young people. It's entirely possible, of course, that the bank just decided it was cheaper to destroy those houses than to keep them up to building code. In some similarly affected parts of the country, the bulldozers may not even be necessary; the homes are collapsing on their own.

At the peak of the building boom, housing was literally being thrown up all over the place. Quality suffered, and many houses put up during the peak are in trouble. In a July 2009 story aptly titled "Cracked Houses—What the Boom Built," the *Wall Street Journal*'s M. P. McQueen told the story of California home owners Robert and Kay Lynn. Early one morning in their new golf-course home in Rancho Murieta, California, the Lynns awoke to the "pop, pop, pop" of what they thought were acorns falling onto the roof. "Little did we know it was the house cracking," Mrs. Lynn told McQueen.[15] As it turned out, their house was shifting toward the golf course. The Lynns say their losses on the house were even more painful than losing their retirement money in the stock market. "The one thing that won't get better is this house, which will always have foundation problems," Mr. Lynn told the *Journal*. "It has driven me from retirement to doing part-time work at the golf course, and I thought I was financially stable for the rest of my life." McQueen writes that "hundreds of thousands of people from California to Georgia say their almost-new homes need costly repairs because of construction defects." Indeed, more than 2 million homes were built annually at the height of the boom. There weren't enough skilled construction workers or quality materials available to keep up with the furious pace of building, but the houses kept on sprouting. There weren't even enough home inspectors to monitor all the new construction. The shoddy workmanship has been tough on home owners whose houses are already underwater. "Because of tumbling real-estate values, those stuck with faulty houses say repairs often cost more than the homes are now worth," McQueen noted. "Many say they can't refinance their mortgages or sell, and they have no equity to leverage for repairs."

Could this be just the tip of the iceberg? Could the once-desirable suburban and exurban communities—with their endless cul-de-sacs and gated McMansions—be on their way to becoming the blighted and abandoned communities of tomorrow? "The future is not likely to wear well on suburban housing," wrote the urban planning expert Christopher Leinberger in an attention-getting essay in the *Atlantic*, "The Next Slum?"[16] Many of the inner-city neighborhoods that began their decline in the 1960s consisted of sturdily built, turn-of-the-century row houses, tough enough to withstand being broken up into apartments and requiring relatively little upkeep. "By comparison, modern suburban houses, even high-end McMansions, are cheaply built," he writes. "Hollow doors and wallboard are less durable than solid-oak doors and lath-and-plaster walls. The plywood floors that lurk under wood veneers or carpeting tend to break up and warp as the glue that holds the wood together dries out; asphalt-shingle roofs typically need replacing after 10 years. Many recently built houses take what structural integrity they have from drywall—their thin wooden frames are too flimsy to hold the houses up."

Some time ago, I asked the Carnegie Mellon urbanist and architect David Lewis what he thought was the biggest issue of urban revitalization of our time. He responded without hesitation that the eventual decline of sprawling, shoddily constructed exurban communities would make even the tough urban cores of cities like Philadelphia or even Detroit—with their compact infrastructure, dense neighborhood footprints, and authentic and historic structures—look downright idyllic by comparison. Not to mention, he added, that the entire boom-bust housing cycle we've just completed amounted to a giant waste of resources and a potential drag on long-run economic competitiveness and prosperity.

Will people continue to wash out of the Sunbelt's once booming cities and regions as fast as they washed in, leaving empty sprawl and its accompanying ills? Will these cities gradually attract more businesses and industries, allowing them to build more diverse and more resilient economies? Or will they subsist on tourism, which may be meager for quite some time, and on the Social Security checks of their retirees? No matter which course they follow, their character and atmosphere are likely to change radically.

■ ■ ■

But not every city in the Sunbelt is in the dumps. A number of them—Atlanta, Dallas, and Houston—were all able to weather the storm reasonably well. So did college towns from Chapel Hill, North Carolina, and Austin, Texas, to Athens, Georgia, and Gainesville, Florida. And as we've seen, Charlotte was able to consolidate its position in the financial industry and diversify its economy to some degree. A close parsing of the data shows that there are two different and distinct Sunbelts. There's the one that's reeling, the sprawling, real-estate-driven, shallow-rooted, housing-wrecked swath of Arizona, Florida, Nevada, and parts of California. And then there's the healthy one, stretching from Colorado and New Mexico to resource-rich Texas and Oklahoma, which has seen more durable growth and had little of the speculative housing boom that wreaked havoc on Phoenix or Las Vegas. Cities such as San Antonio, Texas, for instance, ranked as the nation's "strongest performing," according to Brookings' MetroMonitor, with Oklahoma City and Tulsa; Austin, Houston, Dallas, and McAllen, Texas; Little Rock, Arkansas; Baton Rouge, Louisiana; and Omaha, Nebraska, rounding out the top ten.[17]

Surprisingly, ten of the cities with the fastest population growth in 2008 were in the Sunbelt. But they were anything but centers of real estate sprawl. They were largely technology and talent hubs, such as Round Rock, Texas, a suburb of Austin, which scored as the second-fastest-growing community in the nation. Right behind Round Rock was Cary, North Carolina, a Research Triangle suburb and home to the SAS Institute, while nearby Raleigh tied for sixth on the list.[18]

It is possible for even the most troubled of the Sunbelt cities to make a comeback. The Sunbelt benefits from warm and sunny weather and has spawned its share of big cities and megahubs. Miami is the financial center of Latin America and the hub of the large South Florida megaregion, which includes the entertainment cluster in Tampa and the high-tech and convention industry of Orlando. Phoenix is the center of a large region and has substantial university and technology assets upon which to build. But to do so, it will need to replace housing speculation and overaggressive suburban real estate expansion as a main engine of its economy.

Las Vegas may be the most interesting case of all. The city has economic assets that can make it much more than a city of sand and sprawl. As the economic development specialists Robert E. Lang and Mark Muro note in a February 2009 article in the *Las Vegas Sun*, "Las Vegas, best known for its gambling and entertainment, has also emerged as a deal-making center of world importance."[19] Vegas has become the convention capital of the United States and the world, hosting megaconventions such as the International Consumer Electronics Show (with its 150,000 attendees), the World of Concrete exposition (with some 85,000 attendees), and the National Association of Broadcasters Show (with 110,000 attendees). I can attest to the size of the last one—I gave a keynote address there in winter 2009. It is actually a series of eleven or so conventions linked together that stretches across several city blocks, making what can only be called a city within a city. Las Vegas is the only venue in the world big enough to hold shows like these. "These shows form ad hoc market exchanges that gather whole industries to a common space to make deals," write Lang and Muro. "The irony is that what happens in Las Vegas arguably reaches well beyond the city in terms of business activity. The city's reputation for discretion in personal matters has enhanced its attractiveness as a public space."

In the future, Las Vegas can build on its emergence as a key node in global business networking. "The fact that Las Vegas is especially fun and frivolous—an adult Disneyland—creates even more incentive for people to attend its conferences, which is how it became the nation's preeminent convention destination in the first place," write Lang and Muro. "To all the killjoys who now want to shame people out of a Las Vegas convention visit, we say that a major stimulus for the country remains the social lubricant that Sin City provides business contacts." They're onto something important. Not only has Las Vegas emerged as a center for business interaction, it's also home to a cluster of firms specializing in gaming technology and entertainment staging, both of which have sizable export markets. The proximity of Vegas to the gargantuan southern California megaregion is another advantage as it ties the city to a broader population center and a huge entertainment-technology industrial complex.

Ironically, these genuine strengths of the Las Vegas economy were overwhelmed by the rush to the fictitious wealth of the housing bubble. The question is, which Las Vegas economy will prevail? "Las Vegas's fate now hangs in the balance between its failing real estate industry and more resilient convening/entertainment industries," Lang wrote to me via e-mail. The trick, he added, is for the city to turn its advantages in conventions and business networking into something more than tourist dollars, by generating new industries around them. One possibility, he said, is to leverage the Las Vegas Market and Design Center, a more or less permanent trade show for the interior design and building industry, to attract an architectural and design industry to the city. "Las Vegas is really a lab to see how major 'convening regions' may leverage their now ephemeral advantages as world cities by capturing these exchanges in their year-round economy," he wrote.

Ever since this tiny desert station stop mushroomed into America's sin city in the years after the Second World War, it has stood somehow outside the life of the rest of the country. In Las Vegas, you could escape not just the drudgery of the workaday world but, it seemed, the very rules that society imposes. You could see movie stars, win a bundle of money, or lose a bundle of money. You could even get married, if you had a free half hour. All bets were off in Vegas. The cities own recent ad campaign even seized on this implicit understanding: "What happens in Vegas, stays in Vegas."

Though we've come to see Las Vegas as the exception to everything normal in America, it is possibly the best, most vivid example of what has brought us to this turning point. Vegas is outsized and exaggerated, to be sure, but as any debater will tell you, sometimes you have to exaggerate to make a point. As Muro wrote in a separate commentary in the *Las Vegas Sun*, the city's "gargantuan problems and its necessary way forward mirror and take to an extreme those of our troubled nation as a whole. Southern Nevada may well stand at ground zero of a national economic crisis made massive by speculation, financial game-playing, and insufficient attention to the fundamentals."[20]

Las Vegas left itself open and vulnerable by relying on one basic source of revenue: consumption, whether tourist dollars from gaming, hotels, restaurants, and shops or the flow of borrowed dollars for homes and construction. It was, essentially, a double whammy. As if things weren't bad enough, Muro notes all the cracks in the gleaming veneer: low education levels, woefully insufficient infrastructure, little or no investment in technological innovation.

What next? "Las Vegas epitomized the questions facing the whole nation. Where will the next period of growth come from?" asks Muro. "How can we build a more sustainable new economic order? How will we use the bad times to change and get better?" These questions are exactly the right ones to be asking about Las Vegas and America as a whole.

Part III

**A
NEW
WAY
OF
LIFE**

Chapter Fifteen

The Reset Economy

To anyone who was paying attention over the last several years, this economic crisis was all but inevitable. "I actually think that there was always an unsustainable feel about what had happened on Wall Street over the last 10, 15 years," President Barack Obama told the *New York Times* in the spring of 2009, "and it's not that different from the unsustainable nature of what was happening during the dot-com boom, where people in Silicon Valley could make enormous sums of money, even though what they were peddling never really had any signs it would ever make a profit. That doesn't mean, though, that Silicon Valley is still not a huge, critical, important part of our economy, and Wall Street will remain a big, important part of our economy, just as it was in the '70s and the '80s." He added, "We don't want every single college grad with mathematical aptitude to become a derivatives trader. We want some of them to go into engineering, and we want some of them to be going into computer design."[1] We'd all have to agree with the president on that.

We already intuit that our society is changing in deep and fundamental ways—all of our habits and behaviors, from how we shop and what we buy, to how we spend our free time and to the values that govern our lives. This is what Kurt Andersen means when he talks about a reset in our values.[2] Many argue that we've seen the rise of a "new frugality" as people shift away from conspicuous consumption to simpler, more basic priorities, from a lifestyle where people thought they could purchase their way to happiness to something better and more real. Americans have certainly begun to save more and rely less on credit, at least partly because credit has become much harder to get. To my mind, any move away from the outrageous, over-the-top materialism that went on for far too long is a very good thing. However, a shift in values cannot, by itself, power economic recovery and spur a new round of prosperity. And permanently reduced consumption means less demand and a lower rate of growth.

For the Great Reset to become a bona fide recovery, society needs to come full circle to harness not only emergent and shifting values but also to generate new technologies, new economic systems, and new patterns of consumption. The next Great Reset must ultimately do for our times what suburbanization did for the postwar era—take shape as a new lifestyle and a new economic landscape that can ultimately power new kinds of demand and undergird a new round of growth.

Pundits talk about how change happens at the speed of light in the digital age, but the current Reset will be anything but automatic. "Unlike some recent recessions, this time the economy cannot go back to where it was prior to the recession," writes the economist Mark Thoma, "and the structural change that must occur to move resources out of housing and the financial sector and into other, productive uses will take time to bring about."[3]

I don't have a crystal ball. Nobody can say in advance exactly what this new economy, new way of life, this new spatial fix, will ultimately look like. During the Great Depression, my parents could scarcely have imagined they would be buying a suburban house on what had once been farmland. As we've seen, recovery from both the Long Depression of the 1870s and the Great Depression of the 1930s—the First and Second Resets—took the better part of two or three decades. Trying to paint a detailed portrait of what our economy, society, and daily life will look like once this crash is a piece of history would be like trying to predict the full flowering of postwar suburbanization from the vantage point of Franklin Roosevelt's inauguration day in 1932.

We can, however, begin to identify a set of forces, distilled and documented, playing out in our society that will almost certainly power a real Great Reset and a more sustainable new way of life. They are emerging organically across our economy, rather than resulting from top-down policy or programs. We can see them in new consumption patterns, new ways of organizing and managing businesses, and the factors that determine where and how we live. We need to understand the momentum generated by these forces so that we can nurture and encourage the most promising of them, even as we let go of older, unproductive ways and work to mitigate the most serious costs they entail. To ensure a true, lasting recovery, we'll need to mobilize and guide these shifting forces so that they come together into a workable system. A new spatial fix—a new geography of working and living—will be our only path back to renewed economic growth, confidence, and prosperity.

The financial crash was the event that brought on the economic crisis, but the Great Reset is the consequence of a much deeper and fundamental shift in the underlying engine of our economy. Over the past three decades, our economy has shifted from manufacturing and blue-collar industries to professional, technical, and creative jobs. The United States added some 20 million jobs in the creative, professional, and knowledge sectors of its economy between 1980 and 2006. Wages from these knowledge jobs add up to roughly $2 trillion, amounting to half of all U.S. wages and salaries. The same trend is visible across the advanced countries of northern Europe, Canada, Australia, New Zealand, and Japan, where the ranks of creative workers make up 30 to 40 percent of the workforce.

As I noted earlier, just as the Long Depression was a product of the First Industrial Revolution and the Great Depression a product of the Second Industrial Revolution, the current crisis is bound up with the Third Industrial Revolution—the shift from an economy based on making things to one that revolves around knowledge and creativity.

The financial bubble that developed is a product of this deeper shift—part and parcel of a long historical cycle. The New York University finance expert Thomas Philippon has shown how the financial sector rises and falls in line with major epochs of economic transformation and growth in his detailed research tracking the financial industry's share of GDP from 1860 to the present.[4] The financial sector's share of GDP increased from about 1 to 2 percent before the crash of 1873 and the First Reset. It then jumped from 2 percent to more than 4 percent of GDP in the boom preceding the crash of 1929 and the Second Reset. It then settled back down into the 2 to 4 percent range from the late 1940s through about 1980. It spiked massively between 1980 and the current crash, reaching 8.3 percent of GDP in 2006, double what it was in the 1940s and 1950s and four times the percentage at the turn of the last century. Philippon notes that the finance sector's share is due to fall back from this level and is likely to decline to roughly 7 percent of GDP.[5] I can see it falling further to 6 or even 5 percent, which is more or less in line with its historic level before the run-up of the 1980s and 1990s.

In another study, Philippon and Ariell Reshef from the University of Virginia show that the tremendous rise in the wages, salaries, and bonuses paid to financial professionals boomed in two eras: the 1920s and today.[6] After the Great Depression, once new financial regulations were put into place, the tremendous rewards once paid to financial types declined and talent flowed into other industries. For most of the postwar golden age, the earnings of financial types were in line with those of other professionals. The wages of financial professionals actually declined sharply in the 1930s, according to their analysis, and grew at a normal pace until the 1980s before exploding in recent times. Perhaps they will fall back again today, although the billion dollars in Goldman Sachs bonuses in 2009 might give pause to that thought. "As a society, do we want to put a third of our best brains in the financial sector?" Philippon rhetorically quipped to the *New York Times*.[7] New York University economist Nouriel Roubini echoed a similar concern: "When you have more financial engineers than computer engineers, you know that the brightest minds have gone into something where, probably, the margin was excessive," he told the *New Republic*. "Maybe some of these bright people are going to do something entrepreneurial, more creative, or go into government. I think that's actually a good change."[8] Me, too.

Instead of being caused by the financial meltdown, a number of astute economists argue, the financial crisis is actually a symptom of a much more serious underlying economic malady. It's not just that finance has grown bloated and diverted resources and talent away from much-needed innovation and upgrading of our key industries; the real economy itself has weakened, as productivity and innovation have faltered in both traditional industries and high-tech ones. The strongest voice in this argument belongs to former *BusinessWeek* chief economist Michael Mandel. In a series of articles and postings on his influential blog, Mandel amassed a mountain of persuasive data showing how the past decade was a lost one for both productivity and innovation. Job growth was anemic, and wages for most Americans went nowhere.

"What if outside of a few high-profile areas, the past decade has seen far too few commercial innovations that can transform lives and move the economy forward? What if, rather than being an era of rapid innovation, this has been an era of innovation interrupted?" Mandel asks.[9] The crux of his argument is that many, if not most, of the major new breakthrough innovations in areas from biotech to micromachines have failed to materialize. America's high-tech trade went from a $30 billion surplus in 1998 to a $53 billion deficit by 2008. Such weak performance in technological innovation paved the way for the financial bubble and ultimately the economic collapse. "In the late 1990s most economists and CEOs agreed that the U.S. was embarking on a once-in-a-century innovation wave—not just in info tech but also in biotech and many other technologies," Mandel continues. "Forecasters upped their long-run growth estimates for the U.S. economy. Consumers borrowed against their home equity, assuming their future incomes would rise. And foreign investors lent

America money by buying up U.S. securities, assuming the country would come up with enough new products to pay off the accumulated trade deficit."

We've already seen that innovation tends to slow down in the early phases of economic crises, only to restart during the Resets that follow those crises. American innovation declined twice in the past decade or so—once in the wake of the 2001 tech bubble and again right before the economic and financial crisis.[10] Even so, the overall level of American innovation in 2007—evidenced by the total number of patents or the number of patents per scientific researcher—was significantly higher than a decade earlier. Does that suggest that the U.S. system of innovation is out of the woods and poised to bounce back? Not really, for two reasons.

The geography of innovation has shifted significantly in the past couple of decades. Innovation is up considerably in established high-tech centers from Silicon Valley and Seattle to Austin and North Carolina's Research Triangle. But it is way, way down in America's industrial cities such as Pittsburgh and Detroit, in Sunbelt cities such as Dallas and Houston, and even in big centers such as New York and Chicago. At the same time, foreign inventors have become key players in American innovation. Foreign-born scientists currently make up 17 percent of all bachelor's degree holders, 29 percent of master's degree holders, 38 percent of PhDs, and nearly a quarter of all scientists and engineers in the United States. Anywhere between a third and half of all Silicon Valley start-ups during the 1990s had a foreign-born entrepreneur or scientist on their core founding team.[11] In the past decade, foreign inventors have come to account for almost half of all newly patented innovations. Innovation is no longer a national game but a global one. Anything that might slow the immigration or inflow of foreign inventors or redirect their inventions and patents, for example a backlash against foreign workers, would impede American innovation and the U.S. economy as a whole. It could also slow down economic development elsewhere, as many of those innovations are likely to be actually produced—the factories built and jobs created—outside the United States.

■ ■ ■

Today's Reset will affect our society at a deeper level than did the Resets of the past. We are living through an even more powerful and fundamental economic shift, from an industrial system to an economy that is increasingly powered by knowledge, creativity, and ideas. The crisis itself reflects our inability in the United States and around most of the world to build a durable economic system that can capture these huge new sources of productivity and growth. Instead of reinforcing the economy, the financial system started to undermine it—funneling capital that could have been used to create new technologies and industries into real estate or shaky financial instruments, sucking up scads of talent, and ultimately generating the series of bubbles that got us into this mess in the first place. "At the heart of the current crisis is a fundamental confusion about the nature of wealth," writes the *Economist*. "Were an extraterrestrial to be shown a room full of gold ingots, a stack of twenty-dollar bills or a row of numbers on a computer screen, he might be puzzled as to their function. Our reverence for these objects might seem as bizarre to him as the behavior of the male bowerbird (which decorates its nest with shiny objects to attract a mate) seems to us." Real wealth is based on "the goods and products we wish to consume or of things (factories, machinery, an educated workforce) that give us the ability to produce more such goods and services." Financial assets, on the other hand, "arise from the desire to postpone consumption so that money can be saved, either for precautionary reasons or to invest so that more goods and services can be consumed in the future." Looked at this way, the story concludes, "financial assets are not 'wealth' but a claim on real wealth."[12]

The role of finance changed from being, in the words of William Black, a "servant" of the economy to a "predator."[13] It has grown too large. "The finance sector is an intermediary—essentially a 'middleman,'" he writes. "Like all middlemen, it should be as small as possible, while still being capable of accomplishing its mission." Instead of supporting the real wealth producing parts of the economy, it has become a parasite on them. Rather than putting capital together with enterprise, as a middleman should do, finance itself became the target enterprise, its only product being more capital. "In addition to siphoning off capital for its own benefit, the finance sector misallocates the remaining capital in ways that harm the real economy," he adds. "Because the financial sector cares almost exclusively about high accounting yields and 'profits,' it misallocates capital away from firms and entrepreneurs that could best improve the real economy (e.g., by reducing short-term profits through funding the expensive research and development that can produce innovative goods and superior sustainability)."

Finance also siphons off talent from key parts of the real economy as well. Study after study has shown that the United States suffers from critical shortages of scientists and engineers, and, as we've just seen, it has grown increasingly to depend on foreign talent to fill these gaps. Over the past couple of decades, top graduates in math, science, and technology have been lured to Wall Street by extraordinary salaries. "Individuals with these quantitative backgrounds work overwhelmingly in devising the kinds of financial models that were important contributors to the financial crisis," Black writes. "We take people that could be conducting the research and development work essential to the success of our real economy (including its success in becoming sustainable) and put them instead in financial sector activities where, because of that sector's perverse incentives, they further damage both the financial sector and the real economy."

It's time we stop confusing the practice of moving money around with generating real wealth. If we want to prosper again, we'll need to move the economy away from finance capitalism and back toward the aptly dubbed real economy—investing once again in technology and human capital along with the new infrastructure that can make long-term economic growth possible.

This may already be happening. I'm not talking about the legions of former bankers, traders, and hedge fund managers, featured in countless media stories, who seem to have found their "true selves" by opening a yoga studio, coffee shop, or restaurant. Young people appear to be rethinking their career options now that finance has lost some of its luster. Huge numbers of Harvard grads poured into finance during the 1990s and early 2000s, but all that's changing now, according to annual surveys of graduating seniors conducted by the *Harvard Crimson*.[14] In 2009, half as many Harvard grads said they were pursing finance, falling from 23 percent in 2008 to 11.5 percent in 2009. Consulting also fell off a cliff, with the share of grads dropping from 16 percent to 8.5 percent.

So where were those Harvard grads heading? Health care and education. The share in education increased from 10 to 15 percent of grads, while those in health care increased from 6 to 12 percent. Despite the conventional view that government work, which combines "doing good" with a measure of job security, might become more attractive, the share of grads taking jobs in government fell slightly this year, from 4.5 to 3 percent. The *Crimson* suggests that this is "a paradoxical trend given the Democratic victories in the 2008 elections and the fact that seventy-four percent of Harvard seniors describe themselves as more liberal or considerably more liberal than the average American." Perhaps the student editors should not have been so surprised. Having taught public policy students for the better part of three decades, I've seen a long-running trend away from traditional government work, which many young people perceive as overly hierarchical and bureaucratic. Public service- and cause-oriented students tend to gravitate toward smaller-scale, more flexible nonprofits, where they believe they can have more immediate impact. The *Crimson* reports that nonprofit organizations drew 14 percent of the graduating class, more than ever before. Possibly the most telling result produced by the Harvard survey had to do with grads' dream jobs and careers. When they were asked what career they would choose if finances were not a concern, the top choice was the arts, with 16 percent choosing it as their "dream field," followed by public service (12.5 percent) and education (12 percent). Less than half this number, just 5 percent of grads, named finance and consulting.

We're witnessing a replay of the age-old conflict between "traders" and "builders," as Geoff Beattie, the head of Woodbridge, dubs it. Traders make money off, well, trading things. They create little or no real wealth, because they do not engage in productivity; they profit through trading. Builders, on the other hand, focus on investing in real assets in the real economy. They build wealth for the long term. Personally, I like to think about these as metaphorical labels, about the kinds of enterprises people engage in beyond the realm of money and finance. The industrialists of another age were "builders," giants of innovation and manufacturing: they made steel and cars and railroads, built newspaper empires, or powered the world with electricity, tangibly improving the lives of all. The founders of Apple and Microsoft, Genentech and Google may be cut from that same cloth. But the landscape today is littered with instant tycoons who made their fortunes on tiny upticks in the stock market or by trading shares in other people's debt. For far too many of these "traders," the only product was profit and the only customers were themselves. Clearly, these are extreme examples, but I raise them only to make this point: in either sense—literal or figurative—builders need to take their pre-eminent position back from the traders for the economy of the future to flourish.

Don't think, however, that finance will go away. Obama's right when he says that finance will remain a "big, important part of our economy." It's crucial to channeling capital across the global economy. And my own research shows that it is one of four or five crucial sectors of the economy, alongside business and management; science and technology; and arts, entertainment, and media, that drive the growth of cities and regions. But finance too will have to shift from a trading to a building orientation. Our focus on shoring up and restoring the financial system for its own sake carries with it real risk. The purpose of finance is to support and lubricate the economy, which is what creates goods and services, generates the great bulk of new jobs, and generates real wealth and income for people. I agree completely with economist William Black, who writes, "We must not spend virtually all of our reform efforts on the finance sector and assume that if we solve its defects we will have solved the other fundamental reasons why the real economy has remained so dysfunctional for decades. We need to work simultaneously to fix finance and the real economy."[15]

Insiders began to worry years ago, when day traders and other fast-buck dreamers wrested the financial markets from the hands of thoughtful investors. It wasn't long before the largest institutions, which couldn't turn their backs on the windfall profits generated by the cowboy derivatives traders and currency-swap schemers, institutionalized that gambling mentality. Our economic system needs to stop channeling funds into super-risky, highly leveraged, and speculative areas. Instead, we must return to the original vision and purpose of the financial markets: supporting innovation and the growth of the real economy.

Chapter Sixteen

Good Job Machine

magine yourself living a hundred and fifty years ago, watching your neighbors and relatives packing their belongings and preparing to walk off the family farm forever. It must have been hard to imagine the life to which they were headed and no less difficult to foresee how the economy and society could possibly function if people were no longer around to work the fields. How would these people survive? Where would they live, and how would they eat? Where would their food even come from? How could communities, even whole countries, survive after agriculture ceased to provide a livelihood for most people?

Whole new industries were being born as people harnessed the steam and steel and coal of the new manufacturing era. Factories sprang up everywhere, providing jobs for the tens of thousands of people streaming off the farms and rural areas into urban areas. Wages were low, barely enough for people to subsist on, and factory jobs at the dawn of the Industrial Age were filthy, oppressive, and dangerous. They embodied the evils that those like Marx and others invoked to impugn capitalism. In his poem "Jerusalem," the poet William Blake dubbed England's early factories "satanic mills."[1]

Now flash forward a hundred years, to the middle of the twentieth century. It took more than a few generations, but in time, we left the Agricultural Age and created once-unthinkable forms of work that ushered in a new way of life and engendered a rising standard of living and ultimately a new age of progress. Jobs in the manufacturing sector became some of the most enviable. They were still backbreaking and tedious, but now they came with the promise of reward: high wages, union protection, generous benefits, and unimaginable security. In the golden era, millions of industrial workers were able to put in their time and then retire on their pensions. Factory jobs were not always good jobs; rather, our government and our society took a series of steps to initiate public policies that made them into good jobs.

But the number of factory jobs has been decreasing since the 1950s. Many of those functions have been automated or outsourced, and they're not coming back. The economic crisis has eliminated more than 7 million jobs. We can keep pumping money and energy—and a whole lot of wishful thinking—into a vain attempt to forestall the inevitable, or we can try another route: we can turn more of the jobs in the sectors that are already growing today into good, high-paying jobs.

We've seen very little progress in this arena over the past couple of decades. "This is the only recession since the Great Depression to wipe out all job growth from the previous business cycle," writes Mort Zuckerman, the editor in chief of *U.S. News & World Report*, in an op-ed ominously titled "The Free Market Is Not Up to the Job of Creating Work."[2] Over this time, literally all of the growth in wages and salaries—and income in general—has gone to the highest-earning 1 or 2 percent of the population. Continuing on the present course means the gap between the elite and the rest of us will grow ever wider. Creating a new source of good jobs is a prerequisite for economic recovery. But it's hard to even imagine how to do it. Where will they come from?

There are two kinds of jobs that are growing: higher-paying knowledge, professional, and creative jobs (everything from high-tech engineers and software developers to managers and doctors to graphic designers and entertainment lawyers) and lower-paying routine jobs in the service economy (food service workers, nurses' aides, janitors, home health care workers, and the like). Over the past three decades, the U.S. economy has added 28 million routine service jobs and 23 million knowledge, professional, and creative jobs, compared to just 1 million in manufacturing. Routine service jobs now compose the single biggest area of employment: 45 percent of jobs, 60 million plus in all.. Creative jobs account for 31 percent, and working-class jobs for 23 percent.[3]

These trends will only become more pronounced over the coming decade or so. The United States will add 15.3 million new jobs between 2008 and 2018, according to projections by the Bureau of Labor Statistics. Nearly all of that growth—13.8 million new jobs—will occur in creative and professional jobs on the one hand, and service, administrative, and clerical jobs on the other, which are projected to add 6.9 million new jobs each. Working-class jobs will grow by 1.5 million overall, but most of that growth will be concentrated in construction and transportation. The U.S. economy will shed another 349,000 production jobs, the blue-collar factory jobs that were the mainstay of the industrial economy. And employment in manufacturing industries broadly will decline by 1.2 million jobs, as the so-called goods-producing sector of the economy continues its fall from 17.3 percent in 1998 to 14.2 percent in 2008 and 12.9 percent by 2018.[4]

Both service and creative jobs have been much more resilient in the face of the economic crisis. In September 2009, for example, when the U.S. unemployment rate was roughly 10 percent overall, it was highest, between 15 and 17 percent, for blue-collar workers, 9.5 percent for service workers, and just 5 percent for professional and creative workers. This has been true for decades. Blue-collar workers have felt the brunt of every recession since 1971, with rates of unemployment three or four times greater than those of the creative class. In fact, the unemployment rate for the creative class crossed the 5 percent mark only once—in the current downturn. The unemployment rates faced by service workers have fallen somewhere in between.[5]

The old manufacturing economy honed physical skills such as lifting and manual dexterity. But two sets of skills matter more now: *analytical* skills, such as pattern recognition and problem solving, and *social intelligence* skills, such as the situational sensitivity and persuasiveness required for team building and mobilization. Jobs that demand high analytical skills, such as medicine and bioengineering, and social intelligence skills, such as psychiatry and management, are not only increasing in numbers faster than other jobs but also pay much more. Moving from a job in the bottom quarter of analytical-skill levels to one in the top quarter—from travel agent to, say, accountant—means an average of an additional $18,700 in pay; the gap between jobs that are low and high in social intelligence skills is even greater: $25,100. The reverse is true when it comes to physical skills: moving between a job in the bottom quarter and one in the top quarter of physical demands would be accompanied by, on average, an $8,100 *drop* in wages.[6] The challenge on the jobs front is twofold. It's obvious that we need to grow more jobs that are high in analytical and social skills, but we also need to increase the analytical and social skills of the jobs we have.

But public policy toward the economic crisis seems unaware of this. Less than a month after taking office, the Obama administration unveiled its massive stimulus package—a staggering three-quarters of a trillion dollars aimed at recharging the lagging American economy. In the Senate debate over the arts component of the original stimulus bill, a relatively small amount marked for the National Endowment for the Arts (NEA) was derided as wasteful pork-barrel spending, which strikes me as ludicrous. As Jack Kingston, a Georgia Republican, put it, "We have real people out of work right now, and putting $50 million in the NEA and pretending that's going to save jobs as opposed to putting $50 million in a road project is disingenuous."[7] This is ludicrous. Arts are an important component of the creative economy engine. The economy benefits from considerable spillovers and synergy as art and design expertise combines with technological know-how, producing all kinds of inventive new goods and services. A quick accounting of the products created by this dynamic intersection of art and science in just the last few years includes iPods and video games, blogs and e-books, virtual music studios and online universities. If we want to grow these kinds of technologies and new industries, we need to spend less time and effort bailing out and stimulating the old economy and a lot more on building the new.

But it's not enough just to expand the availability of high-end creative and professional work. It's critical to increase the analytical and social aspect of *all* jobs. This is already happening in some areas. While workers at some manufacturing operations remain stuck with mindless labor, others are engaged in quality circles and statistical training and have more individual authority on the line. Their companies benefit from improved productivity, while the workers benefit from more secure jobs and higher wages.

An enormous potential source of good jobs is right in front of our noses: the service sector, which employs more than four in ten workers. However, many will say these service jobs are among the economy's worst employment alternatives. They pay very little on average, and provide almost no job security. And it isn't just that these jobs offer little hope of long-term financial security; they generally have not fit into the aspirations of most people. They are the jobs that young people perform while they're studying, or what immigrants or others without access to education do while they're waiting for something better to come along. For all these reasons and more, many continue to view them as a poor substitute for the long-run, stable, high-wage jobs that are being lost in manufacturing. "If there is any growth in jobs, it will come mostly from healthcare, education, restaurants and hospitality services," writes Zuckerman. "Healthcare alone made up all the net jobs created in the last decade." He adds that "Such service jobs cannot, however, support growth and innovation." The notion that only manufacturing or high-tech jobs are the source of innovation and growth is precisely what put and currently keeps the economy in its current job-creating rut. From where I sit, service jobs offer lots of potential for innovation, entrepreneurship, and the upgrading of employment opportunities.

While high-flying high-tech start-ups such as Facebook and Twitter get all the coverage, by far the greatest number of new entrepreneurial businesses are in the service sector: restaurants, child care services, landscaping companies, new marketing and delivery services for everything from home-cooked meals to in-home technology consultants. There's an enormous opportunity to nurture these entrepreneurs by providing management assistance and mentoring help, so they can develop stronger, more sustainable businesses.

That still leaves millions of highly standardized service jobs at chain restaurants, supermarkets, rental-car agencies, and photocopy shops. But even these kinds of service jobs can and are being transformed through the same principles that are in operation at the best high-tech companies, such as Google, Cisco Systems, Genentech, and the SAS Institute, and the best manufacturing companies, such as Toyota, which taps its shop-floor workers in continuous innovation and productivity improvement. Some of the most successful service companies follow a similar path, turning jobs that once would have been considered menial into attractive and rewarding employment. In fact, it's service companies, not manufacturing firms, that stand alongside high-tech leaders atop rankings of the best places to work. Service companies from Wegmans Food Markets, Whole Foods Markets, and Starbucks to the recreational equipment retailer REI to Nordstrom, Zappos, and The Container Store make up twenty of the top one hundred places to work in the United States.[8]

For starters, these companies are upgrading compensation. At The Container Store, for example, the typical hourly worker earns about $30,000 a year, still not what a worker on the General Motor's assembly line made in their heyday but about 50 percent more than the average for salary paid to retail workers. Trader Joe's mandates that full-time employees earn at least the median household income in their communities, and store captains, the majority of whom have been promoted from within the organization, can earn six-figure salaries.[9]

We have to move forward from this starting point to make service jobs even more innovative, more productive, and higher paying. We cannot stop until they pay better and afford a better way of life than manufacturing jobs did for a couple of previous generations. But a satisfying workplace involves much more than a bigger paycheck. People want to learn, to develop new competencies, and to grow their capacity and confidence, through training and development and through promotion from within. Four Seasons, for example, has established itself as one of the world's leading luxury hotel chains, in part by treating its employees with dignity and allowing them to move up in the management ranks and to transfer to new openings in various hotels.

A growing number of companies are using team approaches to build community within their workforce and have developed recruitment and selection programs that are more in line with those at manufacturing leaders such as Toyota and high-tech firms such as Apple. At Whole Foods Market, for example, new employees go through a thirty-day initial period, after which the other members of their team actually vote on whether or not the new worker had contributed sufficiently, and fits into the cooperative environment well enough, to stay on. Zappos, the online shoe retailer acquired by Amazon in 2009, has instituted an even more radical policy: paying employees to quit. The company works hard to recruit the right people, but a week after a new person starts, the company offers him or her a $1,000 bonus to quit. It sounds crazy, but management believes this is a highly effective way to weed out workers who won't fit in over the long run. If you're willing to take them up on "The Offer," you've proven that you don't have the commitment the company is looking for.

The service economy offers a tremendous potential for tapping the creative contributions of frontline workers and turning them into improved productivity. One example is Best Buy, which employs 90,000 people and is the largest specialty retailer of consumer electronics in the world, with annual sales of some $25 billion. Taking a page from Toyota's much-lauded management system, employees are encouraged to improve upon the company's work processes. Small changes suggested on the salesroom floor—a teenage sales rep's reworking of an Internet phone calling display or an immigrant salesperson's proposal for ways to target advertising and service to non-English-speaking communities—have been implemented across the company, generating millions of dollars in additional revenue. Best Buy favors promoting from within, so motivated employees are able to move quickly from floor sales to management, where the pay is much better.

This kind of approach is just in its infancy. It can be taken much further. Take janitorial work, for example, which is typically seen as dirty, low-skill, low-status work. But janitorial work can be broadened and the necessary skill level raised so that it becomes a source of important innovations. Why not supplement sweeping floors and washing windows with charging custodial staff to bring about process improvements that make buildings more energy-efficient or more cost-effective to run? Surely the people who maintain a building's furnace or air-conditioning equipment can work on a team that investigates alternatives for systems modernization. Once we recognize service work as a source of innovation and productivity improvement, we can begin to raise wages in sync with the productivity gains these workers generate.

The kinds of work we do and the types of jobs we grow have broader implications for our society and communities. We've already seen how the crisis is devastating factory communities while college towns, government centers, and financial centers remain more resilient. The shift in the economic geography over the past couple of decades has been highlighted by the concentration of high-paying professional work and the clustering of highly educated, highly skilled workers. Thirty years ago, the numbers of people with college or higher degrees, as opposed to those without, were fairly uniform throughout the different parts of the country. Now, however, cities such as Seattle, San Francisco, Austin, Raleigh, and Boston have the concentration of college graduates two or three times that of, say, Akron or Buffalo. Among people with postgraduate degrees, the disparities are wider still. The geographic sorting of people by ability and educational attainment on this scale is unprecedented.

The types of work and jobs that are concentrated in a community have a huge effect on everything from its economic prospects to the happiness and well-being of its residents.[10] We've already seen how working-class communities are plagued by lower levels of income and lower levels of happiness. But communities with high concentrations of service jobs did much better. In fact, they looked a lot like communities with large concentrations of highly paid professional and creative jobs. This might seem surprising, since service jobs pay the least, provide fewer benefits, and are less secure than other types of employment. Regions with higher levels of service jobs, alongside those with large concentrations of creative jobs, showed considerable economic resilience. They had lower rates of unemployment to begin with and have seen smaller increases in unemployment in this recession. Similarly, states with high levels of service jobs, paralleling those with large creative-class concentrations, had consistently higher levels of economic output, income, and innovation. These states had lower levels of divorce, lower levels of stress, and higher levels of happiness. The same thing held for the other countries of the world: nations where service jobs made up a higher percentage of the workforce had higher levels of economic output, productivity, innovation, and new business start-ups and significantly higher levels of happiness and well-being.

This is good news, actually. Many of these service jobs, by their very nature, are less amenable to global competition or to outsourcing. It's hard to outsource the person who cuts your hair, mows your lawn, or takes care of your children or an ailing parent. These kinds of jobs are among the most firmly rooted in specific places. Because the service sector employs so many people and contributes so significantly to the economy, we have little choice but to make these jobs more desirable and more emotionally and financially rewarding.

Upgrading service jobs may be hard to accomplish, however. For one thing, the economic crisis has fallen most heavily on blue-collar men. As a result of the layoffs of blue-collar men, women now make up almost half of the labor force. In fact, the unemployment rate of men has surged past that of women during this crisis, with the gap widening to 3 full percentage points—10.5 percent versus 7.5 percent (for those over sixteen years of age) in spring 2009—due to the concentration of men in manufacturing jobs. Catherine Rampell of the *New York Times* dubs it the "mancession."[11]

The gender division of labor also makes economic adjustment more difficult. Manufacturing jobs are overwhelmingly held by men, while women predominate in service jobs. Margaret Wente of the *Globe and*

Mail argues that broader changes in the economy—the rise of knowledge and service work and the decline of manufacturing work—favor women over men. "The new economy (over the long term) is creating tons of service jobs in retail, customer support, and personal care," she writes. "But no matter how much education and retraining we offer, we are not going to transform factory workers and high-school dropouts into customer-care representatives or nurses' aides any time soon. It's their wives and daughters who will get those jobs." She concludes that "In the new world of work, the old values of working-class men are an anachronism. And what we are really asking of them is not to retrain or upgrade. We are asking them to abandon their very idea of masculinity itself."[12]

From where I sit, she's mainly right. I grew up in that culture. Sexism and racism ran rampant. Fights were almost everyday occurrences; working-class disagreements almost always ended in them. When a Garden State scholarship enabled me to attend Rutgers, I was floored by the relative safety, meritocratic orientation, and personal freedom afforded by middle-class culture. Sure, modern middle-class culture has plenty of faults. And certainly not all working-class men share these retrograde attitudes. Many workers in more modern, high-performance factories (a good many of whom are women) would fit nicely into service or professional work. Still, that old blue-collar male culture remains too much a fixture in too many places.

"Men have worked as essentially shop keepers and store clerks," wrote Lance Mannion, a blogger, "for a lot longer than they have worked on assembly lines. There have been waiters forever. Lawyers are the world's second oldest profession. Teaching was a male-only profession for centuries. The idea that men are and ought to be unreflective, grunting, two-fisted louts is a class thing, not a gender thing and it is imposed upon working class men by a system that needs them to be beasts of burden. Men who reject certain values and behaviors as 'sissy' or 'girlie' are rejecting success, and don't think their bosses aren't grateful."[13]

That strikes a chord with me: When I was a young boy, my father would often take me with him to Newark on Saturdays to buy

Italian bread. We would inevitably pass by a neighborhood beauty parlor where my father would stop for just a minute. "Richard," he would say, "I was so dumb. When your aunt [his older sister] moved to California, she wanted to give me this place. I could have made it work. I enjoy cutting your hair and coloring your mother's. But when I was young, beauticians were considered 'sissies.' So I let my pride take over. Instead of having my own place, being my own boss, and doing something I enjoy, I stayed in the damned factory." The happiest I ever saw him was in the job he took after he retired from the factory, helping out in a health and exercise club. Even though his job was quite a step beneath the managerial position he had worked up to in the factory, he enjoyed it much, much more. He told me regularly how much he enjoyed interacting with people who chose to come there to get or stay in shape—a world of difference from the old ways of the factory.

Some believe that service work cannot be improved. In his book *Shop Class as Soulcraft,* Matthew B. Crawford scoffs at my contention that service jobs, like those I mentioned at Best Buy, can be upgraded. He makes an impassioned case for the skilled trade work that he does in his motorcycle repair shop. He's right to extol the virtues of skilled physical work, which is and has been the source of good livelihoods and much fulfillment to those fortunate enough to be able to do it. The unfortunate truth, however, is that the kind of work Crawford does is available to only a small minority of workers. There are 5.3 million installation, repair, and maintenance workers in the United States, of which only a tiny fraction—16,850—are motorcycle mechanics. That's less than a tenth of the more than 60 million workers who toil in mainly low-skill, low-paid service jobs.

Crawford's own job is particularly enviable. As the owner-operator of his own repair shop, he's not a miserable proletarian by any standard, but an entrepreneur and business owner. What makes Crawford's job a good job—a great one, really—is not just the physical skill he's honed. It's that he is one of a very small minority of workers who has the good fortune to be able to use his full complement of talents and skills—cognitive, physical, and managerial. He has nearly complete control over how his own work is done, and the flexibility to do it how and when he likes—he's his own boss, after all. For these reasons, his work is a source of great pride and obvious joy. Most manufacturing and production work isn't like this. Much of it remains mind-numbing work in which, as countless studies have shown, the content of work has been de-skilled and the pace of work is controlled by machines—a modern version of Charlie Chaplin flailing away as he tries to keep up with the assembly line.

The motorcycle repair jobs that Crawford extols are great, and we would do well to create more of them. But the fact of the matter is that they cannot fill the gaping hole in today's labor market. We can't give up on service jobs, which are among the fastest-growing of all jobs. For the sake of the people who currently toil in the service economy and of our country's long-run prosperity, we must do all we can to turn service jobs into more innovative, more engaging, more fulfilling and much better-paid work.

It's a big mistake to try to elevate one type of work over another. Each and every type of work—shop work, factory work, knowledge work, service work, agricultural work—can be meaningful and special, or it can be mind-numbing, monotonous, and dehumanizing. My greatest hope is that the current Reset can help us fashion a new commitment to work and enable every single person to do work he or she enjoys, that pays well, and that is truly motivating. At the end of the day, it's not what we buy that truly fills our souls and gives us a positive self-image and identity, it's the work we do. Work, after all, is what makes us human. Marx saw factory work as simultaneously exploiting industrial workers and alienating them. He argued that it was their physical labor and their mutual alienation and exploitation that bound them together in a shared social class. But it's not physical work that binds people together; what all of us share is our innate creativity. It's what differentiates us from other species and what makes us all similar. Although we've set up a construct over time in which we compartmentalize work on one side and joyful relaxation on the other, work is key to happiness. We thrive when we do work that is challenging and exciting.

Too much of what led up to the crisis in the old bubble days—the conspicuous consumption, the latter-day Gatsbyism—was fueled by a need to fill a huge emotional and psychological void left by the absence of meaningful work. When people cease to find meaning in work, when work is boring, alienating, and dehumanizing, the only option becomes the urge to consume—to buy happiness off the shelf, a phenomenon we now know cannot suffice in the long term.

If there is indeed a blessing in disguise within this crisis, let it be that we refocus our energy toward enabling people to do work that gives their lives real meaning. The logic of our economy demands it. The great promise of this era is that now, for the first time in human history, further economic development requires the further harnessing of our human creative talents. It's no longer sufficient to pump more resources out of the ground, build bigger factories, or employ more people in physical work. If we want our societies to grow and develop, we'll need to extend the engagement of our full creative talents, not just of a small elite but of each and every worker. The boundaries of the creative economy and the creative class need to expand to everyone who works in a factory or on a farm, in a laboratory or artist's studio, in an office or retail shop, in a restaurant, hair salon, or health club. The places that ultimately emerge from the crisis the strongest and most resilient will be those that recognize the need to—and are able to—build economic and social systems that can harness the full creative capacities of a much broader range of their workforce and stoke the creative furnace that lies within everyone.

Chapter Seventeen

The New Normal

N o economic system is entirely, or simply, about money. Economic systems reflect the way people choose to live and the way societies see themselves. If the mass consumption of the last half of the twentieth century had a catchphrase, it was "keeping up with the Joneses," and in the past decade or two, that has become almost a fearsome mantra. Manufacturers and retailers capitalized on this ethic of identification through acquisition and effectively marketed ready-made taste and status. Were you Armani or L. L. Bean? IKEA or Pottery Barn? ShopRite, Winn-Dixie, Kroger, or Whole Foods? Popular culture became so infected with this brand-name obsession that it became next to impossible to tell the ads from the actual content. I wonder if someone picking up *The Devil Wears Prada* fifty years from now would have any idea what the title means. And what of the women of *Sex and the City*, who uttered the names of their favorite shoe and handbag designers as often as they did the names of their best friends?

Looking back, it doesn't even seem real. Were you—like me—completely amazed at how so many people could afford bigger and bigger homes, New England beach houses and Florida condos, or expensive cars? The answer, according to Ben Funnell, writing in the *Financial Times*, is simple: those things weren't earned but bought on credit. Debt, he writes, is "capitalism's dirty little secret."[1] Cheap mortgages, cheap car leases, and the use of homes as veritable ATMs created fictitious living standards for the middle class and the bulk of the population at a time of low productivity and paltry growth in incomes, when the bulk of the gains in wealth was scooped up by the top fraction of households. "Excessive lending," Funnell adds, "was the only way to maintain the living standards of the vast bulk of the population at a time when wealth was being concentrated in the hands of the elite." The most astonishing thing about all this madness is how it was condoned—in fact, applauded and encouraged—by our political leadership. Who can ever forget George W. Bush, in the days and weeks after the terrorist attack of September 11, 2001, exhorting people not to be afraid, to get out and do the right thing, the patriotic thing, the one thing that could get the economy moving forward again: *start shopping.*

We're all familiar with the phrase "a chicken in every pot and a car in every garage." Even though Herbert Hoover never actually said that, the phrase carries the powerful implication that real prosperity turned on simultaneously improving industrial and agricultural production. A 1928 political ad from the Republican National Committee came close, saying that prosperity turned on "the proverbial 'chicken in every pot.' And a car in every backyard, to boot." And Hoover offered that "the slogan of progress is changing from the full dinner pail to the full garage."[2] To get to the point where there *was* a car in every garage, we first had to make food production cheap enough to have a chicken in every pot.

During the Great Depression and Second Reset, the amount of money families devoted to food fell dramatically, shrinking from nearly half of the average family's budget at the turn of the twentieth century to less than a third by 1950. At the same time, the share of the workforce employed in agriculture dropped from 41 percent in 1900 to 16 percent in 1945. (It's less than 2 percent today.)[3] Cheaper food then freed up disposable income, which was used to buy cars, suburban homes, and everything else that filled them up. This shift in the underlying structure of the economy was necessary to jump-start the much-ballyhooed golden age of postwar prosperity.

A similar seismic shift is a necessary component of the current Reset. It's more than just changing consumer preferences, leading us away from the old housing-auto consumption bundle; it is a deep, structural economic necessity. Over the past half century or so, the amount of money the average American family spends on housing and cars has skyrocketed. From 1950 to the mid-1980s, the amount allotted for housing and cars doubled from 22 percent to 44 percent of its budget. (At the same time, the amount the average American family had to devote to health care rose threefold, from 5.2 percent in the late 1950s to 14.8 percent by the year 2000.) A generation ago, all of life's basic necessities—housing, transportation, health insurance, education, and taxes—accounted for 54 percent of the average family's income; today, they account for 75 percent of it. It's not so much that regular middle-class people are wanton "overconsumers," note Harvard professor Elizabeth Warren and her daughter Amelia Warren Tyagi, it's that we've been trapped by the ever-increasing costs of these necessities.[4]

That's not completely true, of course. Some people did go hog wild, shelling out more and more for pricier cars and houses. Whether they were bigger (McMansions or Hummers) or better (Lexus Hybrids or renovated brownstones) is beside the point; the fact is that they cost more. The concentration of economic activity and talent in certain cities—New York, Washington, San Francisco, and so on—drove up demand, especially in prime, close-in neighborhoods. It wasn't enough to buy a nice house; we'd entered the shelter chic, HGTV era—one needed the full complement of a designer Sub-Zero/Wolf/wine refrigerator kitchen; the humongous master bath with heated floor, massive soaking tub, and overhead rainfall shower; the tricked-out walk-in closet with special shelves and compartments for everything from shoes to shirts and hats; the home entertainment theater with in-ceiling stereo and flat panel on the wall; never mind a wine cellar of your very own. A Toyota or Honda or even an Acura was no longer enough; more and more people thought they "had to" drive a Range Rover or luxury utility vehicle, a Mercedes or BMW sedan, or even a Prius. (Think about the phrase "*luxury utility* vehicle." Like "designer denim," the very notion of it borders on the absurd.) The whole "my-status-depends-on-where-I-live-and-what-I-drive" treadmill got a whole lot steeper. In fact, what separates spenders from savers, according to a detailed 2005 Canadian study, is outlays for housing and especially for cars.[5] While spenders outpurchased savers across the board, spending more on everything from furniture and entertainment to food and drinks to technology and education, they doled out a whopping 54 percent more for their cars and related transportation expenses. If we want to reduce these expenses and have money left over to grow the industries of the future, we'll have to *live* differently. We'll have to prioritize differently.

Even though we may not want to admit it, the challenge we face today is even bigger than that of the 1930s. The Great Depression was a crisis of a mature industrial capitalism, one that economists, business leaders, and policy makers understood fairly well. By the time Keynes published his classic *General Theory of Employment, Interest and Money* in 1936, it was clear that government had to spend money to counter economic decline, but it was also clear *where* that money should be spent: on large-scale infrastructure construction projects such as highways, public works, and even housing. Well before Keynes argued for government spending to stimulate the economy, Henry Ford made the case for a five-dollar working day, so autoworkers could purchase the cars they built. The retail magnate Lincoln Filene—yes, he of Filene's Basement—said the key challenge facing the economy was to boost consumer demand for all sorts of products. Some even interpreted Keynes as implying that the economy would be better off even if all workers did was dig ditches and fill them up again.

But what worked during the Great Depression will not work quite as well now. Today's economy is largely fueled by the idea-driven creative industries that have grown up over the past two or three decades. Restarting economic growth this time around will require a new social and economic framework that is in line with the new idea-driven economy. Sadly, we remain trapped in the mental models of the old industrial economy. The bursting of the high-tech bubble in 2001 held back the emergence of the new order. Scaring investors out of technology, the Internet, and emerging economic sectors, it sent capital flowing out of the creative economy and back into the safety of housing and real estate—from "clicks" back to "bricks," to turn a phrase.

It's ironic that our public discourse is so limited to breathing life back into the old housing-auto complex—bailing out banks, mortgage lenders, and automakers—when these are the very institutions that helped spark the crisis in the first place. It is exactly those products and services that now have to reinvent themselves and become more efficient and more affordable. We need to radically shrink our expenditures on houses, cars, and energy to free up spending for newly emerging goods and services—everything from new biotechnologies and more powerful computers to new forms of personal development and new experiences. Part of this rollback will naturally occur as the real estate bubble deflates and housing prices fall. Still, with the basics sucking up so much of the family budget, the amount of money Americans spend on electronics, a reasonable proxy for high technology, increased from 1 percent in 1959 to just 1.6 percent by 2000, while the amount they spend on entertainment, a proxy for experiences, actually declined from 5.8 percent in 1950 to 3.9 percent in the year 2000.[6]

I'm old enough that I've seen the ethos of society turned on its ear more than once in my lifetime. The 1960s brought a radical shift in cultural perspective and values. The go-go yuppie aggressiveness of the 1980s turned us in a completely different direction. But the paradigm shifts of those eras will pale in comparison to what lies ahead. It's certainly what happened in the 1930s, when the over-the-top age of jazz and flappers and *The Great Gatsby* quickly turned into the era of Woody Guthrie and Studs Lonigan. My parents often spoke of the imprint the Great Depression had left on them and their peers, effectively making them financially conservative their entire lives. They never leased a car and never had a credit card. Will the current crash cause people to consume less and save more? Will it usher in a new era of thrift and introspection, of caution and frugality?

This much is clear: the crash caused American consumers to significantly scale back their spending, to reduce their use of credit, and to save more, and not just in the short run. Spending fell off considerably—more than in any other recent economic downturn—and stayed down for a longer period of time. Consumption remained below prerecession levels nearly two years after the National Bureau of Economic Research declared the onset of recession. In every other recession since 1980, consumption returned to normal in less than nine months.[7] In November 2009, more than a year after the financial markets collapsed—a period when many in the media were talking about pending recovery, consumer spending was a full 20 percent lower than a year before, according to a Gallup survey.[8] Spending was down across every single age-group and generation—Millennials, Generations X and Y, Boomers, and seniors. Seniors, sixty-five and older, understandably saw the biggest cutbacks in spending, reducing their outlays a whopping 32 percent from the previous year. Middle-aged people, in the fifty-to-sixty-four-year-old age group, cut back a sizeable 29 percent. Those in the thirty-to-forty-nine-year-old age range cut back the least, scaling back consumption 15 percent, but even this might have been a blip. In the prime child-rearing years, this group has the most need to buy holiday gifts. Even younger consumers, in the eighteen-to-twenty-nine-year-old age group, with little tying them down and a wide-open future, reduced their consumption a sizeable 23 percent from the previous year.

A separate survey by the consumer research company Yankelovich in summer 2009 found that nearly half of all Americans had given up many of the things they enjoy because of the recession. An even greater number—65 percent—said that they would never again spend as freely as they did before the recession. But not everybody is cutting back—or has been forced to cut back—equally. Of those with incomes under $35,000, 57 percent said they had given up things they enjoy, compared to 36 percent of those earning more than $125,000. And though 73 percent of the first group said they would never again spend money as freely as they had before the recession, only 49 percent of the more affluent group said that was the case.[9]

What exactly are people cutting back on now? A 2009 Ipsos/Reuters survey asked consumers in some dozen countries how they are scaling back their spending. The biggest cutbacks were understandably on discretionary items—such as entertainment, vacations, and luxury goods—on which more than 70 percent of all consumers reported cutting back. Another 30 percent said they were cutting back on their cell phones, and about 20 percent said they were cutting back on cable television. But more than half said they were cutting back on things we commonly see as necessities. More than half said they were scaling back on clothes and energy use, and more than 40 percent said they were cutting back on driving and groceries. Fortunately, only 10 percent said they were cutting back on education.[10]

The sheen may well be coming off some of the core elements of the old suburban-driven lifestyle. The new house, the new car or two, and all the accoutrements no longer hold the incredible sway they once did. Bigger is no longer seen as better. People are downshifting, trading their big houses and big cars for smaller ones. Financial imperatives are part of the reason: energy and gasoline prices spiked before the recession, and people recognize that they're on a long ascent that won't come back down for a long time, maybe ever. But it also reflects a growing energy awareness and the importance to more people of going green. For the first time in more than a decade, the median size of a new single-family home *decreased*, from 2,277 square feet in 2007 to 2,215 square feet in 2008.[11] That's not a whole heckuva lot, but it reverses the decades-long climb in the size of houses.

The appeal of a big suburban house and two or more new cars seems to be waning for younger generations. Jessica Gitner gave up the 1987 Nissan Maxima station wagon she got from her parents when she moved to Washington, D.C. An intern working for National Public Radio, she now takes the Metro and rides her bike. "I'm a recent college graduate, and like many who are in the same boat, I'm struggling to earn enough for rent and living expenses," she told the *New York Times*. "I don't have health insurance. I'd rather spend money on that than a car."[12] The savings are indeed considerable. Those who live in walkable places spend less than 10 percent of their income on transportation, compared to 25 percent for the average American family.[13] I see it in my own life. I am a child of the car culture, but my wife and I have been giving up cars and driving the ones we have longer. It's even more the case in Europe and even Japan, where young men and women, according to one recent report, "are ditching the car as a status symbol."[14]

A 2009 survey by the Pew Research Center provides some interesting insights into our changing consumption priorities. The survey asked respondents to rate various necessities and the change in their rating of them between 2006 and 2009. The highest-ranked necessity was a car: 88 percent of people surveyed named it as a necessity.[15] That may seem like a lot, but in a society where there are two cars or more for every family and where suburban life literally requires a car to accomplish life's most basic tasks, 12 percent of people believing that it's no longer a necessity seems like a substantial number.

The statistics guru Nate Silver, writing in *Esquire*, says there is hard evidence that America's once-great car culture has peaked. Silver performed a statistical analysis to show how much Americans drive based on gas prices and unemployment. He then graphed the results from 1980 to 2009. "Americans should have driven slightly more in January 2009 than they had a year earlier," he found, pointing to sharply lower gas prices as the overriding factor. "But instead, as we've described, they drove somewhat less. In fact, they drove about 8 percent less than the model predicted." Combined with the exceptionally sluggish sales of new cars, Silver concedes that Americans might be "considering making more-permanent adjustments to their lifestyles"—buying fewer cars or buying them less frequently, driving less, and generally "entertaining the idea of leading a car-free existence."[16] A separate study by J. D. Power and Associates, best known for its quality rankings of cars, confirms what young people tell me: after analyzing hundreds of thousands of online conversations on everything from car blogs to Twitter and Facebook, the study found that teens and young people in their early twenties have increasingly negative perceptions "regarding the necessity of and desire to have cars."[17] "There's a cultural change taking place," John Casesa, a veteran auto industry analyst, told the *New York Times.* "It's partly because of the severe economic contraction. But younger consumers are viewing an automobile with a jaundiced eye. They don't view the car the way their parents did, and they don't have the money that their parents did."[18] Whether it's because they don't want them, can't afford them, or see them as a symbol of waste and environmental abuse, more and more people are ditching their cars and taking public transit or moving to more walkable neighborhoods where they can get by without them or by occasionally using a rental car or Zipcar.

Cars are one thing, but many of the appliances that fill our homes also no longer hold the appeal or status they once did. After the crisis, 14 percent fewer people said a dishwasher was a necessity compared to before the recession, according to the Pew Survey; 16 percent fewer people said air conditioners, 17 percent fewer said clothes dryers, and 21 percent fewer said microwaves. "The huge drop in the perceived necessity of clothes dryers, home air-conditioning, and dishwashers is I think partly a response to the economic crisis, but more a response to the bursting of the housing bubble," writes Felix Salmon, an economics blogger; "people don't define themselves by their appliances in the way that they did during the housing boom."[19]

Although spending on tangible goods, especially luxury goods, is demonstrably down, consumers haven't stopped spending completely. Some of the consumer power has been redirected toward more *experiential* purchases: travel, wellness and fitness, entertainment, self-expression, and self-improvement. The creative class is not content to sit quietly in their modest home with the sensible car out front. They will continue to seek out restaurants and cultural events, they will take their families kayaking and skydiving or on "volunteer vacations," they will brew beer and start vegetable gardens and build furniture, powering new markets for new goods and services even as they adopt a more self-sufficient do-it-yourself ethic. This really struck me during a winter visit to Miami Beach in early 2009. The real estate economy was bust, and striking new condo complexes sat vacant with not a single light on at night. Still, mobs of people were eating and socializing in the restaurants, cafés, and bars lining Lincoln Road. They might not have had the cash to buy real estate or even spring for the fanciest hotel, but they were still doing things together, taking a shorter, less expensive weekend getaway, and making sure to find time to get together for a drink or a meal.

It's tempting to imagine people forsaking the lure of trendy new nightspots or the latest fusion cuisine for the pleasures of a home-cooked meal with friends, but let's not lose sight of reality. People will always define themselves through their consumption habits. There will always and inevitably be some element of competitiveness in our consumption that will never die, even if the rules change. If, before, people trumpeted their financial success through their purchases, there's no reason to think they won't continue to show off what righteous and evolved new "citizen-consumers" they've become.

As long as people have been trading money or goods and services, they've been demonstrating their unfailing ability to fall for a clever marketing pitch, and marketers know a good thing when they see it. Witness The Gap's "Buy Red, Save Lives" campaign or a company like Endangered Species Chocolate, which are still designed to get people to buy things they almost certainly don't need but that now play to their newfound identity as responsible citizens of the planet.

We might not like to admit this about ourselves, but it isn't so much material goods themselves that drive our consumption as the perceived status we assign to them. Largely, our material possessions and our perceived status are one and the same thing, but only up to a point. A decade ago, John Seabrook identified a shift away from older forms of conspicuous consumption to new and subtler status distinctions.[20] Green products have become the ultimate status goods. People buying hybrid cars are more driven by the status they confer than the fuel savings and energy efficiency they provide. Toyota Prius owners pay a significant premium over many conventional fuel-efficient cars. When asked about the top motivating factors behind their purchase, the comment "makes a statement about me" was at the top of the list, while "higher fuel economy" came in third and "lower emissions" fifth,[21] according to a July 2007 survey reported in the *New York Times.* (That's probably something we should have intuited. After all, the carmakers figured out long ago that the rush to buy SUVs had less to do with safety or carrying capacity or durability than with buyers' perception that driving an SUV conveyed an image of youth, ruggedness, and adventure.)

A 2009 study by researchers at the University of Minnesota, the University of New Mexico, and Rotterdam School of Management found substantial evidence that green purchases are less about energy savings or cost savings and more about status and image. "[S]tatus motives led people to choose green products over more luxurious non-green products," they found. People were more likely to buy green products when shopping in public, and when those green products cost more than nongreen alternatives. They conclude that green consumers are motivated by status and image—in particular the desire to appear altruistic to others.[22]

This trend looks to be a central element of the new normal—consumers have a new perspective on brand identity as a path to status. Instead of showcasing logos and material bounty as a mark of achievement in life, people—successful, affluent people—are beginning to wear their *lack* of consumption, or at least their capacity for smart consumption, environmentally or politically correct consumption, as a badge of honor. The idea of quality is transmuting. For some, it may be about having the best workmanship or the most authentic products. For others, it may be about complex or exotic components. For still others, it means finding the lowest-priced items that perform as well as the high-end alternatives. And for some, it will mean the value imparted to the world, or the lack of harm done to it, by the purchase.

It's encouraging to think about a consumer environment in which smaller really can be better, where a growing pressure to consume less keeps purchases in check, where the impulse to purchase one's identity off the designer rack has dissipated, and where our shopping is informed by larger and more outward-focused concerns. We're certainly not all the way there yet, but we're making progress. You can sense the shift, especially when compared with the over-the-top bling-bling lifestyles of the 1990s and 2000s.

One of the few good things to come from the crisis is how it took down some of the most egregious forms of conspicuous consumption. "Fire-sale auctions of mansions, yachts, sports cars and other trappings of wealth have become increasingly common as the rich become less rich," wrote *Richistan* author Robert Frank in the *Wall Street Journal*. "Whether unable to pay their bills or loath to appear lavish at a time of national thrift, many millionaires and billionaires are unloading their baubles. In a twist on the estate sales of deceased celebrities, 'living estate sales' have become increasingly popular."[23] Good riddance. It's hard to feel sorry for the ever-striving members of the nouveau riche who have been forced to dump their extravagant purchases.

There are still many out there who want their big cars and big houses. But this kind of thing is losing appeal, and much of the appeal has is of the lurid and voyeuristic type—which also accounts for the popularity of the *Real Housewives* franchise. McMansions are tacky; driving a Hummer, worse than gauche; greedy Gordon Gecko types, simply gross. The social zeitgeist is clearly shifting away from craven materialism—at least outside the south Florida communes that reporters like Frank writes about or Beverly Hills and similar haut-gauche environs. That's a broader social liquidation whose time is long overdue.

It's not at all clear that we're headed completely in the other direction, either. We're not likely to enter a new age of thrift and frugality. The evidence for that "seems more like the product of wishful thinking (there's a palpable longing among pundits for Americans to become more frugal) than anything else," writes James Surowiecki in the *New Yorker*.[24] He notes that after falling off a cliff when the stock market tanked, consumer spending rebounded by spring 2009, just nine months after the initial crash. But we are likely to see a continued evolution in what we consume—we'll need to, in order to spur lasting recovery. And that, in turn, will depend on the evolution of the next spatial fix.

Chapter Eighteen

The Great Resettle

n the spring of 2008, I visited Google's Manhattan office in Chelsea. Gaining access to the building was cumbersome, requiring several advance security clearances. Once inside the old building, I was greeted at reception with a life-size interactive Google map on the wall mimicking my movements. The space had been completely redone as a loftlike flat; LCD screens lined the walls, modern furniture and interesting light fixtures filled the space. Employees fit no common description or dress code. Most were in their twenties and thirties. Jeans, piercings, and even waist-length purple hair were worn with causal flair. As I was escorted to the speaking room, I noticed pullout sofa beds and Ping-Pong tables that made it feel more like a college dormitory than a corporate office. When I rose to speak, I noticed that the majority of the audience was listening in with their laptops open. Several of them were checking out my Web site and Googling me and other references as I spoke. I naively asked the audience if they had a map of where the workers from this office lived. Within seconds, they were showing me laptop screens displaying the answer to my question: Google Maps shot up with dots delineating their homes in middle-class and upscale suburbs of Montclair and Basking Ridge, New Jersey, Westchester County, and the like. But what really struck me was the dense cluster of dots forming a tight band across lower Manhattan, Brooklyn, and once-run-down working-class communities such as Jersey City and Hoboken in New Jersey.

Later, I visited the much larger Googleplex, the company's main campus across the country in Silicon Valley. The digs were even more impressive. I walked across the campus through scads of people eating at outdoor tables and playing soccer and Frisbee. The lunchroom served free food from all over the world—Indian, Chinese, Mexican, reflecting the diversity of Google's employees—at a dozen different food stations. It was packed with not just employees but their spouses, kids, and extended families. The diversity was astonishing—I saw hijabs, robes, ripped jeans, and kippahs. During my speech I asked the same question I had posed to the Googlers in New York: where do they live, and how do they get to work? I learned that Google runs a shuttle bus complete with wireless Internet access that takes employees who live in downtown San Francisco to its Silicon Valley headquarters. Though some endure the longer commute so they can enjoy the urban vibe downtown San Francisco affords, others prefer to live in the closer Silicon Valley suburbs. Regardless, they all work at the same place and are part of the same economic region.

The future of urban development belongs to a larger kind of geographic unit that has emerged over the past several decades: the *megaregion*. People around the globe are crowding into the world's most promising megaregions—the concentrations of population that encompass several cities and their surrounding suburban rings—that have grown swiftly in recent years.

The largest in North America is currently the great "Bos-Wash" megaregion, initially identified by the geographer Jean Gottmann. It stretches down the East Coast corridor, encompassing the cities of Boston, New York, Philadelphia, Baltimore, and Washington, D.C., and is home to more than 50 million people while producing more than $2 trillion in economic activity. Its economic output is greater than that of either the United Kingdom or France and more than double that of India or Canada. The second biggest, which Gottman dubbed "Chi-Pitts," covers more than 100,000 square miles and is home to 46 million people, producing $1.6 trillion in economic output. Other megaregions in North America include:

- Char-lanta: Atlanta, Charlotte, and Raleigh-Durham, 22 million people
- So-Cal: Around Los Angeles, 21 million people
- Tor-Mon-tawa: Toronto, Montreal, and Ottowa, 22 million people
- Nor-Cal: Around San Francisco, 12.8 million people
- So-Flo: Miami, Orlando, and Tampa, 15 million people
- Dal-Austin: Dallas and Austin, 10 million people
- Hou-Orleans: Houston and New Orleans, 9.7 million people
- Cascadia: Seattle, Portland, and Vancouver, 9 million people
- Pho-Tus: Phoenix and Tucson, 4.7 million people
- Den-Bo: Denver and Boulder, 3.7 million people

Around the world, London, Amsterdam, Tokyo, Shanghai, and Mumbai are hubs of giant megaregions. Each of these is a financial and commercial center with tens of millions of people and hundreds of billions of dollars in output.[1]

These megaregions, not nations, really power the global economy. Taken together, the world's forty largest megaregions account for two-thirds of all global economic activity and 85 percent of the world's technological innovation while housing just 18 percent of its population. Megaregions are the strategic power centers of the economy, housing 85 percent of all corporate headquarters in the United States and Canada.[2]

Though many analysts have predicted that the importance of cities—and that of location—would fade with globalization, the reality is that cities and megaregions have become more important economically than ever before. Even as globalization has spread factories, businesses, and laboratories to places such as India, China, Brazil, and beyond, these activities are being concentrated in the megaregions of those countries. Contrary to the notion that the world is flat, the most successful megaregions, in fact, are becoming economically stronger and spikier, not flatter.[3]

Megaregions are to our time what suburbanization was to the postwar era. They provide the seeds of a new spatial fix. They expand and intensify our use of land and space the way that the industrial city did during the First Reset and suburbia did in the Second. As people pour into the world's great megaregions, inner cities and close-in suburbs are being reclaimed and rebuilt. Older suburbs, especially those on transit routes, are being reorganized and rebuilt into denser communities offering more condos and town houses as well as single-family homes. Suburban malls and office complexes are being retrofit-ted and turned into walkable areas with a mixture of housing, shops, and restaurants and in some cases even new parks. Subways and rail transit are being expanded as highways clog.

It's hard for most people to imagine making sudden and radical changes to the way they live. Committed urbanites thrive on the cultural amenities cities have to offer and feed off the hustle and bus-tle of city life. Happy suburbanites wouldn't think of leaving their comfortable homes with spacious yards and double garages full of minivans or SUVs. Both fall into the trap of thinking about future lifestyles as a choice between one or the other, as some sort of conflict between urban versus suburban living. There's no shortage of dyed-in-the-wool urbanists out there predicting the death of the suburbs and a return to denser, urban neighborhoods. It's a lovely, romantic notion, but it's wrong. It's a mistake to consider suburbanization a backward step and impugn it wholesale, with the catchall slur of "sprawl," and to see only more compact, urban-style back-to-the-city development as a path to the future. This is no black-or-white, city-versus-suburb, winner-takes-all battle. Cities and suburbs alike are part of the new spatial fix. Neither our far-flung suburbs, the edge cities with their sprawling office complexes, housing subdivisions, and malls, nor even the distant exurbs will simply vanish. Companies are not likely to abandon the attractive suburban offices they've established, even as more and more are opening offices in more central urban locations. Many people will still commute to work by car, but those who prefer to take public transportation or walk or ride their bikes to work will also be able to.

One of the most promising trends I see is the redevelopment of older suburbs into denser, mixed-use communities. Such developments have sprouted up around Metro stations in Greater D.C. suburbs such as Arlington, Virginia, and Silver Spring, Maryland. And it's happening in suburbs further out as well. Hailed not long ago as the example of a new era of car-oriented edge cities, even Tysons Corner, the giant shopping and business complex in Fairfax, Virginia, has an ambitious plan to reconfigure itself from a car-oriented suburb to a more pedestrian-friendly, live-work-play community located around a new rail line intended to free people from their cars. In Phoenix, a project called Green Street Development has bought a couple dozen foreclosed homes—small ranch houses of about 1,400 square feet—along mass transit lines close to downtown. The project is modernizing them and upgrading them to green building standards. The target market is young professionals who live further out in bigger houses but have tired of long commutes. (The average round-trip commute in the Phoenix area is more than an hour.) "It might be someone who works downtown that wants to have a walkable neighborhood," the developer told NPR's *Morning Edition.* "They can walk to the cafe, a real cool cafe down the street. Or they can walk down to light rail and take it to work or to the ballgame, spend more time at home, drive their car less." The project's designer noted, "I do see a change happening in that people are downsizing and they're making smaller spaces more functional. People are less about trying to impress and more about spaces that function well, that are well priced, that meet their budget."[4]

While it's common to think of suburbs as draining off city assets, today's metropolitan areas, with their urban cores and suburban and exurban rings, are really expanded cities. Up until the early to mid–twentieth century, cities were able to capture peripheral growth by annexing new development, until suburbs figured out they could prosper by becoming independent municipal entities—thus the now-famous concentric-ring or, in some cases, hole-in-the-doughnut pattern of our metro regions. "Most suburban growth is not the result of declining core city populations," writes the urbanist Wendell Cox, "but is rather a consequence of people moving from rural areas and small towns to the major metropolitan areas. It is the appeal of large metropolitan places that drives suburban growth. Larger metropolitan areas have more lucrative employment opportunities and generally have higher incomes than smaller metropolitan areas." As a consequence, "the big urban areas attract people seeking to escape what are often the stagnant or even declining economies in smaller areas."[5] A very Jane Jacobs insight, and one I find compelling. In *The Economy of Cities*, Jacobs controversially argued that virtually all economic growth traces back to cities. In her view, cities actually preceded agriculture. Early cities, according to Jacobs, spurred agricultural development by providing trading centers for agricultural products.[6]

What is true is that after losing population to the suburbs for decades, many cities—and especially the hub cities of great megaregions—are growing again. A July 2009 headline in the *Wall Street Journal* announced the shift this way: "Cities Grow at Suburbs' Expense during Recession."[7] "U.S. cities that for years lost residents to the suburbs are holding onto their populations with a mix of people trapped in homes they can't sell and those who prefer urban digs over more distant McMansions," the story reported. "Growing cities are growing faster and shrinking cities are losing fewer people, reflecting a blend of choice and circumstance." In 1980, the incomes of residents of San Francisco and Seattle were below those of the entire metro area. But by 2008, the incomes of city dwellers in both outpaced those of the metro region by 20 percent.[8] Housing prices tell a similar story: prices in the walkable neighborhoods and close-in suburbs generally held up far better than those in distant suburbs and exurbs. In greater D.C., for example, housing values in the city declined far less than they did in the surrounding suburbs and are now considerably higher than the values of suburban homes.[9]

By 2008, large cities, those with more than 1 million people, had roughly doubled their growth rate over the years 2002–2005. Much of this growth was concentrated in large northern cities such as New York and Chicago, as population growth started to slow and even fall in Sunbelt cities. "This shows cities were reviving at the end of this decade, and they are also surviving a recession that has been a lot harsher for other parts of our landscape," the demographer William Frey told the *Journal*. "Cities are big enough and diverse enough that they are able to survive these ups and downs in the economy a lot better."[10] A major Brookings Institution study of U.S. migration confirmed these trends. Tracking the period 2005 to 2008, it found that migration to exurban and newer suburban counties dropped substantially, creating "unexpected windfall gains" in population for many large urban areas such as New York, Chicago, San Francisco, Boston, and Philadelphia. Likewise, it found that the cities and regions that experienced the "greatest recent migration declines were those that reaped the most migrants during the mid-decade housing bubble."[11] Those trends have become even more pronounced since the economic crash. At the height of the crisis, the Harvard University economist Edward Glaeser found that unemployment was "lowest in those areas that are most centralized."[12]

B ig cities are a huge draw for young, mobile, well-educated people. Guess what city topped the list of a May 2009 of the best places for 2 million–plus college grads to launch their careers? New York City—which eight in ten survey respondents listed as a top destination, despite its financial crisis. Second-place Washington, D.C., was named by 63 percent. Los Angeles, Boston, San Francisco, Chicago, Denver, Seattle, and San Diego rounded out the top ten destinations. Remember, this is a list of the places that are best to find a job, not to have fun, go to great restaurants or clubs, make friends, or get lots of dates. Recall the Harvard survey I mentioned in chapter 15: it also asked graduating seniors where they were going to live. The top three were Boston, New York, and D.C., in that order. My own research shows New York, San Francisco, Washington, Boston, and Los Angeles as the top places for twenty- to twenty-nine-year-olds.[13]

The location decisions made by new college grads have interested me for years. The reason is that they are making choices about what kind of job and career to start off in and where is best to do it. Their choices involve evaluating not just the company they'll work for but the labor market it's located in and what the surrounding area has to offer. Because they are both highly skilled and highly mobile—three to five times as likely to move than, say, a forty-five-year-old—the decisions they make about where to live are likely to leave a lasting imprint on our economic geography.

To get at the factors that attract and keep young Gen Y members, those born between the years 1979 and 1990, in certain places, my colleague Charlotta Mellander and I analyzed the results of a Gallup survey of some 28,000 Americans.[14] Jobs are clearly important. Gen Y members ranked the availability of jobs second when asked what would keep them in their current location and fourth in terms of their overall satisfaction with their community. From this perspective, big cities make sense for them, as they offer more robust labor markets with more and better job opportunities in a wide number of fields. In an age in which corporate commitment has dwindled, job tenure has grown far shorter, and people switch jobs with much greater frequency, career success involves a great deal more than simply finding the right first job. In these highly mobile and economically tumultuous times, career success for young people depends on locating themselves in a thick labor market that offers diverse and abundant job opportunities. Picking an economically vibrant location is an important hedge against economic uncertainty and the risk of layoff.

But remember that jobs were not the highest-ranked factor. Across the board, the survey respondents said that the ability to meet people and make friends was of paramount importance. These young people intuitively understand what economic sociologists have documented: that vibrant social networks are key to landing jobs, moving forward in your career, and securing personal happiness. They not only desire a thick labor market but also seek what I have come to call a thick mating market, where they can meet new people, go out on dates, and eventually find a life partner. They recognize what psychologists of happiness have shown: it's not money per se that makes you happy but rather doing exciting work and having fulfilling personal relationships. What do *you* think is more important to happiness—finding a great job or finding the right life partner? And whereas older Americans see high-quality schools and safe streets for their children as key, Gen Y understandably ranks the availability of outstanding colleges and universities higher. Many are likely to go back to graduate school and want to have good programs nearby. For all these reasons, big cities at the heart of megaregions top the list of their choices.

Megaregions have shown considerable resilience in the wake of the economic crisis. We've already discussed New York, but each of the other major cities in the Bos-Wash megaregion has weathered the storm far better than expected. Washington, as we've seen, has one of the lowest unemployment rates in the nation. Housing prices in all three remain considerably above national levels. And all three—plus Baltimore and Philadelphia—sat atop a 2009 ranking of the nation's smartest cities.[15]

In September 2009, the *Wall Street Journal* published a list of the ten American cities with the best prospects to attract young talent and ultimately to rebound after the crisis. The list was based on a survey of six leading urban experts (disclaimer: I was one of those surveyed). Every city on the list was located in a major U.S. megaregion: Washington, New York, and Boston in Bos-Wash; Chicago, the hub of Chi-Pitts; Austin and Dallas; Seattle and Portland in Cascadia; North Carolina's Research Triangle, part of the Char-lanta megaregion; Silicon Valley in Nor-Cal; and Denver, the hub of Den-Bo megaregion.[16]

Chicago is one city in the Rust Belt that is likely to come out of the crisis stronger than it went in. It has by far the largest share of manufacturing headquarters in the country, and, as we have seen, it has consolidated many of the functions that used to be done in cities such as Detroit and Milwaukee and has drawn off talent from those cities as well. The Chicago offices of the country's fifty biggest law firms grew by 2,130 lawyers from 1984 to 2006, according to William Henderson and Arthur Alderson of Indiana University.[17] Throughout the rest of the Midwest, these firms added a total of just 169 attorneys. San Francisco, the hub of Nor-Cal, is home to Silicon Valley, which will remain the world's leading center of high technology and venture capital long after this crisis has passed. Even though its housing market was initially hit hard, it bounced back quickly. Los Angeles, the hub of the southern California megaregion, is the world's leading center of film, television, and entertainment. While its suburbs in the so-called inland empire have been hard hit by the economic crisis, real estate in West Los Angeles and its environs remains among the most expensive in the nation. Seattle, the hub of Cascadia, is home to the world-class Microsoft, Amazon, Starbucks, and Costco. Its housing market was one of the most stable over the course of the crisis.

Houston is a center of energy production, and Dallas benefits from a diverse high-tech economy. Both held up well even in the face of the economic crisis. Their unemployment rates stayed well below the national average, and their housing markets proved to be among the most resilient in the nation. Atlanta, the hub of Char-lanta, is home to Home Depot, Coca-Cola, and other corporate headquarters, and is a magnet for talented young people and for African-Americans with college degrees. Even Miami, which has been hard hit by the collapse of the real estate bubble, should be able to bounce back, as it remains the commercial center of the So-Flo megaregion and the financial center for much of Latin and South America.

Because of their size, diversity, and regional role, these megaregion hubs have been better buffered from the recent economic crash than other regions, especially manufacturing-dependent areas and places where prosperity was tied to a single transient phenomenon, such as the housing-driven boom of the Sunbelt. These hub cities are connected to the world economy and have benefited from their ability to attract and consolidate various business functions that used to be performed by smaller cities in their regions. They have also emerged as key talent magnets, attracting young and highly skilled people from across their regions and in some cases from other parts of the nation and the world.

Chapter Nineteen

Big, Fast, and Green

Y ou might think that big cities and megaregions would fall victim to their own bigness, that at some point they would become too congested, too dirty, or too expensive to be competitive and lose their edge to smaller, more nimble places. New York has been America's largest city for 149 years. London has been the United Kingdom's largest since before the seventeenth century.[1] And don't forget ancient cities such as Beijing and Mumbai, which continue to persevere. There's a basic logic behind why some cities, metropolitan areas, and now megaregions can become larger and larger and still prosper.

These colossal cities benefit from high rates of innovation and a faster rate of "urban metabolism." That's according to a pioneering theory of the role of cities in economic growth developed by a team of mathematicians, physicists, biologists, and social scientists at the Santa Fe Institute in New Mexico.[2] As you may be aware, the rate at which living things convert food into energy—their metabolic rate—tends to slow as they increase in size. Elephants digest their food and move at a slower rate, per pound, than ants or butterflies. But when the Santa Fe team examined trends in innovation, patent activity, wages, and GDP, they were in for a surprise: they found that the "metabolisms" of successful cities, unlike those of biological organisms, actually get *faster* as the cities grow.

There is something revolutionary about the idea that cities that attract talented people with cultural amenities and a high quality of life will burn even more brightly for it and thereby grow larger, effectively feeding off their own energy. The researchers dubbed this "superlinear" scaling. "By almost any measure," they wrote, "the larger a city's population, the greater the innovation and wealth creation per person." Places such as New York, with finance and media, Los Angeles, with film and music, and Silicon Valley, with high tech, are all examples of high-metabolism places.

Economic growth is increasingly powered not just by the places that have the most raw materials, the biggest ports, or even the best factories but by those with the richest clustering of people. The great urbanist Jane Jacobs first described the powerful impact of talent-clustering on communities. Later, the University of Chicago economist and Nobel laureate Robert Lucas formalized the role of what he called "human capital externalities"—that is, the benefits of talented and ambitious people clustering together—in innovation and economic growth.[3] Talented people who live and interact in dense ecosystems generate ideas and products faster than they can in other places. There is no evidence that globalization or the Internet has changed that. Indeed, as globalization has increased the financial return on innovation (by widening the consumer market), the pull of innovative places, which are already dense with highly talented workers, has only grown stronger. Talent-rich ecosystems are not easy to replicate. To realize their full economic value, talented and ambitious people increasingly need to live within them.

Even in good times, metabolism and talent clustering are important to the fortunes of city-regions. But in tough times, they're essential. It's not that fast-metabolizing cities are immune to the ill effects of economic crises. When bubbles burst, credit freezes up, and a long slump follows, companies can fail unpredictably, no matter where they are. The critical strength of fast-metabolizing cities is that they can overcome business failures more easily, by reabsorbing their talented workers and growing new businesses. As the Reset progresses and recovery sets in, such cities will prosper. Their metabolism rates, already high, will burn even brighter. Conversely, cities that cannot keep up—that become trapped by a dependence on one or two backward-looking industries and a deflated entrepreneurial spirit or by high costs and outmoded organizational and social structures—are likely to lapse and decline.

L arge cities are not only faster and more productive, they're also greener. That may come as a surprise to many. "To most people, big, densely-populated cities look like ecological nightmares, wastelands of concrete and garbage and diesel fumes and traffic jams," writes David Owen, the author of *Green Metropolis*. "But, compared to other inhabited places, cities are models of environmental responsibility." The greenest place in the United States, according to Owen, is none other than New York City, the only U.S. city that "approaches environmental standards set elsewhere in the world." The average New Yorker, Owen notes, generates more greenhouse gases in a year than, say, the average Swede but 30 percent less than the U.S. average. New Yorkers produce less waste, burn less fuel, use less water, and use much less electricity, mostly because they drive less and live in the most energy-efficient residential structures in the world: apartment buildings.[4]

The key to New York's greenness is simple: density, the very same thing that promotes innovation and speed. Manhattan is eight hundred times as dense, in terms of population, as the United States as a whole and thirty times as dense as Los Angeles. Such density enables people to walk, bicycle, or take public transit to accomplish their day-to-day routines. New Yorkers can, and often do, live their daily lives without driving a car. That's true of a handful of other North American cities (it's quite possible in Toronto), but it's impossible in most other places in the United States and Canada. Big, dense cities are also more congested, and that, ironically, creates additional environmental benefits. Congestion and the fear of being stuck in traffic dissuade people from driving their cars. "Traffic jams can actually be environmentally beneficial if they turn subways, buses, car pools, bicycles and walking into more-attractive options," Owen notes.[5]

New York and other large cities make better and more efficient use of existing infrastructure, including everything from buildings and offices to roads, transit lines, and energy lines. The converse is equally true: suburbia and the suburban model of growth waste energy on a grand scale. America's "pro-suburb, pro–big home policies," writes Harvard's Edward Glaeser, "help keep America's households consuming plenty of energy, both inside the home and in the car." On average, he calculates, if a family moves from a home two miles away from the center of the city to one ten miles away, it consumes about a hundred more gallons of gas per year.[6]

The greenness of cities also reflects their fast metabolism. When members of the Santa Fe Institute looked at environmental emissions, they found that the same scaling effect applies to city size: large cities use energy more efficiently and produce fewer carbon emissions. CO_2 emissions—a widely used proxy for energy consumption—grow as the population of a city grows, but at a slightly slower rate. With each increase of 1 percent in population, the growth in carbon emissions is 0.92 percent. And with each 1 percent increase in economic output comes a smaller, 0.79 percent increase in carbon emissions. Even the notoriously smoggy Los Angeles, a metropolitan area of almost 13 million people, produces about half as much CO_2 per person as Yuba City, California, an agricultural economy of 150,000 people. Like biological organisms, the energy metabolism of metropolitan areas slows down as they increase in size: larger regions burn less energy per capita than smaller regions do.[7]

Economic crises tend to reinforce and accelerate the underlying long-term trends within the troubled economy. If there is one constant in the history of capitalist development, it is the ever-more-intensive use of space, and that phenomenon will repeat itself once more as the population shifts from outlying suburbs into the coalescing megaregions. Today, we need to begin making smarter use of both our urban spaces and the surrounding suburban rings—creating comfortable, affordable living space for more people while at the same time providing an improved quality of life. That is going to entail liberal zoning and building codes within cities, to allow more residential development and more mixed-use development in suburbs and cities alike; the in-filling of suburban cores near rail links; new investment in mass transportation; and congestion pricing for travel on our roads. Not everyone wants to live in a city center, and the suburbs are not about to disappear. But at the same time, we cannot facilitate economic recovery by continuing our outward expansion, gobbling up more and more land to build more housing developments. After all, that's largely what brought us to our current crisis.

We can, however, do a much better job of connecting existing suburbs to cities and to one another, using the space already developed more efficiently, and thus allowing regions to grow bigger and denser without losing their velocity. To achieve that end, we'll need to invest in a wide range of transportation options, from rail, subways, and buses to new kinds of development where people can choose to live closer to where they work. Every Great Reset has been spurred on by new infrastructure that can speed the movement of goods, people, and ideas. As the next chapter will show, this one is no different.

Chapter Twenty

The Velocity of You

When my dad started working in Newark, he would walk from his home to his job. Later he took a subway, while my mother took the bus. When they moved to the suburbs, the highways were still uncrowded and his commute took ten minutes. The boundaries of the city and region had expanded, but the car kept everyone and everything connected. It represented quick and easy travel: mobility, comfort, and independence all in one neat package. But as expansion mushroomed into sprawl, the thrill of finding oneself behind the wheel on the open road very soon gave way to the grind of congestion. Today, the highways of major cities and megaregions are veritable parking lots. At the same time, ideas can travel around the world almost instantaneously on a digital highway, and if you're willing to pay enough, you can send a package virtually anywhere overnight. But getting across town, to the next town, or even to the next state for a good job or business opportunity is as difficult as it was a generation ago. A single keystroke can send insight and creativity spreading through society, and that single phenomenon has revolutionized the way we live. The looming challenge is to speed the physical movement of goods, services, and people—the tangible bits of the real world—so that they are more in line with the lightning-fast flow of electronic information in the virtual world.

The history of capitalism and of the two previous resets revolve around the rise of new transportation infrastructure that enabled us to use land more intensively while expanding the borders of where we live and work. They did so by simultaneously speeding the movement of goods, people, and knowledge. Railroads and streetcars accomplished this in the nineteenth century, and auto-based suburbanization did after the Great Depression. The average travel speed in the United States increased from eight miles an hour in 1900 to twenty-five miles an hour in 1950, hitting seventy miles an hour—by car, truck, rail, and air—in the year 2000.[1]

In his book *The Wealth of Cities*, my University of Toronto colleague Christopher Kennedy shows that only wholesale structural changes, from major upgrades in infrastructure to new housing patterns to big shifts in consumption, allow places to recover from severe economic crises and resume rapid expansion. London laid the groundwork for its later commercial dominance by changing its building code and widening its streets after the catastrophic fire of 1666. The United States rose to economic preeminence by periodically developing entirely new systems of infrastructure—from canals and railroads to modern water and sewer systems to federal highways. Each played a major role in shaping and enabling whole eras of growth.[2]

There's been much outcry about the impact of rising fuel costs and even "peak oil"—the notion that the supply of oil has reached its upper limit and will decline and become more expensive—on reshaping our economic landscape.[3] James Kunstler writes that declining oil supplies and rising prices will force us to "downscale and re-scale virtually everything we do and how we do it, from the kind of communities we physically inhabit to the way we grow our food to the way we work and trade the products of our work." The reduced availability of oil will work against the oversized scale that Americans have grown used to in suburbs as well as cities. "Our lives will become profoundly and intensely local," he writes. "Daily life will be far less about mobility and much more about staying where you are. Anything organized on the large scale, whether it is government or a corporate business enterprise such as Wal-Mart, will wither as the cheap energy props that support bigness fall away."[4]

Nobody—except, perhaps, the oil companies—doubts that we'll

have to wean ourselves from oil in coming decades. Still, I view the problem differently. Oil prices are extremely volatile, and they plummeted as soon as this crisis began. (Bear in mind, however, that oil price fluctuations are driven as much by speculators as by actual supply and demand.) In today's idea-driven economy, the cost of time is what really matters. With the constant pressure to innovate, it makes little sense to waste countless collective hours commuting. So, the most efficient and productive regions are those in which people are thinking and working—not sitting in traffic.

The auto-dependent transportation system has reached its limit in most major cities and megaregions. Commuting by car is among the least efficient of all our activities—not to mention among the least enjoyable, according to detailed research by the Nobel Prize–winning economist Daniel Kahneman and his colleagues.[5] Though one might think that the crisis would have reduced traffic (high unemployment means fewer workers traveling to and from work), the opposite has been true. Average commutes have lengthened, and congestion has gotten worse, if anything. The average commute rose in 2008 to 25.5 minutes, "erasing years of decreases to stand at the level of 2000, as people had to leave home earlier in the morning to pick up friends for their ride to work or to catch a bus or subway train," according to the U.S. Census Bureau, which collects the figures. And those are average figures. Commutes are far longer in the big West Coast cities of Los Angeles and San Francisco and the East Coast cities of New York, Philadelphia, Baltimore, and D.C.[6] In many of these cities, gridlock has become the norm, not just at rush hour but all day, every day.

The costs are astounding. In Los Angeles, congestion eats up more than 485 million working hours a year; that's seventy hours, or nearly two weeks, of full-time work per commuter. In D.C., the time cost of congestion is sixty-two hours per worker per year. In New York it's forty-four hours. Average it out, and the time cost across America's thirteen biggest city-regions is fifty-one hours per worker per year. Across the country, commuting wastes 4.2 billion hours of work time annually—nearly a full workweek for every commuter. The overall cost to the U.S economy is nearly $90 billion when lost productivity and wasted fuel are taken into account.[7] At the Martin Prosperity Institute, we calculate that every minute shaved off America's commuting time is worth $19.5 billion in value added to the economy. The numbers add up fast: five minutes is worth $97.7 billion; ten minutes, $195 billion; fifteen minutes, $292 billion.[8]

It's ironic that so many people still believe the main remedy for traffic congestion is to build more roads and highways, which of course only makes the problem worse. New roads generate higher levels of "induced traffic," that is, new roads just invite drivers to drive more and lure people who take mass transit back to their cars. Eventually, we end up with more clogged roads rather than a long-term improvement in traffic flow.

The coming decades will likely see more intense clustering of jobs, innovation, and productivity in a smaller number of bigger cities and city-regions. Some regions could end up bloated beyond the capacity of their infrastructure, while others struggle, their promise stymied by inadequate human or other resources. Government can and must play a role in guiding that growth through intelligent infrastructure and investment. In part, we need to ensure that key cities and regions continue to circulate people, goods, and ideas quickly and efficiently. This in itself will be no small task; increasing congestion is threatening to slowly sap some of these city-regions of their vitality.

Scholars and pundits who describe themselves as futurists tend to reveal a penchant for far-out, high-tech solutions. They envision a city out of *The Jetsons*, where people jet from place to place, if not with jet packs on their backs, then in new kinds of vehicles on digitally enhanced roads. Here's one such account: "You get out, stretch your legs a little, and then start the next phase of your journey by getting into a 20mph Toyota iReal (a three-wheeled, one-seat, personal-mobility concept vehicle) and driving it up onto the elevated Velo-city, which leads out of the port. This dedicated new network of cycle tubes criss-crosses the city—connecting city ports with commuter towns and city-centre attractions. Its low-friction surface allows cyclists and light electric vehicles to travel at surprising speed, while its enclosed nature protects them from the elements. . . . Instead of struggling to find parking, arriving underneath the City Port's sign you find a docking station and move the iReal into a free bay. . . . Once docked, the iReal's front glows red to show the battery is being charged, and when you step out your iPhone beeps to signify your rental has finished."[9] The writer insists that all this is not so far-fetched, that it's actually a combination of three existing concepts. That may be, but I believe that realistic solutions are much closer at hand.

More and more people are choosing to take the subway, train, or bus or even walk or bike to work and go about their daily business—providing they live in an environment that allows for such choices. In Manhattan, 82 percent of workers get to work by public transit or bicycle or on foot. That's ten times the rate for Americans in general, eight times the rate for workers in Los Angeles County, and sixteen times the rate for residents of metropolitan Atlanta. The New York City subway is a remarkably effective technology for moving masses of people around quickly and efficiently. Between eight and nine in the morning on a typical workday, more than 385,000 people use its subway system to commute into the central business district. A subway train carrying 1,050 people crosses into Manhattan's central business district every six *seconds*, compared to 1.2 drivers coming across the East River by car in the same amount of time. According to one calculation, it would take "167 inbound lanes, or 84 copies of the Queens Midtown Tunnel, to carry what the NYC Subway carries over 22 inbound tracks through 12 tunnels and 2 (partial) bridges," and an additional 3.8 square miles of parking, three times the size of Central Park.[10]

Sure, you say, New York is a special place: it's compact and dense, and people can live close to where they work or take the subway. But it's not the only place where this kind of change in commuting and local traffic patterns is occurring. In Washington, D.C., 57 percent of commuters get to work by means other than driving a car—more than a third take public transit, 12 percent walk to work, and 2 percent ride their bikes; just four in ten drive to work alone. In Boston and San Francisco, roughly half of workers get to work without their cars—roughly a third of commuters take transit, and 10 to 15 percent walk to work. In Philadelphia, 41 percent commute without cars and 27 percent take transit. In Chicago, four in ten commuters get to work without cars, and 27 percent get to the office by public transit. In Seattle, 38 percent don't use cars, and 18 percent use the transit system.

Of course, these are mostly older cities, with downtowns that were constructed long before the automobile existed, but the shift away from the car is also seen in other, unexpected places. At least three out of ten commuters in Pittsburgh, Minneapolis, St. Louis, and Baltimore don't use cars. Some smaller cities do well on transit ridership even though they don't have billion-dollar transit budgets. In Boulder, 40 percent of workers don't use cars to commute. Of these, 10 percent use public transit, while 10 percent work where they live. In Iowa City, a third of commuters don't use a car and 16 percent of people walk to work.[11]

If you live close enough, nothing is more efficient than walking or biking to work. Less than 4 percent of Americans walk to work, but 14 percent of Bostonians do, 12 percent of Washingtonians do, and 11 percent of Pittsburghers do—more than in New York City. Former Talking Heads front man David Byrne is a passionate advocate of cycling as a way to get around and get to know cities. He's even written a book on it. When I lived in Boston, the news channel ran a special about once a year: it compared the time it took to get to work for bike, car, and train commuters. On many routes the bike commuters won. Nationally, just .5 percent of people commute to work by bike. But 6 percent of those in Portland, Oregon, do, as do 4 percent of people in Minneapolis and 3 percent in San Francisco and Seattle.[12]

These numbers may seem like a drop in the bucket. But 60 percent of Americans surveyed in 2005 said they want to live in walkable communities with shops, restaurants, movie theaters, schools, and churches nearby.[13] We're already seeing the shift as increasing numbers of people move to walkable communities closer to where they work. That will clearly expand in coming decades. And as the next chapter will show, we'll need to enable it by creating more flexible forms of housing that can reduce the time and distance between home and work.

For the time being, most Americans remain behind the wheel. Today, more than three-quarters of Americans drive to work alone. They have no other choice. There are, however, other things we can do to ease congestion and take more cars off the road. Employers can offer more flexible schedules and the ability to work from home or telecommute. But as we've already seen, in many cities traffic is not just a rush-hour problem. The only alternative left is to price the roads. We pay for everything else: we pay to take the subway, ride the bus, or take the train, we pay to drive through the Lincoln and Holland Tunnels or over the George Washington Bridge. Why should the roads be essentially free? If we want to make traffic better, we have little choice other than to make people pay for the roads they drive on. Economists call it congestion pricing. It's been introduced in London and in Stockholm, where it's cut down on traffic and congestion significantly. "Congestion pricing is basic economics," writes David Owen. "The idea is that if you have a sporadically scarce commodity, such as space in automobile lanes, you can eliminate distribution bottlenecks by adjusting prices in counterpoint to variations in demand. Hotels do this by raising room rates when travel is popular and lowering them when travel is not. That helps to smooth fluctuations in reservation rates, enabling the hotels to make better use of their existing rooms and to increase total revenues without building new capacity, much of which would end up being empty except during periods of peak travel."[14]

There's no reason why we couldn't apply the same principles to making automobile traffic more manageable and efficient. Owen supports the basic idea of congestion pricing, while pointing out the potential environmental drawbacks. He worries that drivers will detour around the higher-priced congestion and actually end up driving more. "There's nothing green about fighting congestion if, by distributing traffic more efficiently, it results in an overall increase in traffic volume and extra miles driven by vehicles avoiding the fee areas." Owen essentially favors a no-holds-barred assault on driving in cities, suggesting high fees for *all* automobile access and public parking. He even believes that cities should reduce the number of automobile lanes on their streets, giving drivers even less room to maneuver—literally. Owen believes that keeping drivers frustrated is a good way to keep them off the road. He's right.

All this can help unclog our roads in and around big cities, but how to reduce the time it takes to get from city to city or even across our sprawling megaregions? That will require a new kind of infrastructure. By increasing velocity and compressing the time of travel, shipping, and communication, new infrastructure can increase productivity. And as we've seen, new infrastructure also opens up new territory for development and enables redevelopment of older cities and suburbs. The one technology on the horizon that fits the geographic scale of megaregions and can help spur more intensive development of those regions is high-speed rail.

Chapter Twenty-One

Faster Than a Speeding Bullet

On the heels of the 2010 State of the Union address, the Obama administration announced that it had pledged $8 billion for high-speed rail. Urbanists, environmentalists, and advocates of energy efficiency greeted the news with outright jubilation. Sure, it's a start, but the United States lags far behind other countries when it comes to high-speed rail. China, for instance, plans to spend more than $300 billion to expand its high-speed rail system, building thousands of miles of new track by 2020. That's enough to cover the distance between Beijing and London and back again. By 2020, China will have more high-speed railway track than the rest of the world combined. France is adding to its TGV system. Spain is planning a large-scale expansion of its high-speed rail system and is set to pass Japan as the country with the most extensive high-speed network. The goal is that nine in ten Spaniards will be within thirty miles of a high-speed rail connection. Little wonder a high-ranking Siemens executive told the *New York Times* that the United States currently looks like "a developing country in terms of high-speed rail."[1]

High-speed rail can get people from place to place much faster than cars or other types of ground transportation and can rival the travel times of planes on some routes because they take people directly from downtown station to downtown station, thus eliminating the long trek out to the airport. Japan's Shinkansen and France's TGV run at speeds of 186 and 155 miles per hour, respectively. Spain's high-speed AVE line from Madrid to

Barcelona clocks in at 210 miles per hour. Shanghai's maglev train to the airport is the world's fastest, with a top speed of more than 250 miles per hour. This compares to 82 miles an hour on Amtrak's Acela express train, which runs along the East Coast corridor from Boston to Washington, D.C. A passenger on Japan's high-speed Shinkansen can get from Tokyo to Osaka in less than three hours. The journey from Madrid to Barcelona takes two and a half hours. In France, a traveler can get across the length of the country from Marseille to Paris in just three hours on the TGV. Many people today prefer to take the Eurostar train through the Chunnel from London to Paris, on which they can travel from station to station in two hours and fifteen minutes.[2]

High-speed rail has its skeptics, who say it costs too much and is ill suited to vast countries with spread out populations like the United States and Canada. In a series of columns for the *New York Times'* Economix blog, Harvard's Glaeser took a close look at the costs and benefits of high-speed rail, noting that he "would be delighted to share the president's optimism about high-speed rail, but if benefits do not exceed the costs, then America will just be living through a real-life version of 'Marge vs. the Monorail,' where the residents of the Simpsons' Springfield were foolishly infatuated with a snazzy rail project oversold in song by Phil Hartman's character." Glaeser marshals estimates developed by the U.S. Government Accountability Office (GAO), which put the costs of high-speed rail at somewhere from $22 million per mile for a route from Las Vegas to Victorville, California, to $132 million a mile for connecting Baltimore and Washington, to construct his own detailed cost and benefit estimates for a high-speed rail line connecting Houston and Dallas. Even after taking an estimated $29.7 million in annual environmental benefits into account, he finds that the Houston-to-Dallas high-speed rail line would operate at an annual loss of somewhere in the range of $400 million to $500 million.[3]

Building out a truly national high-speed rail system that would connect the major cities of our megaregions is estimated to cost between $140 billion and $500 billion. That's a lot of money by any stretch of the imagination. But it's not out of line with what we spent on infrastructure in past epochs. The U.S. highway system cost the equivalent of $429 billion dollars in 2009 dollars, on top of which cities, states, and the federal government spend another $80 billion to $100 billion every year on roads and highways.[4]

The U.S. government—the Federal Railroad Administration, that is—has designated eleven likely high-speed rail corridors across the United States. Most of them correspond to the large megaregions. There's the existing Acela corridor from Boston through New York and D.C. On the West Coast, there's a proposed route connecting the Bay Area to Los Angeles and San Diego. In the Midwest, there are proposed links running across Chi-Pitts from Minneapolis to Chicago and over to Cleveland, Detroit, and a host of other cities. There are other proposed routes for Miami, Orlando, and Tampa in southern Florida; Seattle, Portland, and Vancouver in Cascadia; Dallas, Austin, and San Antonio; Houston and New Orleans; Atlanta, Charlotte, and Raleigh in Char-lanta. In Canada, a route running from Windsor to Toronto and west to Ottawa, Montreal, and Quebec City has been proposed.[5]

High-speed rail can provide the connective fiber that enables megaregions to function as truly integrated economic units. It would dramatically reduce travel times between the major cities of North America's megaregions.[6] Philadelphia would become a veritable suburb of New York City, its commuting time shrinking from nearly two hours to slightly more than a half hour. Washington to New York City and Boston to New York City would become hour-and-a-half trips. San Diego would become a bedroom suburb of Los Angeles. And commuting times across Cascadia's main cities would shrink considerably: the time to get from Portland to Seattle would be cut in half to just over an hour, while travel between Seattle and Vancouver would be reduced to less than an hour. It would take only slightly longer than an hour and a half to get from Charlotte to Atlanta. The commutes between Dallas and Houston and Dallas and Austin would shrink to ninety minutes or less. And commuting by train, where you can read the paper or a Kindle, talk to colleagues or friends, and get work done is far more productive and enjoyable than sitting stuck in traffic behind the wheel of a car.

High-speed rail could be a veritable lifeline for the drowning Rust Belt communities, connecting them to bigger cities like Chicago or even Toronto. As we have seen, Chicago has sucked up scads of economic functions that used to be done by other second- and third-tier midwestern cities. The commute from Milwaukee to Chicago would shrink to just a little more than a half hour. Detroit to Chicago could be done in under seventy-five minutes. Even Pittsburgh to Chicago, now a seven-and-a-half-hour drive, would shrink to less than three hours. Pittsburgh could also be better connected to Washington, D.C. When I lived between the two cities, the drive was four-plus hours, just enough to make it a chore. But high-speed rail would make that a manageable ninety-minute trip.

I don't envision people making these commutes every day. But in the future, as flexible working hours, working from home, and telecommuting become even more common than they are today, high-speed rail holds the promise of connecting declining places to thriving ones, greatly expanding the economic options and opportunities available to their residents. Instead of stumbling along inefficiently as functionally distinct centers, they can become part of a much larger area of interconnected supply and demand, production and consumption.

Momentum is building in Canada for a high-speed rail link from, say, Windsor, just outside Detroit, through Toronto, over to Ottawa and on to Montreal and Quebec City. This would be a way of gluing together Canada's largest megaregion and spurring in-fill development along its corridors. With new residents and new immigrants continuing to flood into greater Toronto, a functioning rail link would stretch out the development frontier while building size and scale across the entire corridor. It could also help the auto-producing region around Windsor and across the river in Detroit. My wife, who is from greater Detroit, and I make the drive from Toronto to the Motor City regularly; it takes us about four hours. But high-speed rail would reduce that to roughly ninety minutes. Even if cross-border issues hold up a Toronto-Detroit high-speed rail line, a Toronto-Windsor link might very well do the trick: downtown Detroit can be easily connected via subway across the tunnel to Windsor.

The blogger and urbanist Ryan Avent sees an important parallel between the revitalization of the Rust Belt and what's occurred across the Bos-Wash corridor. "Along the northeastern corridor, there are cities that made the jump from industrial to postindustrial economy fairly successfully," he writes, "namely, those that had developed knowledge-intensive industries like finance or technology even as industry was beginning to leave center cities. In between these successful cities are interspersed others that were heavily reliant on industry, and which didn't fare nearly as well over the past half century." The reason for the turnaround, he argues, is transportation, which increases connectivity and proximity to thriving markets. "One of the chief lessons of economic geography," he adds, "is that a good way to get rich is to be near other rich places; remoteness is costly."[7]

That's exactly right. A key element of this transition has been fast, reliable train service, notably Amtrak's express Acela line. Though it's not nearly as fast as high-speed rail in Europe or Japan, the Acela line has connected cities along the Bos-Wash corridor. In doing so, it has made the corridor itself a much more integrated economic unit. In the 1960s and 1970s, as New York–area companies expanded, they were able to shift some key economic functions to take advantage of talent pools and cost advantages across the tristate area. But today those same functions can easily be shifted to Philadelphia, Baltimore, and even Washington D.C. Faster rail connections shrink the effective distance between cities within megaregions and enable secondary cities to cash in on economic functions that were once the sole province of the central hub.

Think of it as shrinking distance, borrowing proximity, and building scale. The speed and ease of high-speed rail brings once-distant cities into closer reach of one another. It may be the single best way the federal government can help rebuild the once-great industrial corridors of the Great Lakes, which have lost much of their previous economic function and where distances are currently too great to commute from one city to the next. Chicago and Toronto stand as the twin pillars of the region, with strong, growing economies. But what if we could bring other cities in closer time proximity to them and knit the region together as an economic unit? "If we could shift all the cities in the Midwest closer to each other," writes Avent, "and then pick them up and move them nearer to the northeastern corridor, we would go a long way toward restoring the economic viability of many Midwestern cities." And here is the role of high-speed rail. "We can't literally do that," he adds, "but we can effectively accomplish something similar by improving physical links within the Midwest and between it and other regions. We could decongest highways and airports with congestion charges, for instance, and plow the proceeds into high-speed passenger and freight rail connections among Midwestern cities and between the Midwest and the northeastern corridor as well as healthy Canadian metropoles."

High-speed rail offers a mechanism for breathing life back into great industrial cities. It not only shrinks the time it takes to get back and forth between these cities, it also provides a framework for future in-fill development along its corridors. Just as development filled in along the early streetcar lines and the postwar highways, high-speed rail will encourage denser, more compact and concentrated development filling in along its routes over time. Spain's new high-speed rail link between Barcelona and Madrid has not only slashed commuting times between these two great Spanish cities, it has also helped revitalize several troubled locations along the line. Imagine that sort of revitalization happening along the lines of a new Great Lakes high-speed rail network.

I believe that investing in high-speed rail systems may be the single most important thing we can do to bring back once-great Rust Belt cities. It would be the first step toward making our most devastated cities part of the new spatial fix, by connecting them to the developing megaregions that represent the next phase of our economy.

It's time to start thinking of transit and infrastructure projects less in political terms and more as a set of strategic investments, as fundamental to the speed and scope of our economic recovery as they are to the emerging shape of the economy, society, and communities of the future. Critics point out the tremendously high cost of high-speed rail and believe that we'll never see a return on the investment. But strict cost-benefit calculations miss the broader economic benefits that come from new infrastructure. Past investments in railroad lines and highways spurred development of real estate and of industries that far outstripped anything we could imagine at the time. Infrastructure is always hugely expensive, and there's no clear way to measure the overall future return on the investment, whether it's in the form of in-novation, development, or new communities and jobs. Infrastructure provides a skeleton on which to grow a new economic model. The infrastructure investments we make now will determine the kind of economy we have in the future.

History shows us that it's even more costly to play catch-up, to wait until there's a crying need for the infrastructure before beginning to assemble it. In the past, the United States led the world in the develop-ment of new infrastructure, which helped secure its economic preemi-nence. Now these investments come mostly in other countries around the globe, from China to Spain and many places in between. Just as civilization sprang up along natural conduits such as rivers, bays, and valleys, towns sprang into existence along the streetcar and rail lines and highways as they were built. The high-speed rail lines will enable the fill-in I described, but they need to be in place first. *If you build it, they will come.* That may be an older, slightly hackneyed phrase that's often used to deride new investment, but in the case of infrastructure it holds more than a grain of truth. In some ways, infrastructure is analogous to government support for basic research in medicine or the sciences. Such investments, which are either too large or too risky for private companies to undertake, offer a significant social rate of return that can drive future invention, productivity, and growth. We can't always justify them on the grounds that their immediate short-run benefits will outweigh their costs, and we can't fully estimate their long-run benefits, but they are critical for prolonged prosperity. Just as in the past, infrastructure provides a critical platform for growth and a framework on which to build a new kind of economy.

Chapter Twenty-Two

▪

Renting the Dream

n 1931, in the depths of the Great Depression, the historian James Truslow Adams introduced the expression "the American Dream," defining it as the "dream of a land in which life should be better and richer and fuller for everyone, with opportunity for each according to ability or achievement."[1] For the past half century, ownership of a single-family home has been one of the cornerstones of that dream. A home of one's own, a yard, a picket fence, a car or two in the driveway: an important step on the road to happiness and security and part of the gospel for generations. But a whole slew of recent research indicates that it ain't necessarily so. One detailed study by Grace Wong Bucchianeri, an economist at the University of Pennsylvania's Wharton School of Business, found that after controlling for income and demographics, home owners are no happier than renters. Less surprisingly, home owners report considerably higher levels of stress than renters. That makes perfect sense: their financial burden is higher, and upkeep of a home is a chore.[2] There's a reason people refer to their houses as "money pits." They are *time* pits as well.

Historically, one of the greatest allures of home ownership was that it represented wealth. A house was like a savings account that just kept growing over time. It was an investment. If you bought a house and hung on to it for twenty or thirty years, you could sell it at a big enough profit to fund your retirement. The U.S. tax code even allowed for this eventuality by granting a onetime exemption from capital gains taxes on home sales if the seller is over age fifty-nine and a half.

Of course, that era ended when the housing bubble burst. Now, instead of making money on their homes, millions of people have lost a bundle. And millions more are stuck with homes whose mortgages exceed their value. According to one study, 30 percent of people age forty-five to fifty-four and 18 percent of those between fifty-five and sixty-four were underwater in their homes in 2009.[3] Except for some exceptional boom periods, housing has never been a good financial investment. Yale University's Robert Shiller, the world's leading student of bubbles, housing and otherwise, found that from "1890 to 1990, the rate of return on residential real estate was just about zero after inflation."[4]

Even if a house isn't underwater, chances are good that its owners are house poor in the traditional sense: too much of their income is being sucked up by house payments and house-related expenses. The rule of thumb—at least this is what our parents told us—used to be that you should spend 25 to 30 percent of your household income on housing. But as average house prices climbed faster and higher than average wages, that percentage ballooned. In some places, people were spending—and many continue to spend—50 percent or more of their income on housing, never mind shelling out for cars and life's other necessities. For these reasons, you might start to think that renters may actually be financially better off than comparable home owners, especially those who bought near the height of the market during the boom. Indeed, that's what one study has found: among people of similar financial status, those who chose to rent in 2004 had more wealth in 2009 than those who bought their homes.[5]

Home ownership does bring with it important social benefits. It generally instills in people a deeper emotional commitment to their community. Still, it can be very costly to the economy as a whole.[6] A 1998 study by the Federal Reserve Bank of Dallas, undertaken well before the boom, provided detailed empirical evidence that the United States has overinvested in housing relative to other forms of capital since 1929. "The general pattern has been that we have invested more in housing relative to other kinds of capital goods than we would in an economy in which the tax system and credit institutions did not tilt the playing field at all," wrote the MIT economist James Poterba. In other words, the housing sector drained off precious capital that could otherwise be spent on productivity improvement, innovation, medical technology, software, or alternative energy—the sectors and products that could drive U.S. growth and exports in the coming years. The demand for bigger houses also skewed residential patterns, leading to excessive low-density suburban growth, which in turn proved expensive in terms of energy consumption and infrastructure building for the economy as a whole. Or, as the economist Edmund Phelps succinctly puts it, "It used to be the business of America was business. Now the business of America is homeownership."[7] "To recover and grow again," he adds, "America needs to get over its 'house passion.'"

M obility and flexibility are key principles of the modern economy. Home ownership limits both. According to one important study, cities with higher home ownership rates also suffer from higher unemployment rates. The study, by the economist Andrew Oswald, found that across European cities, a 10 percent increase in home ownership correlated with a 2 percent increase in unemployment. Home ownership, the study found, is a more important predictor of unemployment than rates of unionization or the generosity of welfare benefits.[8] If you've invested in a house, you're less likely to pack up and move when times get tough, either because of the investment you've made in the community and the social roots you've established there or, more simply, because you're unable to sell your house at a price you consider reasonable.

Americans' mobility hit record lows during the crisis. In 2008, fewer people moved, as a percentage of the population, than in any year since the Census Bureau started tracking address changes, in the late 1940s: less than 12 percent in 2008, compared to more than 20 percent during suburbia's golden years. "[T]he U.S. population, often thought of as the most mobile in the developed world," the Brookings

Institution demographer William H. Frey told the *New York Times*, "seems to have been stopped dead in its tracks due to a confluence of constraints posed by a tough economic spell."[9] It is bitterly ironic that housing, for so many Americans, has gone from being their *shelter* to being their *burden*.

A Reset like the current one is the absolute worst time to lose the ability for people to move around. The economy is going through a broad structural shift; this is no typical, predictable business or economic cycle. It is not, for instance, just a period of temporary layoffs of manufacturing workers, who will be picked up again as the economy recovers. This is a moment of significant creative destruction; older manufacturing firms, jobs, and industries are being destroyed, and new industries, occupations, and firms are being created. In this kind of situation, it's much harder for workers, particularly low-skilled ones, to find jobs where they live. In today's economy and the economy of the future, geographic mobility is required to match workers and their skills to appropriate jobs.

We cannot escape the reality of the conflict of two great dreams: the dream of unlimited economic opportunity and the dream of owning a single-family home. We've seen the ways in which the importance of home ownership became overblown and began to undermine the economy; how it consumed an ever-larger share of income for far too many, constraining their lifestyle and sometimes even bankrupting them; and how it encouraged massive, unsustainable growth in places where land was cheap and the real estate economy dominant. We could well look back on this moment in history as a time when people lived like indentured servants, with their own homes as lord and master. For too many, the dream of home ownership turned into an economic trap, one of our own making. The most staggering damage caused by the housing crisis may not be the impact on the financial markets; it may be the long-run competitive disadvantage caused by the inability to relocate the labor force to where the jobs of the future lie. It's not that home ownership per se is bad, it's that home ownership on the scale it has grown to is plainly ill suited to today's postindustrial economy. Letting go of it as the centerpiece of our collective aspirations might be among the healthiest, most liberating steps we can take.

We are already beginning to see some signs of a shift toward renting. With all the turmoil in the housing markets, many people have put off buying. And with tightened credit standards (requiring a modest down payment and a reasonable credit rating), it's become much harder for those who don't have their financial house in order to buy. A December 2009 *Wall Street Journal* story chronicled the many Americans who were giving up, or being forced out of, their homes and moving into rentals, summing up the situation with the headline "American Dream 2: Default, then Rent."[10] As the rate of home ownership has charted its biggest decline in two decades, falling from its peak of 69.2 percent in 2004 to 67.6 percent in September 2009, it has dropped the most for younger Americans. The home ownership rate for Americans under age thirty-five slipped by 2 percent between 2008 and 2009. Across the United States, some 36 million people are renters. About a third of all occupied homes are rentals. The ongoing movement of higher-paid and higher-skilled talented people to megaregions and talent magnets is accelerating the demand for rental housing. Even though prices have declined somewhat, it's still very expensive to buy a home in many of these places. More people have no choice but to rent in those cities. Renting is much more prevalent in metro areas such as New York, where 66 percent of residents are renters, as well as D.C. and Chicago, where more than half (56 and 51 percent, respectively) rent their homes.[11]

The housing crisis creates additional opportunities for rental housing. Across the country, there is an accumulation of foreclosed homes and failing condo projects that could be turned into rentals. With prices down 30 or 40 percent or more in some places, this kind of conversion increasingly makes economic sense. It becomes possible to assemble large numbers of units and capitalize on economies of scale. New building technologies and materials, as well as new energy-saving technology, offer long-run cost savings, while new strategies for delivering and managing rental housing hold even greater promise.

Tata, the huge Indian conglomerate that led the way in low-priced automobiles with its $2,000 Nano car, is moving in the same direction in the housing sector. At a time when most developers in big Indian cities such as Mumbai are putting up luxury high-rises and suburban mansions to attract the newly wealthy of India's blossoming economy, Tata is building Nano housing. According to *BusinessWeek*, it's putting up whole communities of small, highly energy-efficient, inexpensive apartments in the industrial areas where decent lower-income housing is scarce.[12] You may not think this concept has a much of a future in the land of McMansions, but I'm old enough to remember when Americans scoffed at Japan's tiny "shoe-box" cars. I'm not saying that typical American families will go for 250-square-foot Nano houses, but certainly these principles could be applied to the development of larger, but still affordable, rentals more in line with their tastes. At the other end of the spectrum, upscale hotel chains such as the Four Seasons, the Ritz-Carlton, and the St. Regis are already in the condo business in a big way, offering complete amenities and soup-to-nuts service for their residents.

This kind of approach can be extended to more affordable rental housing. In fact, it already has been. Korman Communities, for example, is building new kinds of flexible rental communities in New Jersey, Pennsylvania, and suburban Virginia, according to a *New York Times* report. The AVE complexes offer furnished and unfurnished rental units that come with condo-style amenities and hotel-style service. Furnished units are leased on a monthly basis, but unfurnished units are leased for a minimum of six months and, more ordinarily, a year. AVE communities also have movie theaters, pools and other entertainment facilities, organized social events, meeting rooms, and business facilities. Originally designed for people and families in transition—perhaps recently unemployed or divorced—this kind of approach also has the potential to serve mobile people.[13]

The kind of future I'm imagining is one where you sign up with a large-scale provider of rental housing. You select the place you like and specify the paint colors and fixtures you like. If you get a new job or simply want to move, no problem: you send in your notice and go through the list of properties in the new city. It's plug-and-play housing, if you will, that will facilitate the flexibility and mobility today's economy needs.

There are several things government can do to encourage the shift from owning to renting. Though well intentioned, the Obama administration has gone way overboard with its plan to stabilize housing, stem the tide of foreclosures, and breathe life back into the paralyzed mortgage market. It makes absolutely no sense—in fact, it's just plain reckless—for the administration to propose foreclosure relief that will extend mortgage terms to forty years and reduce monthly payments to 38 percent—or even 31 percent—of income.[14] That will simply continue the enslavement of people to houses they couldn't afford in the first place. And estimates are that more than half of those who have their mortgages refinanced under such programs ultimately end up defaulting on their mortgages.[15] The administration's quest to reinvigorate home ownership actually works against the flexibility and affordability needed for economic recovery. Why not take the houses off the owners' hands and rent them back to them at a much more affordable rate? Fannie Mae has taken a step in this direction by enabling home owners who have defaulted on loans that it holds to transfer their deeds to the agency and then rent their homes back. Some 1,200 former home owners became renters under the program in the first half of 2009, though this was just 2 percent of the 57,000 foreclosures Fannie Mae made during that time.[16]

The government could extend this kind of approach, working with banks and real estate companies to offer to rent each home to the owner at a market rate, which would typically be lower than the mortgage payments, for a certain number of years. At the end of that period, the former home owner could be given the option to repurchase the home at the prevailing market price. And what about the home owners already forced into foreclosure? Again, the government could help banks and large real estate companies turn these homes into rental properties, helping to clean up neighborhoods while providing affordable rental housing.

American housing policy massively subsidizes owners over renters. The federal government provided some $230 billion in home ownership subsidies in 2009, nearly four times the $60 billion that went to renters, according to the Congressional Budget Office.[17] But guess who needs it more? The report notes that renters bear a higher burden of housing costs. In 2007, 45 percent of renters devoted more than 30 percent of their income to housing—a percentage that typically indicates that housing is unaffordable when other household needs are taken into account—compared to 30 percent of home owners.

It's time for housing policy to change. It no longer makes economic sense to provide massive subsidies, tax advantages, and incentives for owning a home. Edward Glaeser is among a growing number of economists who says it's time to kill, or at least somehow limit, the tax deduction for interest paid on mortgages. "The Great Depression provided an opportunity to rethink old policies in a major way," he writes. "In the current morass, everything should, once again, be open for debate. One sacred cow that has long been in need of a good stockyard is the home mortgage interest deduction."[18] The deduction promotes inefficient use of scarce economic resources. On top of that, the bulk of the benefits go to fairly rich households, "people who are overwhelmingly in single-family detached houses," notes Glaeser, who "would be likely to own that house with or without the home mortgage interest rate deduction." He's describing me, for instance; I own a single-family home in Canada, where no such deduction exists. He suggests "gradually reducing the upper limit" on the deduction to loans of up to $300,000.

But it should not stop there; the current Reset provides the opportunity to rethink and restructure the housing system more broadly. We need to envision an overhaul as sweeping in scope as the one that brought us the modern system of housing finance of the Second Great Reset. That means bringing mortgage-lending practices into line with those of other advanced countries, such as Canada, Sweden, or most of the rest of Europe. It means larger down payments and stricter lending standards. The American tolerance of allowing borrowers to essentially mail in the keys and walk away from their loans is disastrous and needs to end. I can't do it in Canada, and neither can borrowers in most other parts of the world, where if you decide to stop paying your mortgage the bank comes after your earnings and savings. What kind of financial sense does it make to encourage people to buy homes, let them do so with virtually nothing down, and, if the home loses value, well, they can simply send the keys back? Just as government incentives, with the cooperation of private lending institutions, spurred a massive increase in home ownership after the Second World War, it can facilitate the expansion of new, more flexible forms of rental housing today, allowing people the freedom to move as their job, career, and lifestyle prospects change. Such a shift would stabilize the lives of countless individuals and the economy as a whole.

New forms of housing have always been crucial to Great Resets. The modern mortgage and the single-family house powered the spatial fix of the past era. They were the right developments for their time and absolutely contributed to the long-term dynamic of recovery and postwar prosperity. In hindsight, however, we can see how those same factors contributed to a massive misallocation of resources away from growing industries and productive assets. Our overwhelming reliance on suburban-style single-family home ownership is an experiment that has outlived its usefulness and is well past its sell-by date. It is now readily apparent that not everyone should own a home and that the mortgage system is a big part of what got us into the current financial mess. It's also clear that home ownership ties people to locations, making it harder for them to move to areas of economic prosperity. Now, as we move into the second decade of the twenty-first century, the bursting of the bubble has created an opportunity to remake the housing system into one that is more in tune with the knowledge-driven economy's need for flexibility and labor mobility.

Chapter Twenty-Three

■

Resetting Point

We're a hurried people, living in an anxious time. We've grown impatient, accustomed to instant gratification. We want the economic crisis to just be over. We want our pension funds, stock portfolios, and college savings accounts to be healthy and growing; we want our jobs back; we want to be able to go out to eat or buy ourselves a treat without panicking about the household budget. And we want all of it right now.

Resets, however, take time. If the past is any guide, they are complex processes that unfold over two or three decades—the better part of a generation. None of us can know exactly what our economy or society will look like a generation or two from now. We can't predict with any certainty what the next economic landscape and spatial fix will look like when they are fully formed. But we can try to find emerging patterns and to recognize and understand the positive trends that exist even in these difficult times. And we can make use of what we've learned from the experience of previous generations.

One thing is for certain: government is not the prime mover in Great Resets. Government can certainly take action to mitigate the most onerous effects of a crisis and to establish regulatory frameworks to prevent future ones. But though government can patch up some holes to keep the economy afloat for a short time, it lacks both the means and the resources to generate the enormous level of demand needed to power sustained growth. As I've tried to demonstrate, Great Resets evolve organically: new innovations emerge, new systems of technology and infrastructure are put in place, and new patterns of living and working gradually take shape and begin to remake the economic landscape. Government's central task is to enable and accelerate these shifts by helping to create the fertile environment in which they can grow and develop. Resets—like most everything else—are a delicate combination of nature and nurture.

Great Resets are the pivot points of economic history, in the nineteenth century, the twentieth century, and now. They are the great transformative moments when new technologies and technological systems arise, when the economy is recast and society remade, and when the places where we live and work change to suit new needs. However, not all Resets are the same. We focus today on the Great Depression era and the New Deal as historical touchstones, and hope to find in those historical experiences the wisdom to deal with our current crisis. We may not want to admit it, but the challenge we face today is much more daunting than that of the 1930s. The shovel-ready stimulus that built highways and roads worked so well during the Great Depression and its aftermath because it helped generate demand for the products of the industrial assembly line. Pouring money into public works and infrastructure literally paved the way for suburbanization, which then stimulated exactly the kind of industrial production that the economy needed to get moving again. Today's economic troubles share much more with the Long Depression of the late nineteenth century, the period I call the First Reset. Now as then, we are in the midst of a tectonic shift to a fundamentally new economic order: the shift from an agricultural to an industrial economy then, the shift from an industrial to an idea-driven creative economy now. The challenge is to accelerate the transition from the old to the new order and, at the same time, to spur the transition to a new geographic framework in which new living habits and work habits can take shape.

Our efforts must concentrate on actively building the economy of the future. Instead of infusing scarce capital into the very banks and financial system that brought us to the brink in the first place, or trying to reinvigorate the housing and mortgage markets that pushed us over the edge, and instead of bailing out mismanaged old-economy companies, we must use whatever resources are available to accelerate the transition to an idea-driven economy, while improving the jobs that have survived or are now being created. Though it's impossible to paint an accurate, detailed portrait of the post-crash economy and society, I can outline some basic guiding principles culled from our examination of past Resets that can help us move toward a more sustainable and prosperous future.

A simple, undeniable first principle is that every single human being is creative. Each and every effort and policy initiative we undertake can be measured by this simple yardstick: how do they increase the ability of people, organizations, places, and companies to mobilize human creative capabilities? No, not all of us can paint, write novels, make movies, compose symphonies, develop new software, build new energy-efficient systems, or invent new biotechnologies. But we all have something we're good at, our own creative spark, and there's little in life more satisfying and rewarding than the chance to exercise that talent. The real key to economic growth lies in harnessing the full creative talents of every one of us.

There's an urgent need to create new good jobs—lots of them. I've shown how the economy, even as it sheds manufacturing jobs, is actively creating new knowledge work and lower-skill service jobs. We cannot stop the clock of history from ticking and we can't magically bring back the old industrial economy. We need to support the growth of higher-paying knowledge, professional and creative jobs, and make sure that greater numbers of workers are prepared for them. But that will only get us part of the way there. As service jobs continue to grow and be point-of-entry jobs for many, we need to make them into better, higher-paying jobs. This cannot wait any longer. We need a major effort to upgrade these jobs, and make them more innovative and productive. We did it before with manufacturing jobs, we need to do it now with service jobs, which can offer a much better way of life for many people and contribute meaningfully to the productivity and prosperity of our economy.

In this light, we can see more clearly than ever the need to over-haul our education system. Tinkering at the margins will no longer do. We need a learning and development system that is in sync with the new creative economy. Here again, the two previous Resets are instructive. New and improved education systems were indispensable to these past Resets and will again be vital for the current Reset. The First Reset gave us the modern system of public schools and laid the foundations of the modern university and college education system, as well as modern engineering education. The Second Reset expanded higher education, among other things sparking the creation of the modern research-intensive university. Those giant strides forward are but small steps compared to the changes required today.

We need a system of learning and human development that mobilizes and harnesses human creative talent en masse. Bill Gates, among others, says the current school system is "broken." The system arose during the shift from an agricultural to an industrial economy and served the needs of that time, pumping out literate, skilled, docile factory workers. But the development of the educational system has not kept pace with subsequent changes in the society and the economy. In the context of today's knowledge-based economy, ironically, it feels more than antiquated, as if it had been designed specifically to squelch creative thought. We've mythologized the histories of entrepreneurs such as Gates or Steven Jobs or Michael Dell, constantly retelling the stories of those go-getters starting new businesses in their dorm rooms or garages in their spare time. Yet nobody ever asks the obvious questions: Why were they doing those things in their *spare* time? Why isn't the education system structured so that this kind of activity is the very goal? Humans have always essentially learned by doing. The idea that school is the only, or even the main, source of education is a relatively recent development. We need to understand that classroom education is merely one phase of a continuous process of learning, discovery, and engagement that can occur anywhere and anytime. We need a learning system that fuels, rather than squelches, our collective creativity.

A new kind of social compact is also required. Much has been made of the need to upgrade health care in America and to address mounting inequality, but this is only part of the story. The social compact needs to be reworked in light of the demands and challenges of today's knowledge-driven economy. The old industrial order was organized around enormous companies that provided long-term, stable employment, and government that provided a social safety net. Big companies continue to play an important role, but they no longer define our economy and society, as they did for the last fifty years or so. In our more mobile and flexible economic system, people change jobs much more frequently than in the past. Such economic flexibility requires a safety net that is similarly flexible and allows people to have portable benefits that are not tied to specific employers. A new safety net must also ensure that those who are truly disadvantaged are provided adequate living standards. And it must go even further: even countries such as Sweden, Denmark, and Canada, which do this very well, need to do more. The key is to expand the very concept of a social safety net, from one that provides just material well-being to one that provides real opportunity for every person. A true social compact for our times starts from the principle that each individual should have the basic right to develop and utilize his or her creative talents fully—in ways that generate a livelihood for the individual and foster productivity for society as a whole.

Earlier Resets saw massive investments in new infrastructure systems, from railroads, streetcars, and subways to telephone lines and interstate highways, which helped set economic growth in motion. We need to build the infrastructure of the future, not just patch up that of the past. Failure to do so will only stall the current Reset and hold back recovery. We must make intelligent investments in new infrastructure that can move beyond the constraints of our current energy-inefficient, environmentally destructive, time-devouring infrastructure. We need to increase the velocity of moving people, goods, and ideas.

The history of economic development has been a history of greater expansion and more intense use of land and space. The First Reset saw the transition from small cities and an agricultural society to dense industrial cities. The Second Reset gave us the sprawling suburbs and great metropolitan areas that defined recent times. The current Reset is premised on the rise of a new and even larger economic landscape defined by megaregions that spread across multiple cities, several states and provinces, and, in some instances, national borders. Those regions will have a hard time forming without the infrastructure necessary to bring people and ideas together. Instead of building more highways, we'll need to invest in high-speed rail that can knit these megaregions together, speed movement across them, and enable new infill development and greater density. Such infrastructure will also help create the context for new modes of living and working that enable people to live closer to where they work and shrink their commutes. By raising our economic metabolism and providing the density and interaction that leads to innovation, it will enable future prosperity.

For too long, we've equated urban centers with concentrations of poverty and disadvantage. Now we must recognize them as important drivers of economic growth. Governmental structures, too, will need to adapt. While national governments in the United States and around the world are mired in ideological conflict, partisan gridlock, and bureaucratic stasis, political leaders in cities, counties, and states around the world are crafting new, pragmatic solutions to pressing social and economic problems. The economist Alice Rivlin long ago argued that the right place to make decisions about productivity and economic development was the local level, because local actors had the deepest knowledge about their economies.[1] This is essentially the same principle that motivates leading companies to give individual workers and teams of workers the autonomy to solve problems and propose innovative new solutions. We need to revamp our governmental institutions and governance structure to fit these realities, with less authority at the top and more at the local and regional levels.

Resets always carry with them new ways of living and working, giving birth to new habits of consumption. This one is no different. The colossal debt we collectively amassed, as we bought ever-bigger houses, cars, more goods and gadgets, eventually crushed us. We're already starting to move away from our addiction to acquisition. That's a very good thing. People are shopping smarter, buying less, saving more, and focusing more on using their money to enrich the experiences of their lives, rather than fill their homes with stuff. It makes tremendous sense to rid ourselves of overly burdensome possessions—huge mortgages or car payments, money-pit houses filled with oversize appliances—if we want to gain the mobility and flexibility required in this Reset. The traditional notion of ownership itself may well be outmoded. Ironically, the once-vaunted ownership society appears to be giving way to a new form of rentership society. Car purchases which long ago gave way to car leases are now being replaced by access to Zipcars. More and more people are choosing to rent their homes, and growing numbers of homeowners are shifting to rentals.

The promise of the current Reset is the opportunity for a life made better not by ownership of real estate, appliances, cars, and all manner of material goods, but by greater flexibility and lower levels of debt, more time with family and friends, greater promise of personal development, and access to more and better experiences. All organisms and all systems experience the cycles of life, death, and rebirth. Forest fires destroy the landscape but perform a necessary function, clearing the dense and choked ground for new growth. In fall, the grass turns brown and the leaves fall from the trees, but in spring, the leaves return and the trees have grown taller and stronger. Our leaders will have to make smart decisions about how much time and resources we spend trying to save companies and business that might be better left to go the way of all things, especially when that effort could serve people far better by preparing them for something new and easing their path to more sustainable livelihoods. Education and infrastructure, creativity, and connectivity—these are things we can address, things we must improve and ensure to see this Reset through and build a new prosperity.

That's the role I see for government as we move toward the future. Government has its most important and legitimate role to play in establishing the enabling framework for a new era of shared prosperity, and it squanders precious resources that could support such future-oriented, prosperity-boosting efforts when it chooses to bail out old industries, breathe life back into outmoded institutions, or place Band-Aids on problems. Such approaches may or may not stop the bleeding, but they won't keep us from falling again. And they will do little to set us on the path to a better future.

Let's stop treating the symptoms. Let's stop confusing nostalgia with resolve. It's time to turn our efforts, as individuals, as governments, as a society, to putting the necessary pieces into place for a vibrant, prosperous future.

Acknowledgments

Looking back, this book originated with a phone call from Don Peck of the *Atlantic*. The stock market had just crashed, and Don wanted to know if I'd write something on the crisis and its effects on New York City. We set a date to meet in Washington, D.C., about a month later, where we sketched out the basic ideas for what would become my *Atlantic* cover story "How the Crash Is Reshaping America," which appeared in March 2009. My deepest thanks go to Don, who helped me hone and refine the original idea and worked as a true collaborator in fashioning the final piece. The article generated more attention than I ever dreamed, and so I thought: why not turn it into a book?

I'm grateful to several key people who made that happen. My literary agent, Jim Levine, helped shape and guide the project and to find great publishers. I thank Hollis Heimbouch at HarperCollins in the United States and Anne Collins at Random House Canada for believing in this project and for being thoughtful and supportive editors. David Sobel helped shape and edit the manuscript. Beth Fisher at Levine Greenberg made sure the book would reach a global audience, lining up great publishers around the world.

A book like this is a team effort, and I'm deeply grateful to each and every member of mine. Patrick Adler was my go-to person from the start, working tirelessly to scour historical sources, dig up data, perform analyses, and do whatever background research was needed. Charlotta Mellander, with whom I have collaborated on numerous projects, provided her usual deft hand at number crunching and commented on various drafts of the manuscript. Kevin Stolarick, the research director at the Martin Prosperity Institute (MPI), helped in myriad ways: by developing data, contributing to analysis, reading over the manuscript, and overseeing our terrific research team. Ian Swain, Ronnie Sanders, Scott Pennington and Adrienne Ross provided invaluable research assistance. Kim Silk, our data librarian, helped track down sources and assisted with fact-checking, copyediting, and bibliographic details. Laura Anderson of the Rotman School's Business Information Centre also helped with references and queries. Erik Calonius edited drafts of several early chapters. Craig Pyette of Random House Canada also provided editorial assistance.

The ability to do creative work depends on having other people to take care of management and administration. Jim Milway, our executive director, takes care of much of that, with the support of Kim Ryan and the very capable staffs of the MPI and Rotman School. Marisol D'Andrea, who supports my work on a day-to-day basis, assisted with fact-checking and editing of the manuscript. The MPI is an incredible environment in which to think, research, and write. I'd like to thank Roger Martin, dean of the Rotman School of Management, for his original vision; Geoff Beattie for his ongoing support; and our funders, Joe Rotman, the Province of Ontario, the Royal Bank of Canada, Manulife, and Jim Fleck, for their generosity.

I'm grateful to my team at the Creative Class Group (CCG)— Reham Alexander, Steven Pedigo, and Elizabeth McGolerick—for supporting my speaking, blogging, and writing.

I am fortunate to have a large extended family that is the source of great comfort and joy: my brother, Robert, his wife, Ginny, and my nieces Sophia and Tessa and nephew Luca; the Kozouz clan: Ruth, Reham, Markis, and Adiev Alexander; Dean and Ruba Alexander; Leena, Adam, Christian, Melia, and Sophia Hosler; Tarig, Anastasia, and Zachary; Ramiz and Christina; and my DeCicco cousins too numerous to mention.

My deepest debt of gratitude is to my wife, Rana. She runs our business and is my partner in everything I do. She helps focus and sharpen my ideas, edits what I write, and deals with the details large and small. She's the love of my life and fills every day with fun, passion, and boundless energy.

References

Chapter 1: The Great Reset

1. Emanuel told CBS's *Face the Nation*, "Rule one: Never allow a crisis to go to waste. They are opportunities to do big things." Quoted in Jeff Zeleny, "Obama Weighs Quick Undoing of Bush Policy," *New York Times*, November 9, 2008. Thomas Friedman reports that Romer said this to him in "9/11 and 4/11," *New York Times*, July 20, 2008.
2. Speech to the annual conference of Business for Social Responsibility, November 8, 2008, retrieved from www.marcgunther.com/2008/11/06/an-emotional-social-economic-reset.
3. The concept originates with David Harvey, "The Spatial Fix—Hegel, Von Thunen and Marx," *Antipode* 13, no. 2 (1981): 1–12; Harvey, *The Limits of Capital* (New York: Oxford University Press, 1982); Harvey, *The New Imperialism* (New York: Oxford University Press, 2003).
4. Michelle Maynard, "Is Happiness Still That New Car Smell?" *New York Times*, October 21, 2009.

Chapter 2: The Crisis Most Like Our Own

1. Scott Reynolds Nelson, "The Real Great Depression: The Depression of 1929 Is the Wrong Model for the Current Economic Crisis," *Chronicle of Higher Education: The Chronicle Review* 55, no. 8 (October 2008): B98.
2. Alfred Kleinknecht, *Innovation Patterns in Crisis and Prosperity: Schumpeter's Long Cycle Reconsidered* (New York: St. Martin's Press, 1987). Also see Jacob Schmookler, *Invention and Economic Growth* (Cambridge, Mass.: Harvard University Press, 1966).

3. My discussion of technological innovation during the First Reset is based on the following key sources: Joel Mokyr, *The Lever of Riches: Technological Creativity and Economic Progress* (New York: Oxford University Press, 1992), and Mokyr, *Gifts of Athena: Historical Origins of the Knowledge Economy* (Princeton, N.J.: Princeton University Press, 2004). See also David Landes, *The Wealth and Poverty of Nations: Why Some Nations Are So Rich and Others Are So Poor* (New York: W. W. Norton, 1999).

4. David Hounshell, *From American System to Mass Production, 1880–1932: The Development of Manufacturing Technology in the United States* (Baltimore: Johns Hopkins University Press, 1985).

5. Joel Mokyr, "The Second Industrial Revolution, 1870–1914," in Valerio Castronovo, ed., *Storia dell'economia mondiale* (Rome: Laterza Publishing, 1999), 219–245.

6. Christopher Freeman, *The Economics of Industrial Innovation* (London: Routledge, 1997); Gerhard Mensch, *Stalemate in Technology: How Innovations Overcome the Depression* (New York: HarperCollins, 1983).

7. "Interview with Edmund Phelps," The Daily Beast, July 17, 2009, retrieved from www.thedailybeast.com/blogs-and-stories/2009-07-13/interview-with-edmund-phelps.

8. Thomas P. Hughes, *Networks of Power: Electrification in Western Society, 1880–1930* (Baltimore: Johns Hopkins University Press, 1983); Hughes, *American Genesis: A Century of Invention and Technological Enthusiasm* (Chicago: University of Chicago Press, 2004).

9. Mathew Josephson, *Edison: A Biography* (New York: John Wiley and Sons, 1992), 314, retrieved from www.nps.gove/nr/twhp/wwwlps/lessons/25edison/25edison.htm/

10. Paul Israel, "Inventing Industrial Research: Thomas Edison and the Menlo Park Laboratory," *Endeavor* 26, no. 2 (June 1, 2002), retrieved from www.sciencedirect.com.

11. Mokyr, "The Second Industrial Revolution."

12. The quote is from *Telegraphic Journal and Electrical Review* 20 (1887), p. 349, as cited in Hughes, *Networks of Power*, 105.

13. A terrific study of this process is Naomi R. Lamoreaux, Margaret Levenstein, and Kenneth L. Sokoloff, "Mobilizing Venture Capital during the Second Industrial Revolution: Cleveland, Ohio, 1870–1920," *Capitalism and Society* 1, no. 3 (2006), retrieved from www.bepress.com/cas/vol1/iss3/art5. Richard Florida and Mark Samber, "Capital and Creative Destruction: Venture Capital and Regional Growth in U.S. Industrialization," in *The New Industrial Geography, Regions, Regulation and Institutions*, Trevor Barnes and Meric Gertler, eds. (London: Routledge, 1999), 265–287.

14. Harper quote and discussion of early urban transit systems is from Mary Bellis, "History of the Streetcar, " retrieved from http://inventors.about.com/library/inventors/blstreet.htm.

15. See Brian Cudahy, *Cash, Tokens and Transfers: A History of Urban Mass Transit in North America* (New York: Fordham University Press, 1990).

16. Mokyr, "The Second Industrial Revolution."

17. Data on school attendance are from Williams Sonnenberg, "Elementary and Secondary Education," chapter 2 of Thomas Snyder, *120 Years of American Education: A Statisticanl Portrait* (Darby, Pa.: Diane Publishing, 1993), 25–62.

18. Though the percentage of Americans attending college was just 2 percent; see Thomas Snyder, *120 Years of American Education: A Statistical Portrait* (Darby, Pa.: Diane Publishing, 1993).

19. On the rise of engineering education in the United States, see Roger Geiger, *To Advance Knowledge: The Growth of American Research Universities, 1900–1940* (New York: Oxford University Press, 1990); David Noble, *America by Design: Science, Technology and the Rise of Corporate Capitalism* (New York: Oxford University Press, 1977); Nathan Rosenberg and Richard Nelson, "American Universities and Technical Advance in Industry," *Research Policy* 23, no. 3 (1994), 323–48.

Chapter 3: Urbanism as Innovation

1. The figures on rural and urban population are from U.S. Census, *Selected Historical Decennial Census Population and Housing Counts, Urban and Rural Populations, Population 1790–1900* (1993), retrieved from www.census.gov/population/www/censusdata/files/table-4.pdf.

2. "Figures on Urban Population, Population of the 100 Largest Urban Places: 1860, Table 9" (1998), retrieved from www.census.gov/population/www/documentation/twps0027/tab09.txt.

3. There are a huge number of studies of this process, but see, e.g., David Gordon's classic "Capitalist Development and the History of American Cities," in *Marxism and the Metropolis: New Perspectives on Urban Political Economy*, William K. Tabb and Larry Sawers, eds. (New York: Oxford University Press, 1984), 21–53.

4. Population data for American cities are from Campbell Gibson, "Population of the 100 Largest Cities and Other Urban Places in the United States: 1790 to 1990," U.S. Census, June 1998, retrieved from www.census.gov/population/www/documentation/twps0027/twps0027.html. Data on manufacturing employment are from Gordon, "Capitalist Development and the History of American Cities."

5. Mancur Olson, *The Rise and Decline of Nations: Economic Growth, Stagflation and Social Rigidities* (New Haven, Conn.: Yale University Press, 1984).

6. Statistics on immigration and immigrants during the First Reset are from Campbell J. Gibson and Emily Lennon, "Historical Census Statistics on the Foreign-born Population of the United States: 1850–1990," U.S. Census, February 1999, retrieved from www.census.gov/population/www/documentation/twps0029/twps0029.html.

7. See the broader discussion of the role of foreign-born entrepreneurs in U.S. industrialization in my *The Flight of the Creative Class: The Global Competition for Talent* (New York: Harper Business, 2005).

8. Immigrants made up 42 percent of the population in New York, 41 percent in Chicago, and 40 percent in Detroit.

9. Data on average travel speeds are from Randal O'Toole as cited in Neil Reynolds, "America's Fast Track to Wealth," *Globe and Mail,* October 9, 2009.

10. Lewis Mumford, *The City in History* (New York: Harcourt, Brace and World, 1964), 458, as cited in Patrick Ashton, "Urbanization and the Dynamics of Suburban Development under Capitalism," in *Marxism and the Metropolis: New Perspectives in Urban Political Economy*, William K. Tabb and Larry Sawers, eds. (New York: Oxford University Press, 1984), p. 55.

11. On early industrial suburbanization, see Richard Walker and Robert D. Lewis, "Beyond the Crabgrass Frontier: Industry and the Spread of North American Cities, 1850–1950," *Journal of Historical Geography* 27, no. 1 (January 2001): 3–19.

12. So dubbed by the urban historian Sam Bass Warner in *Street Car Suburbs: The Process of Growth in Boston, 1870–1900* (Cambridge: Harvard University Press, 1978). See also Kenneth Jackson, *Crabgrass Frontier: The Suburbanization of the United States* (New York: Oxford University Press, 1987).

13. This is all documented in Claude Fischer, "Changes in Leisure Activities, 1890–1940," *Journal of Social History* 27, no. 3 (1994): 453–475.

14. Roger Miller, "The Hoover in the Garden: Middle-Class Women and Suburbanization, 1850–1920," *Environment and Planning D: Society and Space* 1, no. 1 (1983): 73–87.

15. These figures were compiled from Eva Jacobs and Stephanie Shipp, "How Family Spending Has Changed in the U.S.," *Monthly Labor Review* 113, no. 3 (1990): 20–27; Larry Moran and Clinton McCully, "Trends in Consumer Spending, 1959–2000," *Survey of Current Business* (2001): 15–21; and Ben J. Wattenberg, *The Statistical History of the United States* (New York: Basic Books, 1977).

Chapter 4: The Most Technologically Progressive Decade

1. There are scores of histories of the economic and cultural dimensions of the Great Depression. See, e.g., John Kenneth Galbraith, *The Great Crash of 1929* (New York: Mariner Books, 1997); Robert McElvaine, *The Great Depression: 1929–1941* (New York: Three Rivers Press, 1993); and David Kyvig, *Daily Life in the United States, 1920–1940: How Americans Lived through the Roaring Twenties and Great Depression* (Chicago: Ivan R. Dee, 2004).

2. Noah Mendel, "When Did the Term Great Depression Receive Its Name (and Who Named It)?" History News Network, June 19, 2009.

3. Alexander Field, "The Most Technologically Progressive Decade of the

Twentieth Century," *American Economic Review* 39, no. 4 (September 2003): 1399–1413.

4. Alexander Field, "Technological Change and U.S. Productivity Growth in the Interwar Years," *Journal of Economic History* 66, no. 1 (2006): 203–236.

5. Their research is based on a detailed data set of new books published that defined and described new technology. At the time, books were the best, if not the only, way to inform people about such new technologies and so are a reliable indicator of the rate of innovation. These researchers went a step further and tracked the impacts of the various technologies covered by those books; they were able to confirm that the innovations helped accelerate the general economic recovery. Michelle Alexopoulos and Jon S. Cohen, "Measuring our Ignorance, One Book at a Time: New Indicators of Technical Change, 1909–1949," *Journal of Monetary Economics* 56, no. 4 (2009): 450–470; and Alexopoulos and Cohen, "Believe It or Not! The 1930s Was a Technologically Progressive Decade," University of Toronto, Department of Economics, January 2007, retrieved from www.chass.utoronto.ca/~malex/believeitornot.pdf.

6. These figures are from David Mowery and Nathan Rosenberg, "Twentieth Century Technological Change," *The Cambridge Economic History of the United States*, vol. 3, ed. Stanley Engerman and Robert Gallman (Cambridge: Cambridge University Press, 2000), 803–906. Also see their book *Technology and the Pursuit of Economic Growth* (Cambridge: Cambridge University Press, 1989).

7. Thomas Snyder, *120 Years of American Education: A Statistical Portrait* (Darby, Pa.: Diane Publishing, 1993).

8. Data are from U.S. Census Bureau, Current Population Survey, retrieved from www.census.gov.

Chapter 5: Suburban Solution

1. Megan McArdle, "Home Economics," *Atlantic*, July–August 2009, retrieved from www.theatlantic.com/doc/200907/home-economics.

2. Benjamin Schwarz, "Life In (and After) Our Great Recession," *Atlantic*, October 2009. retrieved from www.theatlantic.com/doc/200910/middle-class.

3. From 27 percent in 1917–1919 to 30 percent in 1934–1936. Eva Jacobs and Stephanie Shipp, "How Family Spending Has Changed in the U.S.," *Monthly Labor Review* (March 1990), 24.

4. I've been studying the role of housing policy in postwar suburbanization since my twenties. I wrote my undergraduate honors thesis at Rutgers and my doctoral dissertation at Columbia on this, as well as several of my earliest published papers. See Richard Florida and Marshall Feldman, "Housing in U.S. Fordism," *International Journal of Urban and Regional Research* 12, no. 2 (1988): 187–210; Richard Florida and Andrew Jonas, "U.S. Urban Policy:

The Postwar State and Capitalist Regulation," *Antipode* 23, no. 4 (1991): 349–384.

5. Data on average travel speeds are from Randal O'Toole as cited in Neil Reynolds, "America's Fast Track to Wealth," *Globe and Mail,* October 9, 2009.

6. Jacobs and Shipp, "How Family Spending Has Changed in the U.S.," 23.

7. The exact figures are as follows. Expenditures on food fell from 46.4 percent in 1901 to 32.5 percent in 1934–1936 to 19.4 in 1986–1987. Spending on "home furnishings and equipment" increased from 4.6 in 1934–1936 to 7.1 percent in 1950. "Vehicle expenses" climbed from 5.9 percent in 1934–1936 to 12 percent in 1950 and 22.9 percent by 1972–1973. Basic needs includes combined expenses on "food and alcoholic beverages," "shelter," and "apparel and services." Such spending fell from 76 percent of expenditures in 1901 to 49 percent by 1960. Data ibid.

8. Frank Hobbs and Nicole Stoops, "Demographic Trends in the Twentieth Century: Census 2000 Special Reports," Series CENSR-4, November 2002, retrieved from www.census.gov/prod/2002pubs/censr-4.pdf.

9. Ibid., 18.

10. Between 1950 and 1990, the West grew by 170 percent and the South by 81 percent, far outpacing the Midwest at 34 percent and the Northeast at 29 percent. Ibid.

Chapter 6: The Fix Is In

1. He discusses this in a series of books and articles. See David Harvey, "The Spatial Fix—Hegel, Von Thunen, and Marx," *Antipode* 13, no. 3 (December 1981): 1–46; Harvey, *The Limits to Capital* (New York: Oxford University Press, 1982); Harvey, *The New Imperialism* (New York: Oxford University Press, 2003); Harvey, "Globalization and the Spatial Fix," *Geographische Review* 2 (2001): 23–30.

2. Erica Schoenberger, "The Spatial Fix Revisited," *Antipode* 36, no. 3 (2004): 427–433.

3. Alexander Field, "Uncontrolled Land Development and the Duration of the Depression in the United States," *Journal of Economic History* 52 (December 1992): 785–805.

Chapter 7: Unraveling

1. Reuven Glick and Kevin Lansing, "Global Household Leverage, House Prices, and Consumption," FRBSF Economic Letter, January 11, 2010.

2. Scott Pelley, "Where's the Bottom? Fears of a Second Mortgage Crisis Coming to Bear Soon," *60 Minutes,* December 14, 2008.

3. Federal Reserve Bank of San Francisco, "U.S. Household Deleveraging and Future Consumption Growth," FRBSF Economic Letter, May 15, 2009.

4. These figures are from "Rebalancing the World Economy: America, Dropping the Shopping," *Economist*, July 23, 2009, retrieved from www.economist.com/businessfinance/displaystory.cfm?story_id=14098372. (Fee-based access.)

5. Matthew Slaughter, "Time to Tackle America's Widening Inequality," *Financial Times*, October 6, 2009.

6. Federal Reserve Bank of San Francisco, "U.S. Household Deleveraging and Future Consumption Growth."

7. There were 1,046,449 bankruptcies filed between January and September 2009, compared to 773,810 in the same period the year before. Sara Murray, "Personal Bankruptcy Filings Soar," *Wall Street Journal*, October 2, 2009.

8. Rudolf Hilferding, *Finance Capital: A Study in the Latest Phase of Capitalist Development* (London: Routledge and Kegan Paul, 1985).

9. Yves Smith, "Why You Should Hate the Treasury Bailout Proposal," Naked Capitalism, September 21, 2008, retrieved from www.nakedcapitalism.com/2008/09/why-you-should-hate-treasury-bailout.html.

10. In August 2009, the U.S. unemployment rate was 9.8 percent. A third of metro regions had unemployment rates of 10 percent or more, while unemployment stayed below 7 percent in almost one-fifth of them. U.S. Bureau of Labor Statistics, Local Area Unemployment Statistics, retrieved from www.bls.gov/lau.

11. See the S&P/Case-Shiller Home Price Indices, available online.

Chapter 8: Capital of Capital

1. The exact figure was 96,739 private-sector jobs and 35,986 finance and insurance jobs lost between August 2008 and August 2009. See Christine Haughney, "Bloomberg Has Added Jobs, and Lost Some, Too," *New York Times*, October 14, 2009. Also see Mary Pilon, "From Ordering Steak and Lobster to Serving It," *Wall Street Journal*, June 1, 2009. The 10.3% unemployment rate and 450,000 figure is from Patrick McGeehan, "Unemployment Hits 10.3% in New York City," *New York Times*, September 19, 2009. Also see Andrew Beveridge, "New York's Now Beleaguered Financial Workforce," *Gotham Gazette*, August 3, 2009.

2. Marcus Gee, "Centre of the Financial Universe Could Soon Be Shifting East," *Globe and Mail*, October 8, 2008.

3. Michael Lind, "The Next Big Thing: America," *Foreign Policy*, May–June 2009, retrieved from www.foreignpolicy.com/story/cms.php?story_id=4848.

4. Youssef Cassis, *Capitals of Capital: A History of International Financial Centres, 1780–2005* (Cambridge: Cambridge University Press, 2007).

5. Amsterdam was listed in twenty-fourth place. See Mark Yeandle, Jeremy Horne, and Nick Danev, "The Global Financial Centres Index—4," City of London Corporation, 2009.

6. Ibid.
7. As noted in Cassis, *Capitals of Capital*, 265.
8. Haughney, "Bloomberg Has Added Jobs, and Lost Some, Too."
9. Based on an analysis of U.S. Bureau of Labor Statistics data by Charlotta Mellander.
10. Ibid.
11. Elizabeth Currid, *The Warhol Economy* (Princeton, N.J.: Princeton University Press, 2008).
12. Jane Jacobs, *The Economy of Cities* (New York: Vintage, 1970); Jacobs, *Cities and the Wealth of Nations* (New York: Vintage, 1985).
13. Patrick McGeehan, "After Reversal of Fortune, City Takes a New Look at Wall Street," *New York Times*, February 22, 2009.
14. Fred Siegel and Harry Siegel, "Can Bloomberg's 'Luxury' City Survive?" *Wall Street Journal*, October 14, 2009.

Chapter 9: Who's Next?

1. As quoted in Helle Dale, "Best and Worst . . . Political Quotes of 2008, *Washington Times*, retrieved from www.washingtontimes.com/news/2008/dec/31/the-best-and-worst.
2. Quoted in Edmund Andrews, "World Bank Head Expects Dollar's Role to Diminish," *New York Times*, September 29, 2009.
3. As outlined in his now-classic book: Paul Kennedy, *The Rise and Fall of Great Powers* (New York: Vintage, 1989).
4. Fareed Zakaria, *The Post American World* (New York: W. W. Norton and Company, 2008).
5. John Pender, "War, Peace and Financial Hubs," *Financial Times*, May 12, 2009.
6. Angus Maddison, *Chinese Economic Performance in the Long Run* (Paris Organization for Economic Cooperation and Development, 1998).
7. "Shanghai as World Financial Capital? Maybe Next Century," China Digital Times, May 31, 2009, retrieved from www.chinadigitaltimes.net/2009/05/shanghai-as-world-financial-capital-maybe-next-century.
8. Helmut Reisen, "Shifting Wealth: Is the US Dollar Empire Falling?," June 20, 2009, retrieved from www.voxeu.org/index.php?q=node/3672.
9. Jeffrey Garten, "Amid Economic Rubble, Shangkong Will Rise," *Financial Times*, May 10, 2009.
10. Quote is from Youssef Cassis, *Capitals of Capital: A History of International Financial Centres, 1780–2005* (Cambridge: Cambridge University Press, 2007), 281
11. OECD, *Economic Survey of Japan 2006*, retrieved from www.oecd.org/document/47/0,3343,en_2649_34601_37130991_1_1_1_1,00.html.
12. Peter Ford, "Will Asian Financial Centers Overtake Wall Street?," *Christian Science Monitor*, October 10, 2008.

13. See "Today in Lehman Poaching: Barclays and UBS," *Wall Street Journal*, October 8, 2008, retrieved from http://blogs.wsj.com/deals/2008/10/08/ today-in-lehman-poaching-barclays-and-ubs; "China's Sovereign Wealth Fund Seeking Talent," Reuters, June 17, 2009, retrieved from http://money .cnn.com/2009/06/17/news/international/CIC_hiring.reut; "Wall Street's Job Losses May be Asia's Gain," Reuters, Trading Places, September 19, 2008, retrieved from http://blogs.reuters.com/trading-places/2008/09/19/ wall-street-job-losses-may-be-asias-gain; Gavin Finch and Poppy Trowbridge, "Nomura, Barclays Lure Bankers as Rivals Cut Jobs, Cap Bonuses," Bloomberg, November 6, 2009, retrieved from www.bloomberg.com/apps/ news?pid=newsarchive&sid=aGY5f6XsWveE.

14. Michael Pettis, "Bigger Than Ever: Why the Crisis Will Only Help Ny-Lon," *Newsweek*, May 23, 2009, retrieved from www.newsweek.com/id/199100.

Chapter 10: Fire Starter

1. Daniel Bell, *The Coming of Post-Industrial Society* (New York: Harper Colophon Books, 1976); Thierry Noyelle and Thomas Stanback, *The Economic Transformation of American Cities* (Totowa, N.J.: Rowman and Allanheld, 1984).

2. Eric Janszen, "The Next Bubble: Priming the Markets for Tomorrow's Big Crash," *Harper's*, February 2008, retrieved from www.harpers.org/ archive/2008/02/0081908.

3. Analysis by Charlotta Mellander based on Bureau of Economic Analysis, Regional Economic Accounts, retrieved from www.bea.gov/national/index .htm#gdp.

4. E-mail communication with Deborah Strumsky of the University of North Carolina, Charlotte, January 15, 2010.

Chapter 11: Big Government Boomtowns

1. Mac Margolis, "The New Boomtowns," *Newsweek*, March 14, 2009.

2. "The Role of Metro Areas in the U.S. Economy," report for the U.S. Conference of Mayors, Global Insight, 2006. Washington, D.C.: U.S. Conference of Mayors.

3. Richard Florida, "A Creative Crossroads," *Washington Post*, May 7, 2006, retrieved from www.washingtonpost.com/wp-dyn/content/article/2006/05/05/ AR2006050501750.html; Florida, "Where the Brains Are," *Atlantic*, October 2006.

4. Richard Florida, *Who's Your City?: How the Creative Economy Is Making Where to Live the Most Important Decision of Your Life* (New York: Basic Books, 2008).

5. Richard Florida, *Who's Your City?: How the Creative Economy Is Making Where to Live the Most Important Decision of Your Life*, Canadian edition (Toronto: Random House Canada, 2008).

6. Kelly Evans, "Why College Towns Are Looking Smart," *Wall Street Journal*, March 24, 2009.

7. I provide figures on these trends in Richard Florida, "Town, Gown, and Unemployment," *Atlantic*, May 20, 2009, retrieved from http://correspondents .theatlantic.com/richard_florida/2009/05.

8. Edward L. Glaeser, "How Some Places Fare Better in Hard Times," *New York Times*, March 24, 2009.

Chapter 12: Death and Life of Great Industrial Cities

1. Robert Pirsig's classic *Zen and the Art of Motorcycle Maintenance: An Inquiry into Values* (New York: HarperPerennial Modern Classics, 2008); Matthew Crawford, *Shop Class as Soulcraft: An Inquiry into the Value of Work* (New York: Penguin Press, 2008); Richard Sennett, *The Craftsman* (New Haven, Conn.: Yale University Press, 2008).

2. Data are from the Bureau of Labor Statistics, retrieved from www.bls.gov/ces/tables.htm.

3. Michael Mandel, "The Failed Promise of Innovation in the U.S.," *BusinessWeek*, June 3, 2009, retrieved from www.businessweek.com/magazine/content/09_24/b4135000953288.htm?chan=top+news_top+news+index+-+temp_top+story.

4. Paul Krugman, "Southern Discomfort," *New York Times*, December 22, 2008, retrieved from http://krugman.blogs.nytimes.com/2008/12/22/southern-discomfort.

5. See "Motor City's Woes Extend Beyond Auto Industry," Associated Press, December 20, 2008, retrieved from www.msnbc.msn.com/id/28327490.

6. Andrew Leonard, "137 Pages of Wayne County Foreclosures," Salon, November 18, 2008, retrieved from www.salon.com/tech/htww/2008/11/18/wayne_county_foreclosures/index.html.

7. Mike Wilkinson, "Nearly Half of Detroit's Workers Are Unemployed," *Detroit News*, December 16, 2009, retrieved from: www.detnews.com/article/20091216/METRO01/912160374/1409/METRO/Nearly-half-of-Detroit-s-workers-are-unemployed.

8. As quoted in "Motor City's Woes Extend Beyond Auto Industry."

9. Louis Aguilar, "48 Vacant Buildings Blight Downtown Detroit," *Detroit News*, August 17, 2009.

10. Kevin Krolicki, "Detroit Housing Auction Flops for Urban Wasteland," Reuters, October 25, 2009, retrieved from www.detnews.com/article/20090817/METRO01/908170334/48-vacant-buildings-blight-downtown-Detroit (fee-based access). Also see Jonathan Oosting, "48 Vacant Buildings in Downtown Detroit," Mlive.com, August 17, 2009, retrieved from www.mlive.com/news/detroit/index.ssf/2009/08/report_48_vacant_buildings_in.html.

11. Jonathan Mahler, "GM, Detroit, and the Fall of the Black Middle-Class," *New York Times Magazine*, June 24, 2009, retrieved from www.nytimes.com/2009/06/28/magazine/28detroit-t.html.

12. James R. Gaines, "Detroit's Second Life: An Urban Planner's View," FLYP, February 19, 2009, retrieved from www.flypmedia.com/content/detroits-second-life-urban-planners-view.

13. In April 2009, the unemployment rate for the Detroit metropolitan area was 13.6 percent in April 2009, compared to Flint at 14.2 percent and Monroe at 14.3 percent. In Ohio, the unemployment rate was 9.8 percent in Akron, 11.5 percent in Canton, 12 percent in Toledo, 12.8 percent in Youngstown, and 13.2 percent in Mansfield. Data from the Bureau of Labor Statistics, retrieved from www.bls.gov/news.release/metro.t01.htm.

14. Martin Kenney and Richard Florida, *Beyond Mass Production: The Japanese System and Its Transfer to the U.S.* (New York: Oxford University Press, 1993); Daniel Gross, "Big Three, Meet the 'Little Eight': How Foreign Car Factories Have Transformed the American South," Slate, October 13, 2008, retrieved from www.slate.com/id/2206525/pagenum/all.

15. For a realistic account of Pittsburgh's economic transformation, see Franklin Toker, *Pittsburgh: A New Portrait* (Pittsburgh: University of Pittsburgh Press, 2009).

16. Howard Fineman, "What Pittsburgh (Don't Laugh) Can Teach Obama," *Newsweek*, June 6, 2009.

17. Aaron Renn, "Detroit: Urban Laboratory and the New American Frontier," New Geography, November 4, 2009, retrieved from www.newgeography.com/content/001171-detroit-urban-laboratory-and-new-american-frontier.

18. John G. Craig Jr., "To: Detroit, From: Pittsburgh," *Washington Post*, March 22, 2009, retrieved from www.washingtonpost.com/wp-dyn/content/article/2009/03/12/AR2009031202480.html.

19. Belinda Lanks, "The Incredible Shrinking City," *Metropolis*, April 17, 2006.

20. Tom Leonard, "US Cities May Have to Be Bulldozed to Survive," *Telegraph*, June 12, 2009. Also see Edward L. Glaeser, "Bulldozing America's Shrinking Cities," *New York Times*, June 16, 2009, retrieved from http://economix.blogs.nytimes.com/2009/06/16/bulldozing-americas-shrinking-cities.

21. For a history of planned shrinkage and benign neglect, see Deborah Wallace, *A Plague on Your Houses* (London: Verso, 2001).

22. My team and I have conducted a wide variety of research on this point. For our city and regional findings, see my "Worsening Unemployment," *Atlantic*, July 3, 2009; "Unemployment's Geography," *Atlantic*, June 5, 2009. For our state-level findings, see Jason Rentfrow, Charlotta Mellander, and Richard Florida, "Happy States of America: A State-Level Analysis of Psychological, Economic, and Social Well-being," *Journal of Research in Personality* 43, no. 3 (December 2009), 1073–1082; and my "Happy States and the Economic Crisis," *Atlantic*, August 17, 2009. For our national-level

findings, see my "Why Class Still Matters," *Atlantic*, May 18, 2009; "Class and the Wealth of Nations," *Atlantic*, May 19, 2009; "Class and Innovation," *Atlantic*, May 20, 2009; "Class and Entrepreneurship," *Atlantic*, May 21, 2009; "Class and the Happiness of Nations," *Atlantic*, May 22, 2009; all retrieved from http://correspondents.theatlantic.com.

23. Edward Glaeser, "How Some Plaes Fare Better in Hard Times," New York Times Economix (online), March 24, 2009, retrieved from http://economix.blogs.nytimes.com/2009/03/24/how-some-places-fare-better-in-hard-times.

24. The Prestowitz quote is from Dana Hedgpeth and Jennifer Agiesta, "Poll of Detroit Residents Finds Grim Conditions but Optimistic Outlooks," *Washington Post*, January 3, 2010, retrieved from www.washingtonpost.com/wp-dyn/content/article/2010/01/02/AR2010010201935.html.

25. As the detailed studies of the economist James Heckman show; see James Heckman, "Schools, Skills and Synapses," *Economic Inquiry* 46, no. 3 (2008): 289–324.

26. These are the key results of the Gallup Organization's Soul of the Community Survey, retrieved from www.soulofthecommunity.org. I discuss this at length in *Who's Your City?: How the Creative Economy Is Making Where to Live the Most Important Decision of Your Life* (New York: Basic Books, 2008), and "Soul of the City," *Atlantic*, October 1, 2009, retrieved from http://correspondents.theatlantic.com.

Chapter 13: Northern Light

1. Crime data are from Statistics Canada. Joshua Zumbrun, "World's Most Economically Powerful Cities," *Forbes*, July 15, 2008, retrieved from www.forbes.com/2008/07/15/economic-growth-gdp-biz-cx_jz_0715powercities.html; "2007–2008 Global Urban Competitiveness Report," retrieved from www.gucp.org/en/news.asp?NewsID=424&BigClassID=2&SmallClassID=20.

2. Data on Toronto's homicide rate are from Marnie Wallace, "Police-Reported Crime Statistics in Canada, 2008," Statistics Canada, July 2009, retrieved from www.statcam.gc.ca/pub/85-002-x/2009003/article/10902-eng.htm.

3. Toronto figures from the Toronto Real Estate Board; see "GTA Housing Market Rebound Continues in September," Toronto Real Estate Board, October 5, 2009, retrieved from www.torontorealestateboard.com/consumer_info/market_news/mw2009/pdf/mw0909.pdf. Across Canada, prices were up 11 percent and sales increased 18 percent, their largest increase on record, in the third quarter of 2009; see Steve Ladurantaye, "Fewer Listings Boost Home Prices," *Globe and Mail*, October 15, 2009.

4. Albert Watson, "A Rare Building Boom up North," *New York Times*, October 14, 2009.

5. Fareed Zakaria, "Worthwhile Canadian Initiative," *Newsweek*, February 16, 2009.

6. Doug Alexander, "Wall Street Cedes to Bay Street as Canada Banks 'Play Offense,'" Bloomberg, October 6, 2009, retrieved from www.bloomberg.com/apps/news?pid=20601109&sid=aNaLwcGrz3.8

7. Data on bank rankings are from the Web site of The Banker, retrieved from www.thebanker.com/cp/57/T1000_Top25.gif.

8. Doug Alexander, "Wall Street Cedes to Bay Street as Canada Banks 'Play Offense.'"

9. J. David Hulchanski, "The Three Cities within Toronto: Income Polarization among Toronto's Neighbourhoods, 1970–2000," University of Toronto, Centre for Urban and Community Studies, Research Bulletin 41, December 2001.

10. Based on the Martin Prosperity Institute's inequality index rankings, which compare the ratio of wages in creative occupations to those in more routine fields of work.

Chapter 14: Sun Sets on the Sunbelt

1. The figures are: Las Vegas, 26.6 percent; Miami, 26.1 percent; Phoenix, 25 percent. Based on 2006 data from the Bureau of Economics Research, analysis by Charlotta Mellander.

2. David Streitfeld, "Amid Housing Bust, Phoenix Begins a New Frenzy," *New York Times*, May 23, 2009.

3. Quoted in Kris Hudson, "Phoenix Bears the Brunt of Hotel Market's Steep Downturn," *Wall Street Journal*, June 3, 2009.

4. Quoted in Dennis Wagner, "Pain on Main Street: Timing Proves Bad for Phoenix," *USA Today*, December 20, 2008.

5. Daniel Gross, "Who is Killing America's Millionaires?" Slate, July 24, 2009; Gross cites a Capgemini study as the source of these data. Overall, the number of high-net-worth individuals in the United States fell from 3.02 million in 2007 to 2.46 million in 2008, a decline of 18.5 percent. He cites Capgemini's Ileana van der Linde as saying "We've been doing this report for 13 years and haven't seen this kind of loss of wealth since we started."

6. At the time, 21.9 percent of homes nationally were identified as being underwater. The exact figure for Las Vegas was 67.2 percent. See Ruth Simon and James Haggerty, "House Price Drops Leave More Underwater," *Wall Street Journal*, May 6, 2009, based on data from www.zillow.com.

7. This was up more than 50 percent from the previous year (late 2007) according to a *New York Times* analysis based on based on data from the research firm DataQuick. See Streitfeld, "Amid Rubble of Housing Bust, Phoenix Begins a New Frenzy."

8. See Shelley Dreiman, "Using the Price to Income Ratio to Determine the Presence of Housing Bubbles," no date, retrieved from www.fhfa.gov/webfiles/1071/Focus4Q00.pdf. A nice chart tracking the historical level of housing price to

income ratios is retrieved from CalculatedRisk, "House Price-to-Income Ratio," November 25, 2008, retrieved from www.calculatedriskblog.com/2008/11/house-price-to-income-ratio.html. Our calculations and map can be found at Richard Florida, "Bubble Cities," *Atlantic*, May 24, 2009, retrieved from http://correspondents.theatlantic.com/richard_florida/2009/05/bubble_cities.php.

9. Income is a broad measure that includes not only how much somebody earns at work but other forms of wealth that accrue from other sources, such as stocks and bonds, interest, and rent. Wages, on the other hand, are a more direct and meaningful representation of the money that's earned in a region and thus a more realistic gauge of how housing prices relate to the underlying productivity of a location. My team and I calculated this housing-to-wage ratio for every U.S. metro region in 2006 at the height of the bubble. The housing-to-wage ratio was high in New York (9.4), greater D.C. (8.7), and Boston (8.1), where housing price appreciation was tied, to a greater degree, to regional economic growth and rising demand, as opposed to the speculative, housing-driven growth of the Sunbelt. The best housing-to-wage ratios were found in Dallas (3.5), Houston (3.2), Pittsburgh (3), and Buffalo (2.8) where housing prices didn't appreciate much.

10. Brookings MetroMonitor tracks the economic performance of the one hundred largest metropolitan areas, ranking them from strongest to weakest on six key indicators: employment, unemployment rates, wages, gross metropolitan product, housing prices, and foreclosure rates. See "MetroMonitor: Tracking Economic Recession and Recovery in America's 100 Largest Metropolitan Areas," Brookings Institution, September 2009, retrieved from www.brookings.edu/reports/2009/06_metro_monitor.aspx.

11. The Stress Index for greater Phoenix grew from 5.1 at the onset of the recession in December 2007 to 12.7 in March 2009, while the stress index for greater Las Vegas grew from 10.5 to 19.5.

12. Haya El Nasser and Paul Overberg, "America's New Landscape," *USA Today*, December 23, 2008.

13. Damien Cave, "After Century of Growth, Tide Turns in Florida," *New York Times*, August 30, 2009. The *New York Times* reported that Florida's population declined by 58,000 people from April 2008 to April 2009, according to the University of Florida's Bureau of Economic and Business Research. This was the first time since at least 1900 that this had occurred save for the exceptional periods around World Wars I and II. The *Times* notes that "Florida grew from 2.8 million people in 1950 to 6.9 million in 1970, and by about three million people each decade after that. Even during stagflation in the '70s, Florida added about 200,000 people a year. More recently, from 2004 to 2006, Florida added about 1,100 people a day."

14. The original video via Diana Olick, Reality Check, "Are Bulldozers the Best Neighbors?" CNBC.com, May 5, 2009, retrieved from www.cnbc.com/id/30580830. Also see Richard Florida, "The Suburban Bulldozer," *Atlan-*

tic, May 11, 2009, retrieved from http://correspondents.theatlantic.com/richard_florida/2009/05/the_suburban_bulldozer.php. The phrase "federal bulldozer" originates with Martin Anderson's book *The Federal Bulldozer: A Critical Analysis of Urban Renewal, 1942–1962* (Cambridge, Mass.: MIT Press, 1964).

15. M. P. McQueen, "Cracked Houses—What the Boom Built," *Wall Street Journal*, July 13, 2009.

16. Christopher Leinberger, "The Next Slum?," *Atlantic*, March 2008, retrieved from www.theatlantic.com/doc/200803/subprime.

17. "MetroMonitor: Tracking Economic Recession and Recovery in America's 100 Largest Metropolitan Areas, Brookings Institution, September 2009, retrieved from www.brookings.edu/reports/2009/06–metro–monitor.aspx.

18. Patrik Jonsson, "Fastest Growing Cities Seek to Beat Recession Soonest," *Christian Science Monitor*, July 1, 2009.

19. Robert E. Lang and Mark Muro, "What Happens in Vegas . . . Stimulates the Economy," *Las Vegas Sun*, February 25, 2009.

20. Mark Muro, "Las Vegas' Dilemma: America's, Only More So," *Las Vegas Sun*, October 25, 2009.

Chapter 15: The Reset Economy

1. David Leonhardt, "After the Great Recession," *New York Times*, April 29, 2009.

2. Kurt Andersen, *Reset: How the Crisis Can Restore Our Values and Renew America* (New York: Random House, 2009).

3. Mark Thoma, "FRBSF: U.S. Household Deleveraging and Future Consumption Growth," Economist's View, May 19, 2009, retrieved from http://economistsview.typepad.com/economistsview/2009/05/frbsf-us-household-deleveraging-and-future-consumption-growth-.html.

4. Thomas Philippon, "The Evolution of the Financial Industry from 1860 to the Present: Theory and Evidence," Working Paper, New York University, November 2008.

5. Thomas Philippon, "The Future of the Financial Industry," Stern on Finance, October 16, 2008, retrieved from http://sternfinance.blogspot.com/2008/10/future-of-financial-industry-thomas.html.

6. Thomas Philippon and Ariell Reshef, "Wages and Human Capital in the U.S. Financial Industry: 1909–2006," National Bureau of Economic Research, January 2009, retrieved from www.nber.org/papers/w14644.

7. Floyd Norris, "In Finance, Wages Are Due for a Fall," *New York Times*, February 2, 2009.

8. Julia Ioffe, "Prophet Motive," *New Republic*, June 3, 2009.

9. Michael Mandel, "The Failed Promise of Innovation in the U.S.," *BusinessWeek*, June 3, 2009. Also see Michael Mandel, "The GDP Mirage," *BusinessWeek*, October 29, 2009, retrieved from www.businessweek.com/magazine/

content/09_45/b4154034724383.htm.

10. With the help of my research team, I tracked the trend in patents for the better part of the century, patents by major cities, and the relative importance of American- versus foreign-born inventors in generating new patented innovations.

11. See Vivek Wadhwa, AnnaLee Saxenian, Richard Freeman, and Gary Gereffi, "America's Loss Is the World's Gain: America's New Immigrant Entrepreneurs, Part 4," March 2, 2009, retrieved from http://ssrn.com/abstract=1348616; Richard Florida, *The Flight of the Creative Class: The New Global Competition for Talent* (New York: HarperCollins, 2005).

12. "The Nature of Wealth," *Economist*, October 8, 2009, retrieved from www.economist.com/businessfinance/displaystory.cfm?story_id=14587262.

13. William Black, "How the Servant Became a Predator: Finance's Five Fatal Flaws," New Deal 2.0, October 12, 2009, retrieved from www.newdeal20.org/?p=5330; Peter Goodman, *Past Due: The End of Easy Money and the Renewal of the American Economy* (New York: Times Books, 2009); "The Nature of Wealth," *Economist*; Benjamin Friedman, "Overmighty Finance Levies a Tithe on Growth," *Financial Times*, August 26, 2009.

14. Obviously, this is a biased sample, but it's also a very interesting one, as it tracks graduates from arguably the world's leading university. As such, it provides useful signals about the kinds of jobs and the kinds of career paths that highly motivated, highly mobile young talent is choosing. Paras D. Bhayani, "Surveying the Class," *Harvard Crimson*, June 1, 2009.

15. Black, "How the Servant Became a Predator: Finance's Five Fatal Flaws."

Chapter 16: Good Job Machine

1. In his poem "Jerusalem," the exact line is "Among these dark Satanic mills?"; retrieved from http://theotherpages.org/poems/blake01.html.

2. Mort Zuckerman, "The Free Market Is Not Up to the Job of Creating Work," *Financial Times*, October 18, 2009.

3. Richard Florida, *The Rise of the Creative Class*, as updated by the Martin Prosperity Institute (New York: Basic Books, 2002).

4. Employment projections are from Bureau of Labor Statistics, "Employment Projections, 2008–18," U.S. Department of Labor, Bureau of Labor Statistics, December 10, 2009, retrieved from www.bls.gov/news.release/pdf/ecopro.pdf.

5. "Unemployment on the Rise: Who's Hit Most by the Recession?" Martin Prosperity Institute, Rotman School of Management, University of Toronto, June 21, 2009.

6. Richard Florida and Roger Martin, "Ontario in the Creative Age," Martin Prosperity Institute, Rotman School of Management, University of Toronto, 2009.

7. As quoted in Scott Lilly, "Arts Bashing," Center for American Progress (online), February 6, 2009, retrieved from www.americanprogress.org/

issues/2009/02/arts_bashing.html.

8. Annual rankings from the Great Places to Work Institute, which finds that the best places to work significantly outperformed the S&P 500 between 1998 and 2009, retrieved from www.greatplacetowork.com.

9. These case studies and examples are being developed as part of an ongoing project on upgrading service jobs at the Martin Prosperity Institute; see www.strengthinservices.org.

10. With number-crunching help from Charlotta Mellander, I looked at how three main types of work—manufacturing, service work, and creative work—affect everything from income and unemployment, innovation and entrepreneurship, to rates of marriage and divorce and our stress and well-being. We did this analysis for all U.S. metropolitan areas, the fifty U.S. states, and a hundred or so countries around the world. For our state-level findings, see Jason Rentfrow, Charlotta Mellander, and Richard Florida, "Happy States of America: A State-level Analysis of Psychological, Economic, and Social Well-being," *Journal of Research in Personality*, 43, no.6 (2009): 1073–1082; and my "Happy States and the Economic Crisis," *Atlantic*, August 17, 2009. For our national-level findings see my "Why Class Still Matters," *Atlantic*, May 18, 2009; "Class and the Wealth of Nations," *Atlantic*, May 19, 2009; "Class and Innovation," May 20, 2009; "Class and Entrepreneurship," *Atlantic*, May 21, 2009; "Class and the Happiness of Nations," *Atlantic*, May 22, 2009; all retrieved from http://correspondents .theatlantic.com.

11. Catherine Rampell, "The Mancession," *New York Times*, August 10, 2009, retrieved from http://economix.blogs.nytimes.com/2009/08/10/the-mancession.

12. Margaret Wente, "We Are Witnessing the Passing of Working-class Masculinity," *Globe and Mail*, May 22, 2009.

13. Lance Mannion, "Male Values Don't Include Patience?," May 24, 2009, retrieved from http://lancemannion.typepad.com/lance_mannion/2009/05/male-values-dont-include-patience.html.

Chapter 17: The New Normal

1. Ben Funnell, "Debt Is Capitalism's Dirty Little Secret," *Financial Times*, June 30, 2009.

2. The Herbert Hoover Presidential Library and Museum clarifies the matter; retrieved from http://hoover.archives.gov/info/faq.html#chicken.

3. The share of household spending on food declined from 47 percent in 1901 to 32 percent in 1950. See Eva Jacobs and Stephanie Shipp "How Family Spending Has Changed in the US," *Monthly Labor Review*, March 1990. Figures on the share of agricultural employment are from Carolyn Dimitri, Anne Effland, and Neilson Conklin, "The 20th Century Transformation of U.S. Agriculture and Farm Policy," U.S. Department of Agriculture, Economic Research Service, Electronic Information Bulletin, no. 3 (2005), retrieved

from www.ers.usda.gov/publications/eib3/eib3.pdf.

4. Elizabeth Warren and Amelia Warren Tyagi, "What's Hurting the Middle Class: The Myth of Overspending Obscures the Real Problem," *Boston Review*, September–October 2005, retrieved from http://bostonreview.net/ BR30.5/warrentyagi.php.

5. Raj Chawla and Ted Wannell, "Spenders and Savers," *Perspectives*, Statistics Canada, March 2005.

6. Figures based on the following: 1950 figure for entertainment spending is from Eva Jacobs and Stephanie Shipp, "How Family Spending Has Changed in the U.S.," *Monthly Labor Review* 113, no. 3 (1990): 20–27; 1959 and 2000 figures for entertainment and electronics are from Larry Moran and Clinton McCully, "Trends in Consumer Spending, 1959–2000," *Survey of Current Business*, 2001, 15–21.

7. These figures are from Mark Thoma, "Will Consumption Growth Return to its Pre-Recession Level," Moneywatch.com, November 30, 2009, retrieved from http://moneywatch.bnet.com/economic-news/blog/maximum-utility/ will-consumption-growth-return-to-its-pre-recession-level/265.

8. Dennis Jacobe, "Upper Income Spending Reverts to New Normal," Gallup Organization, December 10, 2009, retrieved from www.gallup.com/poll/124634/ Upper-Income-Spending-Reverts-New-Normal.aspx?CSTS=alert.

9. Yankelovich/The Futures Group, "A Darwinian Gale: 2010," November 12, 2009, retrieved from www.darwiniangale.com.

10. Michelle Nichols, "Exclusive Exclusive: Global Consumer Confidence Stabilizing," Reuters, June 2, 2009, retrieved from www.reuters.com/article/ousiv/ idUSTRE5512L720090602.

11. Mark J. Perry, "Average New Home Size Falls for the Frst Time since '94," Seeking Alpha (online), March 8 2009, retrieved from http://seekingalpha.com/article/124684-average-new-home-size-falls-for-first-time-since-94.

12. Micheline Maynard, "Is Happiness Still That New Car Smell?" *New York Times*, October 22, 2009.

13. Christopher Leinberger, "Car Free in America/Bottom Line: It's Cheaper," *New York Times*, online symposium, May 12, 2009, retrieved from http:// roomfordebate.blogs.nytimes.com/2009/05/12/carless-in-america/?hp

14. Yuri Kageyama, "Car-Free: In Japan, That's How a Generation Rolls," Associated Press, January 6, 2009.

15. Rich Morin and Paul Taylor, "Luxury or Necessity? The Public Makes a U-Turn," Pew Research Center, April 23, 2009, retrieved from http://pewsocialtrends.org/pubs/733/luxury-necessity-recession-era-reevaluations.

16. Nate Silver, "The End of Car Culture," *Esquire*, May 6, 2009, retrieved from www.esquire.com/features/data/nate-silver-car-culture-stats-0609.

17. Martin Zimmerman, "Rebel without a Car?" *Los Angeles Times*, October 8, 2009, retrieved from http://latimesblogs.latimes.com/uptospeed/2009/10/

james-dean-.html.

18. Micheline Maynard, "Is Happiness Still That New Car Smell?"

19. Felix Salmon, "Chart of the Day: Necessity," Reuters (blog), April 28, 2009.

20. John Seabrook, *Nobrow: The Culture of Marketing, the Marketing of Culture* (New York: Vintage, 2001).

21. According to a *New York Times* survey. Micheline Maynard, "Say 'Hybrid' and Many People Will Hear 'Prius,'" *New York Times*, July 4, 2007.

22. Vladas Griskevicius, Joshua M. Tybur, and Bram Van den Bergh, "Going Green to Be Seen: Status, Reputation, and Conspicuous Conservation," University of Minnesota, Carlson School of Management, retrieved from www .carlsonschool.umn.edu/assets/140554.pdf.

23. Robert Frank, "At Estates of the Fabulously Rich, Gilded Age Is Going, Going, Gone," *Wall Street Journal*, May 19, 2009.

24. James Surowiecki, "Inconspicuous Consumption," *New Yorker*, October 12, 2009.

Chapter 18: The Great Resettle

1. Jean Gottmann, *Megalopolis: The Urbanized Northeastern Seaboard of the United States* (New York: Twentieth Century Fund, 1961). For a more detailed discussion of how we define and identify megaregions, see Richard Florida, Tim Gulden, and Charlotta Mellander, "The Rise of the Mega-Region," *Cambridge Journal of Regions, Economy and Society* 1, no. 3, (2008), 459–476, and Richard Florida, *Who's Your City?: How the Creative Economy Is Making Where to Live the Most Important Decision of Your Life* (New York: Basic Books, 2008).

2. "Head-Office Clustering in the Mega-Regions," Martin Prosperity Institute, June 5, 2009.

3. Friedman himself writes that the inspiration for his best-selling book *The World Is Flat* came from a conversation with the CEO of a high-tech company in Bangalore, India, an agglomeration of more than 6 million people at the center of India's software industry and a key part of the Bangalore-Mumbai megaregion. Thomas Friedman, *The World Is Flat* (New York: Farrar, Straus and Giroux, 2005). See also Edward Leamer, "A Flat World, A Level Playing Field, a Small World after All, or None of the Above? Review of Thomas L. Friedman, *The World Is Flat*," *Journal of Economic Literature* 43, no. 1 (2007): 83–126; Richard Florida, "The World Is Spiky," *Atlantic*, October 2006, retrieved from www.theatlantic.com/images/issues/200510/world-is-spiky .pdf.

4. Adam Hochberg, "In Ariz., Luring Suburbanites to Greener, Urban Life," *Morning Edition*, National Public Radio, October 23, 2009, retrieved from www.npr.org/templates/story/story.php?storyId=113816643.

5. Wendell Cox, "Suburbs and Cities: The Unexpected Truth," New Geography, May 16, 2009, retrieved from www.newgeography.com/content/00805-suburbs-and-cities-the-unexpected-truth.

6. Jane Jacobs, *The Economy of Cities* (New York: Vintage, 1970; first edition 1969).

7. Conor Dougherty, "Cities Grow at Suburbs' Expense during Recession," *Wall Street Journal*, July 1, 2009.

8. Calculation by the blog Discovering Urbanism, "Charting the Reinvestment in Central Cities," October 5, 2009, based on Census data, retrieved from http://discoveringurbanism.blogspot.com/2009/10/charting-reinvestment-in-central-cities.html.

9. Discovering Urbanism, "Charting the Reinvestment in Central Cities."

10. Quoted in Conor Dougherty, "Cities Grow at Suburbs' Expense During Recession."

11. William H. Frey, *The Great American Migration Slowdown: Regional and Metropolitan Dimensions*, Washington D.C., The Brookings Institution, December 2009.

12. Edward L. Glaeser, "How Some Places Fare Better in Hard Times," *New York Times* Economic blog, March 24, 2009, retrieved from http://economix.blogs.nytimes.com/2009/03/24/how-some-places-fare-better-in-hard-times.

13. The one other type of place that my research shows does well with this demographic is great college towns near the heart of megaregions such as Austin, part of the Dal-Austin megaregion; Boulder, part of the Denver-Boulder megaregion; and Raleigh-Durham in Char-lanta. Andrew Strieber, "Starting Out: The 10 Most-Popular Cities for First-Time Job-Seekers," Careercast.com, May 2009, retrieved from www.careercast.com/jobs/content/ten-best-cities-college-graduates-jobs-rated; Florida, *Who's Your City?*

14. Roughly between eighteen and twenty-nine years of age at the time the survey was carried out. Richard Florida, "Why Certain Cities Attract Gen Ys," *Business Week*, June 2009, retrieved from www.businessweek.com/managing/content/jun2009/ca2009069_660226.htm.

15. Boston was third, D.C. seventh, Baltimore tenth, Philadelphia eleventh, and New York thirteenth. "America's Smartest Cities—from First to Worst," Daily Beast, October 4, 2009, retrieved from www.thedailybeast.com/blogs-and-stories/2009-10-04/americas-smartest-cities---from-first-to-worst.

16. Sue Shellenbarger, "The Next Youth Magnet Cities," *Wall Street Journal*, September 30, 2009.

17. William Henderson and Arthur Alderson, "The Changing Economic Geography of Large U.S. Law Firms," paper presented to the 3rd Annual Conference of Empirical Legal Studies Papers, May 16, 2008. Retrieved from http://papers.ssrn.com/sol13/papers.cfm?abstract_id=1134223.

Chapter 19: Big, Fast, and Green

1. On New York, see Edward Glaeser, "Urban Colossus: Why New York is America's Largest City," *Federal Reserve Bank of New York Economic Policy Review* 11, no. 2 (2005): 7–24. For London, see the entry, "London (England)," Encarta Online Encyclopedia 2009, retrieved from http://encarta.msn.com.
2. Luís M. A. Bettencourt. José Lobo, Dirk Helbing, Christian Kühnert, and Geoffrey B. West, "Growth, Innovation, Scaling, and the Pace of Life in Cities," PNAS 104, no. 17 (2007): 7301–7306.
3. Jane Jacobs, *The Economy of Cities* (New York: Vintage, 1970; first edition 1969); Robert Lucas, "On the Mechanics of Economic Development," *Journal of Monetary Economics* 22 (1988): 3–42.
4. David Owen, *Green Metropolis: Why Living Smaller, Living Closer, and Driving Less Are the Keys to Sustainability* (New York: Riverhead, 2009); Owen, "Sustainable Cities," Project Syndicate, October 5, 2009, retrieved from www.project-syndicate.org/contributor/1661.
5. David Owen, "How Traffic Jams Help the Environment," *Wall Street Journal*, October 9, 2009.
6. Edward Glaeser, "With a Tax Break, a Big Carbon Footprint," *Boston Globe*, November 5, 2009.
7. "Cities and CO2: Bigger Is Better," Martin Prosperity Insights, October 14, 2009, retrieved from www.martinprosperity.org/insights/insight/cities-and-co2-bigger-is-better.

Chapter 20: The Velocity of You

1. Figures on average travel speed are from Randal O'Toole as cited in Neil Reynolds, "America's Fast Track to Wealth," *Globe and Mail*, October 9, 2009.
2. Christopher Kennedy, *The Wealth of Cities* (Toronto: University of Toronto Press, forthcoming).
3. The literature on the subject is vast. Peak oil was first predicted by M. King Hubbert. See Kenneth Deffeyes, *Hubbert's Peak: The Impending World Oil Shortage* (Princeton, N.J.: Princeton University Press, 2001); James Kunstler, *The Long Emergency: Surviving the End of the Oil Age, Climate Change, and Other Converging Catastrophes* (New York: Atlantic Monthly Press, 2005); Paul Roberts, *The End of Oil: On the Edge of a Perilous New World* (Boston: Houghton Mifflin, 2004); Michael Ruppert, *Crossing the Rubicon: The Decline of the American Empire at the End of the Age of Oil* (Gabriola Island, Canada: New Society Press, 2005); Matthew Simmons, *Twilight in the Desert: The Coming Saudi Oil Shock and the World Economy* (Hoboken, N.J.: Wiley & Sons, 2005); Christopher Steiner, *$20 Per Gallon: How the Inevitable Rise in the Price of Gasoline Will Change Our Lives for the Better* (New York: Grand Central Publishing, 2009); Jeff Rubin, *Why Your World Is About to Get a Whole*

Lot Smaller: Oil and the End of Globalization (New York: Random House, 2009).

4. James Kunstler, "The Long Emergency," *Rolling Stone*, March 24, 2005.

5. Daniel Kahneman, Alan B. Krueger, David A. Schkade, Norbert Schwarz, and Arthur A. Stone, "Survey Method for Characterizing Daily Life Experience: The Day Reconstruction Method," *Science* 306, no. 5702 (2004): 1776–1780.

6. Data from the U.S. Census Bureau, American Community Survey, summarized in Population Resource Center, "The Great Recession: A View from the American Community Survey," September 22, 2009, retrieved from www.facebook.com/note.php?note_id=140544004586.

7. Texas Transportation Institute, *2009 Urban Mobility Report*, Texas A&M University, 2009, retrieved from http://mobility.tamu.edu/ums.

8. Estimates by Kevin Stolarick and Patrick Adler of the Martin Prosperity Institute. The measure is calculated by taking the amount of time saved in minutes as a percentage of the total workday. It then calculates economic value by multiplying this percentage by earnings. It also takes into account the type of commute.

9. Joe Simpson, "Digital Cities: The Transport of Tomorrow Is Already Here," *Wired UK*, November 2009, retrieved from www.wired.co.uk/wired-magazine/archive/2009/11/features/digital-cities-the-transport-of-tomorrow-is-already-here.aspx.

10. "What's Capacity Got to Do with My City?" Frumination, August 9, 2009, retrieved from http://frumin.net/ation/2009/08/whats_capacity_go_to_do_with_m.html.

11. Data on commuting patterns here and above are from Kaid Benfield, "Which US Cities Have the Greenest Commuting Habits?" National Resources Defense Council, October 2, 2009, retrieved from http://switchboard.nrdc.org/blogs/kbenfield/which_us_cities_have_the_green_1.html.

12. "2008 Bike Share Rankings," The Wash Cycle, September 23, 2009, retrieved from www.thewashcycle.com/2009/09/2008-bike-share-rankings.html.

13. Susan Handy, James F. Sallis, Deanne Weber, Ed Maibach, and Marla Hollander, "Is Support for Traditionally Designed Communities Growing? Evidence from Two National Surveys," *Journal of the American Planning Association* 74, no. 2 (2008): 209–221.

14. David Owen, "How Traffic Jams Help the Environment," *Wall Street Journal*, October 9, 2009, retrieved from http://online.wsj.com/article/SB100014240527466045744615723048428410.html.

Chapter 21: Faster Than a Speeding Bullet

1. As cited in Chris Nelder, "High Speed Rail: A No-Brainer," GetRealList, October 5, 2009, retrieved from www.getreallist.com/high-speed-rail-a-no-

brainer.html; Robert Wright, "New Age of Train Offers Route out of Recession," *Financial Times*, October 6, 2009; Jamil Anderlini, Beijing's Ambitions Eclipse 'Golden Age,'" *Financial Times*, October 6, 2009; Giles Tremlett, "Spain's High-Speed Trains Win over Fed-Up Flyers," *Guardian*, January 13, 2009.

2. Maximum high-speed rail speeds are based on figures from Vukan R. Vuchic and Jeffery M. Casello, "An Evaluation of Maglev Technology and Its Comparison with High Speed Rail," *Transportation Quarterly* 56, no. 2 (2002): 33–49, retrieved from http://thetransitcoalition.us/LargePDFfiles/maglev -EvalandComparisonHSR.pdf. Shinkasen times are from www.japanrail .com, TGV/Eurostar times from www.raileurope.ca.

3. Edward Glaeser, "Is High-Speed Rail a Good Public Investment?," July 28, 2009; Glaeser, "Running the Numbers on High-Speed Trains," August 4, 2009; Glaeser, "How Big Are the Environmental Benefits of High-Speed Rail"; Glaeser, "What Would High-Speed Rail Do to Suburban Sprawl"; all at *New York Times*, retrieved from http://economix. blogs.nytimes.com.

4. Current dollar conversions based on data in Wendell Cox and Jean Love, *The Best Investment a Nation Ever Made: A Tribute to the Dwight D. Eisenhower System of Interstate & Defense Highways* (Philadelphia: Diane Publishing Company, 1998).

5. A map with full descriptions of all eleven proposed U.S. routes can be found at "High Speed Rail Corridor Destinations," Federal Railroad Administration, retrieved from www.fra.dot.gov/us/content/203. On the proposed Canadian line, see SNC-Lavalin and Delcan, Quebec-Ontario High Speed Rail Project: Preliminary Routing Assessment and Costing Study, Final Report," March 1995, retrieved from www.bv.transports.gouv.qc.ca/mono/0985915.pdf.

6. These calculations are based on the distance between hub cities based on current top high-speed rail speeds from *Transportation Quarterly*. Driving time estimates are from Google maps. See Richard Florida, "Mega-Regions and High-Speed Rail," *Atlantic*, May 4, 2009, retrieved from http:// correspondents.theatlantic.com/richard_florida/2009/05/mega-regions_ and_high-speed_rail.php.

7. Ryan Avent, "Why Railroads Will Make Us Richer," Seeking Alpha, May 5, 2009, retrieved from http://seekingalpha.com/article/135297-why-railroads-will-make-us-richer.

Chapter 22: Renting the Dream

1. James Truslow Adams, *The Epic of America* (Simon Publications, 2001).
2. Grace W. Bucchianeri, "The American Dream or the American Delusion? The Private and External Benefits of Homeownership," Wharton School of Busi-

ness, University of Pennsylvania, December 1, 2008, retrieved from http://real
.wharton.upenn.edu/~wongg/research/The%20American%20Dream.pdf.

3. David Rosnick and Dean Baker, "The Wealth of the Baby Boom Cohort after the Collapse of the Housing Bubble," Center for Economic Policy Research, February 2009.

4. Jason Zweig, "Shiller: Mr. Worst-Case Scenario," *Money*, July 6, 2007.

5. Rosnick and Baker, "The Wealth of the Baby Boom Cohort after the Collapse of the Housing Bubble."

6. See Stephen Slivinski, "House Bias: The Economic Consequences of Subsidizing Homeownership," *Region Focus*, Fall 2008, 1–4; Poterba is cited therein. Lori Taylor, "Does the United States Still Overinvest in Housing?," Federal Reserve Bank of Dallas, *Economic Review*, Second Quarter 1998, 10–18.

7. As quoted in Amity Shlaes, "America's Obsession with Housing Hobbles Growth," Bloomberg, August 20, 2009, retrieved from www.bloomberg .com/apps/news?pid=newsarchive&sid=a5LoEiJ0IyAo.

8. Andrew Oswald, "The Housing Market and Europe's Unemployment: A Non-technical Paper," in *Homeownership and the Labour Market in Europe*, Casper van Ewijk and Michiel van Leuvensteijn, eds. (New York: Oxford University Press, 2009).

9. Sam Roberts, "Slump Creates Lack of Mobility for Americans," *New York Times*, April 22, 2009.

10. Mark Whiteman, "American Dream 2: Default, Then Rent," *Wall Street Journal*, December 10, 2009, retrieved from http://online.wsj.com/article/ SB126040517376983621.html.

11. Figures for the number of renters in 2007 are from the American Community Survey. The percentage of renters is from American Community Survey; metro-level data are from U.S. Census, "2005–2007 American Community Survey 3-Year Estimates," retrieved from http://factfinder.census.gov/ servlet/DatasetMainPageServlet?_program=ACS. Home ownership rates are from U.S. Census Bureau, "Housing Vacancies and Homeownership, 2nd Quarter 2009," retrieved from www.census.gov/hhes/www/housing/hvs/ qtr209/q209ind.html.

12. Prashant Gopal, "Tata's Nano Home: Company Behind the World's Cheapest Car to Sell $7,800 Apartments," *BusinessWeek*, May 7, 2009, retrieved from www.businessweek.com/the_thread/hotproperty/archives/2009/05/first_ it_came_o.html.

13. Antoinette Martin, "The Divorced Find a Housing Niche," *New York Times*, December 12, 2008.

14. Mark S. Smith and Alan Zibel, "Obama Unveils $75 Billion Mortgage Relief Plan," *USA Today*, February 18, 2009.

15. Fifty-five percent of those whose mortgages were renegotiated redefaulted within twelve months, according to figures compiled in U.S. Department of

the Treasury, "OCC and OTS Mortgage Metrics Report, 2009," retrieved from www.occ.treas.gov/ftp/release/2009-118a.pdf.

16. Alan Zibel, "Fannie Mae Offers Borrowers Option to Foreclosure," Associated Press, November 5, 2009, retrieved from http://finance.yahoo.com/news/Fannie-Mae-offers-borrowers-apf-3320393724.html?x=0.

17. Congressional Budget Office, "An Overview of Federal Support for Housing," November 3, 2009, retrieved from www.cbo.gov/ftpdocs/105xx/doc10525/11-03-HousingPrograms.pdf. Also see Justin Fox, "Almost $300 Billion in Housing Aid (and Only $60 Billion of It for Renters)," *Time,* November 3, 2009, retrieved from http://curiouscapitalist.blogs.time.com/2009/11/03/almost-300-billion-in-housing-aid-and-only-60-billion-of-it-for-renters/#ixzz0WTk6zVHH.

18. Edward L. Glaeser, "Killing (or Maiming) a Sacred Cow: Home Mortgage Deductions," *New York Times,* February 24, 2009, retrieved from http://economix.blogs.nytimes.com/2009/02/24/killing-or-maiming-a-sacred-cow-home-mortgage-deductions.

Chapter 23: Resetting Point

1. Alice Rivlin, *Reviving the American Dream: The Economy, the States & the Federal Government* (Washington, D.C.: The Brookings Institution, 1992).

Index

Westinghouse, George, 12, 14
Westinghouse Electric Company,
 14–15
Whole Foods, 121, 122
Who's Your City (Florida), 67–68
Whyte, William, 41
work
 First Reset and growing distinction
  between home and, 21–22
 as key to happiness, 127–128

Yankelovich survey, 134

Zakaria, Fareed, 55, 89–90
Zappos, 121, 122
Zoellick, Robert, 55
zoning codes, 22
Zuckerman, Mort, 117, 120
Zurich, Switzerland, 50, 56